for ♥

Block Warriors
600 BLOCK South

GEORGE JONES

NOT TO BE
RESOLD

EMPLOYEE
BOOK SALE

About the Author

Bob Allen is a freelance writer, originally from Sykesville, Maryland, and now residing in Nashville, Tennessee. His articles have appeared in *Esquire, Playboy,* the Atlanta *Journal, Rolling Stone,* and *Billboard.* He is a former editor of *Country Music Magazine* and *Nashville!* magazine. He has also worked as a writer and consultant for Time-Life Records.

GEORGE JONES

The Saga
of an American Singer

BOB ALLEN

A DOLPHIN BOOK
DOUBLEDAY & COMPANY, INC.
Garden City, New York
1984

I would like to thank the following for use of their photos: Luther Nalley, Starday Records, Keith Kolby, the Country Music Foundation Library, *The Music City News*, Les Leverett, Fred Goodwin, Jim Fitzgerald, Jill Krementz, Owen Cartright/Nashville *Banner*, Charlyn Zlotnik, Bill Jarnigan, Kathy Gangwisch, Robin Hood, Bill Thorup/ Nashville *Banner*, Wide World Photos, J. Clark Thomas, John Yearwood/Woodsman Publishing Company.

"Give Me the Roses While I Live" by A. P. Carter. Copyright © 1980 by Southern Music Publishing Co., Inc.
Used by permission. All rights reserved.

"The Window Up Above" by George Jones. Copyright © 1960, 1961, Fort Knox Music Company and Glad Music Company.
Used by permission. All rights reserved.

"A Drunk Can't Be a Man" by George Jones and Earl Montgomery. Copyright © 1976, Uncanny Music Company.
All rights administered by Tree International.
International copyright secured, all rights reserved.
Used by permission.

"A House of Gold" by Hank Williams. Copyright © 1950 by Fred Rose Music, Inc.
Copyright renewed 1977, assigned to Fred Rose Music, Inc., and Hiriam Music, Inc., for the U.S.A. only.
All rights outside the U.S.A. controlled by Fred Rose Music, Inc.
Used by permission of the publisher. All rights reserved.

Library of Congress Cataloging in Publication Data

Allen, Bob.
　　George Jones: the saga of an American singer.

　　1. Jones, George, 1931– . 2. Singers—United States—Biography. 3. Country musicians—United States—Biography. I. Title. II. Title: The saga of an American singer.
ML420.J756A7　1984　　784.5′2′00924　[B]　　84-1541
ISBN 0-385-27906-X

Copyright © 1984 by Bob Allen
All Rights Reserved
Printed in the United States of America
First Edition

FOR:

My mother, ANNE CARR ALLEN (1924–73),
for my love of the written word . . .

And for my uncle, LAWRENCE MONROE ALLEN (1923–75),
for turning me on to the music.

Acknowledgments

I would first like to thank those individuals (including some who are not mentioned in the text) who were particularly generous in sharing their time and memories with me: Gordon ("Bax") Baxter, Sonny Burns, Linda Craig, Harold W. ("Pappy") Daily, Alfred Edwards, Jimmie and Anne Hills, Herman and Evalina Jones, Ruth Jones, George ("Buster") Maddox, Earl ("Peanut") and Charlene Montgomery, Gerald Murray, Luther Nalley, Don Pierce, George Riddle and Linda Welborn. Also special thanks to the Joneses, Pattersons, Marcontells and other kind people of the Big Thicket of Texas for their hospitality and generosity.

Thanks also to: Russ Barnard and the staff at *Country Music* magazine; Rick Blackburn, Cynthia Leu, Debbie Banks, Mary Ann McCready and all the guardians of the Xerox machine at CBS Records, Nashville; Rick Bolsom; Margaret Dawson and Charles McCardell at Time-Life Books & Records, Inc.; Joan Dew; Richard ("Rock") Harbert ("the New York connection"); Bill Jarnigan and the Muscle Shoals (Alabama) Music Association; Rich Kienzle ("phantom of the late-night, long-distance lines"); Aunt Eunice and Uncle Elias ("Dutch") Koontz; Pete Loesch; Bob Millard; Annie Moser; Alanna Nash; the "Oermax twins" (Robert K. Oermann and John Lomax III); the Reverend Clyde Patton; Bob Pinson; Ronnie Pugh; Lola Scobey; Billy Sherrill; Edward Shipper; Elizabeth Thiels; Nick

("Leave a Message") Tosches; Ardelle Upchurch; Charles K. Wolfe; and Bobby Womble.

Additional thanks and credit where credit is due, to the following organizations and institutions: the Big Thicket Museum in Saratoga, Texas; the Country Music Hall of Fame and Foundation Library in Nashville, Tennessee; the Texas Division of the United Daughters of the Confederacy; and WSMV Channel 4 News, in Nashville.

I would also like to acknowledge the following books and publications: *The Big Thicket Legacy* by Campbell and Lynn Loughmiller; *Country Music U.S.A.* by Bill Malone; *Country Song Round-Up; The Illustrated History of Country Music* edited by Patrick Carr; the Kountze *News-Visitor; The Music City News;* the Nashville *Banner;* the Nashville *Tennessean; Stand By Your Man* by Tammy Wynette and Joan Dew; *Tales from the Big Thicket* edited by Francis E. Abernethy; and *Texas Monthly* magazine.

Also special gratitude to my agents, Joyce Frommer and Diana Price, and to my editor, James Fitzgerald at Dolphin/Doubleday for their unwavering patience and endurance in seeing me through this project, from beginning to end.

And last, but certainly not least: thanks to the source of my inspiration, George Glenn Jones, the prodigal singer himself, with his voice, a font of lonesome truth and desolate beauty that calls out, like a crying in the night, to all of us who listen and take heed—all of us who hear it and know that there is a little bit of George Jones in us all.

Contents

There are vicious boxers in the rings of Montreal and there are dog fights and chicken fights and bullfights and many out there think these spectacles epitomize cruelty. Meanwhile, the good ole boys and the businessmen and all of us go home and worry about the lines in our faces and our wives getting fat. In small rooms everywhere we slice and destroy each other, we pull each other apart while George Jones sings the soundtrack in the background. . . .

Tom Russell

All my life it seems I've been running away from something. . . . If I knew what it was, maybe I could run in the right direction.

George Jones

GEORGE JONES

Prologue

LEGION

Sleep pulled him down into its bottomless depths, like still waters claiming a drowning man. When he opened his eyes and looked around him, the world was bathed in a spectral twilight, and he was unsure if he was waking or dreaming. He felt a great crushing weight of loss and confusion descend upon him. He raised his head and looked toward the television set in the motel room where he lay, and saw that there emanated from it a blinding luminescence that filled the shadowy room and flowed outward in rays that were as many as the colors of the rainbow. He was made to understand that each of these rays represented a good deed that was yet undone. These rays were like a halo, like raiment for the smiling, beckoning face of Jesus Christ that slowly took shape in their midst.

Slowly, the face of Jesus grew brighter, until its resplendent, overpowering lucency threatened to turn the utter darkness of night into day. The prodigal singer blinked his eyes and rubbed them. He felt a nauseous spasm of cold fear stab at his insides, like the sharp jagged stab of icicles. Reaching for the Bible that was there in the drawer of the small nightstand, he held it in his hands and was suddenly overcome with joy and amazement: he could see that this was the Bible that his mama had given him before she died, the Bible that he was sure he'd lost years ago, lost for all eternity.

Muttering softly to himself, repeating broken, disjointed fragments of scripture, he flipped frantically through the yellowed, timeworn pages, searching feverishly for that one passage that had eluded him for so many years—the one passage that would surely be the key to understanding this eternal light, and would surely be the key to his deliverance from the horrible travail and misfortune that now swirled madly around him, threatening to engulf him.

Eventually, he came across the familiar passage in Mark, the one about the man at Gadara who dwelt in the tombs and was called Legion, because of the host of "unclean spirits" that dwelt within him—a man he knew some preachers in their sermons had even likened him to. This was not it. The passage he needed so badly to find still continued to elude him; once more, he realized that his search was in vain.

The light in the room grew still more intense and all-consuming. Now the face of Jesus smiled and beckoned brighter, until it was as horrible and terrifying as the deepest darkness of night; and it burned his eyes and then his hands as he raised them to his eyes to shield his face. The small room filled with the muffled sounds of his own screams, like the sounds of a drowning man gasping desperately for air.

Then he awoke and looked toward the TV. He no longer saw the face of Jesus—just the aging, unreassuring face of Johnny Carson, with his snake-oil smile that did not beckon. In his hands, he still clutched the Bible and he saw that it was not the lost Bible that his dead mama had given him, after all, but just a standard-issue Gideon Bible, the likes of which are found in motel rooms everywhere. In his anger and frustration, he ripped viciously at its pages, and hurled it furiously against the wall. It came to rest on the floor, its pages outspread, like the wings of a dead, bedraggled moth.

He rubbed his eyes, poured himself a tall drink and flipped restlessly across the late-night television channels. Confusion seemed to swallow him up; he puzzled over the meaning of this strange vision which had come to him many times before, in lonely motel rooms in Nashville, Arkansas, Alabama . . .

As he hurriedly downed his drink and poured himself another, like a morning mist lifting, he suddenly remembered: it was late 1981, and chaos reigned. A few days earlier, on October 12, a warm day in Nashville when sullen skies obscured the resplendent hues of autumn that were beginning to fall across the Middle Tennessee landscape, he'd been presented, for the second year in a row, with the Country Music Association's prestigious Male Vocalist of the Year award. In no less a disoriented and bewildered state than he was in now, he'd accepted the award on national television, via the CBS network's live, prime-time broadcast of the association's awards show, a gaudy, star-studded pageant in which Nashville's music industry pays annual fealty to its two icons of the late twentieth century: TV and money.

Things had not gone too smoothly for George Glenn Jones the day of the CMA Awards show. Not gone smoothly at all. From the time he got up, he'd been drinking Jack Daniel's and 7-Up at a rate that was far too fast for his own good. By late morning, he'd already worked himself into a seething and dangerous state of emotional disequilibrium. When he left the small second-floor seventy-five-dollar-a-night room that he was sharing with his on-and-off-again fiancée, Linda Welborn, in the ornately gabled $29 million Opryland Hotel (just a short distance from the Grand Ole Opry House, where the evening's show was to be held), he was in a quiet but sinister rage.

Late that morning he'd told Linda that he was going to get his hair cut. By midafternoon, he'd still not returned. Linda and those minions whose job it was to watch over the troubled singer were mindful of his bitter, anguished objections over having to attend the awards ceremony that night and be put on display on national TV. They were also only too familiar with his penchant for pulling sudden disappearing acts under such circumstances. Their concern rose until, finally, members of his band and his temporary management team were enlisted into a makeshift posse that fanned out to scour the Music City bars, motels and barbershops that were known to be "the Possum's" infamous and favorite hiding places. When they finally located him, nine and a half miles away, in a dimly lit corner of the seedy Hall of Fame Motor Inn Lounge in South Nashville, he was still furiously knocking back double whiskeys, hoping to wash away his anger and bitterness, hoping to assuage the wild beasts that he could feel summoning their strength within him.

After much persuasion, he'd allowed them to take him back to his hotel. Once there, he'd merely headed for the downstairs bar, where he'd managed to find another dark corner and knock back a few more doubles. It was forty-five minutes before show time when he was half led, half carried back to his room again. He'd fallen so deeply under the combined spell of strong drink, nervousness and exhaustion that his hands shook too badly for him even to shave himself with his electric razor. He even needed help getting changed into the open-collar shirt and casual Western-style suit that he insisted on wearing instead of a tuxedo.

By the time George and his small entourage left the hotel for the show, the light clouds had cleared and a full moon hung in the night sky. The prodigal singer's condition had not improved. He avoided the crush of waiting photographers in the lobby and was picked up at a side entrance by the limousine hired by his record company to carry him the half mile or so to the Opry House from the hotel. When he'd arrived backstage, he'd done his best to convince those in charge that he was not to be summoned to the stage, under any circumstances.

Late in the show, when, through his whiskey numbness, he'd heard his own name announced for an award, he knew that there was no escape from the inevitable. He rose from his seat and moved unsteadily down the aisle, under the harsh, unrelenting glare of the television cameras. With all eyes in the packed 4,400-seat auditorium fixed on him, those who knew George feared that he might actually fall on his face. His movements were like those of a trapped animal treading on dangerously thin ice. His usually immaculate hair was now drooping and tousled and dangled loosely in his face.

Even in his dislocated frame of mind and his disheveled physical condition, George Jones, the prodigal singer, seemed to shine like a scarred, tarnished diamond in the rough whose brilliance was lost and strangely out of place amidst this glittering, ersatz, fool's-gold sea of fancy hairdos, imitation jewelry, rented tuxedos and carefully rehearsed country politeness.

As the wayward singer staggered onstage and was caught in the spotlight, all the pain and hard times of his fifty years of living could be seen etched into the gnarled contours of his pale and haggard face. As he accepted the shiny, artillery-shell-shaped trophy before thirty-five million television viewers, he showed no elation. Inwardly he was consumed by vertigo—lost in the sickly, dizzying heights of a worldly fame that mystified him. Utterly alone in the dark depths of his deep mortal confusion, he stood there, the confusion and madness of it all swirling around in his brain like the vile writhing of poisonous serpents. He stared into the TV cameras and delivered a brief, semi-incoherent acceptance speech, while his close-set eyes swirled crazily, like the eyes of one who stares giddily into the depths of a dark, bottomless well.

Not that all this grief was anything new. It was just the same old bullshit, really. Hell, the year before he'd swept these same awards —he'd had a hand in winning nearly a half dozen of them: "Male Vocalist of the Year," "Song of the Year," "Single of the Year" and so on and so forth, and he hadn't even bothered to show up for the ceremonies. He'd tried his damnedest to get out of it again this year, tried his damnedest to break and run, like he'd done so many times before. It was with a sickening shudder that he'd been forced to admit to himself that *this* time he'd been too weak even to do that. Now, it seemed like a damned shame, almost, that they'd put him through all this agony just to give him one paltry award—the last thing in the world that he really needed.

Hell, he'd won a truckload of these awards in the last couple of years—sold millions of records—not that he'd ever asked anybody for *any* of it. Sometimes he couldn't help but wonder to himself just where in the hell all these smiling, smooth-talking awards presenters had been during the last twenty-five years, when he'd been beating his brains out night after night, year after year, singing to strangers in strange cities, squandering his peace of mind, and all the while, slowly but surely, battering himself into the emotional wreck that he'd now become. "If you don't spend half your time [in Nashville] bowing and scraping and kissing ass, you don't get the awards"—he knew that.

No, that had never been his way of doing things. He'd done it the hard way. Like a cat with nine lives, he had, in his own peculiar and compulsively reckless way, outlasted—and in many cases, outlived —his contemporaries. Along the way, though, he'd set his own personal record as the only country singer to have scored a number one single in four consecutive decades.

Coming as it did against the backdrop of his own strife-ridden personal life—the frequent hospitalizations for drug abuse, alcoholism and exhaustion; the numerous arrests on charges ranging from drunken driving to assault with intent to murder—all this belated fame and adulation which had finally come his way meant little to George.

In fact, at times it all seemed downright pointless. Despite all the awards, gold records and a gross annual income that once ran as high as $2 million a year, and despite the fact that everyone and his brother kept telling him how he was the greatest country singer who ever lived, he still had precious little to show for it all. One way or another, he'd managed to let himself be fast-talked or snake-oiled out of most everything he'd ever earned. As far as he knew, he no longer even owned his own legend, his own dark shadow: in a careless moment, he'd even signed away the rights to his own life story. What few worldly possessions he had managed to hold on to were, for the most part, gone, too. They had been stolen, or merely lost and scattered, like his memories, across the three different states—Tennessee, Texas and Alabama—where he'd tried futilely to find a home for himself in the past few years. As he walked off the stage that night, clutching his award as carelessly as an empty whiskey bottle, his total net worth amounted to what it had been when he'd first fought his way out of East Texas obscurity and got his first fragile toehold in this unrelentingly harsh and demanding music profession nearly three decades earlier: just the loose change that jingled in his pocket.

"For a man who's won all the awards I'm supposed to have won and achieved all the things I'm supposed to have achieved, I have nothing to my name," he'd lamented bitterly to reporters just a couple of months earlier. Nothing, nothing, nothing. Nothing but the shirt on his back and the coins in his pocket.

The only thing that he did have left, the only thing they hadn't been able to take away from him, was that voice of his: that remarkable voice which—despite all the abuses of whiskey, cocaine and chain-smoked cigarettes that he'd heaped on it over the years—remained a priceless and powerful instrument. As always, that voice of his still rang clear, still resonated with a timbre that was hauntingly full of desolate beauty and painfully raw truth and conviction —like the desperate cry of a fallen angel who teeters precariously at the brink of the yawning precipice between the transcendent brightness of the everlasting light and the black, bottomless pit of damnation.

Hell no! He'd never kissed ass and he never would—especially not tonight. When he arrived back at the hotel, he jumped so hurriedly from the limousine that he forgot his award, left it lying haphazardly on the back seat. Avoiding the gaggle of television camera crews and reporters who'd gathered in the hotel's resplendently carpeted lobby, he fled through the shadowy corridors, back to the room that he was sharing with Linda Welborn. He flopped unceremoniously down on the bed. Linda, who'd accompanied him to the awards ceremony, quickly mixed him the fresh tumbler of double Jack Daniel's and 7-Up that he'd requested. When she handed him the drink, he did not look up, but merely drank deeply from it, sank further into his festering rage and despair and stared darkly into the flickering TV, which he always kept on, night or day, whether he was awake or sleeping. The TV whose pale iridescent light now cast eerie shadows around the small darkened hotel room.

In his eyes, Linda could now see the steely glint of impending violence.

"I shoulda won more," he snarled in a low, menacing growl that was full of outrage and self-pity. "It ain't fair," he added sullenly as he raised his drink to his lips once more. "It ain't right."

"But George," Linda replied softly, hoping to soothe his frayed sensibilities and quell the demons that she knew were gathering their cold forces within him. "You should be proud of the one you got tonight. There's some people that didn't win anything tonight."

For an instant, the anger in his eyes seemed to soften. "You're right," he sighed forlornly. "What the hell! I've had it all. I been there. I don't give a damn! I shouldn'ta won nothin'."

But the icicles of rage and hopelessness suddenly shot their cold, torturous blades through the pit of his stomach once again. He smashed his glass against the wooden bedstead, sending whiskey, 7-Up, ice cubes and bits of shattered glass flying everywhere.

"I'm so goddamn sick and tired!" he screamed as he held the sharp, jagged base of the broken glass at arm's length and studied the gnarled, snakelike configurations of the veins in his wrist. He shifted his cold gaze slightly and stared ominously into the patterns made by the flickering light from the TV as it caressed the jagged ends of broken glass. "I think I oughta just end it all . . . now . . . right here."

He rose from the bed where he'd been sitting and flung the ruined drink glass against the wall. His hands tightened into fists and lashed out at Linda, as if she were the source of all the dark restiveness seething within his now trembling body.

Having felt the sting of the flat of his hand against her face more than once before, she quickly stepped out of his reach, then fled from the room. Hurrying downstairs to the lobby, she summoned a cab and disappeared into the night, leaving the tormented singer to wrestle with his demons alone.

In the now empty room, George lay back on the double bed, stared back into the TV, and sank into his eerie, unendurable solitude once again. The hours passed. Night became day and then turned to night again. Now, here he was, alone again, in another strange motel room, with the horrible silence of the night seeping through the cracks in the windows and around the door, invading his solitude, filling the room with an invisible ether that carried in its wake all the sorrow of a lifetime of suffering, all the loneliness and sadness of the world, all the troubling memories that always seemed to return in twisted, disjointed fragments to haunt him on nights like these.

When the silence again became unbearable, he rose from the bed and turned on the radio and flipped frantically, yet aimlessly across the static-ridden electronic chaos of the crowded nighttime AM airways. Through the pestilent hum of the interference, he listened to somebody on a phone-in talk show in Cleveland running his mouth off about flying saucers, until the signal faded off into static silence. He heard a backwoods preacher somewhere in Mississippi hollering about money and salvation; he listened until his pronouncements, too, were swallowed up by the gray silence. A rock station in Chicago was beaming out the news of a plane crash, more static and another preacher, this one with an "uptown"-sounding voice, broadcasting from a mission house in New Orleans with a whole other brand of salvation. Then he heard a weaker, more distant signal, from some low-wattage backwater country station somewhere far to the south; he heard the sound of his own voice—youthful and confident—singing a song that he had recorded many years ago. With his ear up against the radio, he listened intently, but gradually that signal, too, faded out amidst the garble of wildly bouncing radio signals. Like another scattered, misplaced piece of his own troubled past, it, too, became lost in the darkness of the night.

He shut the radio off and turned the TV up even louder. The silence still made him shiver. He fixed himself another tall glass of whiskey and hurriedly gulped it down.

It did no good. The blinding light of the face of Jesus still burned like a beacon through the searing moil of guilt, anger and confusion that swirled within him. He picked up the whiskey bottle from the bedside table and poured himself yet another drink, and seeing that the bottle was nearly empty, tilted his head and took the last swallow of the 90-proof whiskey straight down—from the bottle itself. He then sent the bottle—agonizing reminder of emptiness that it was— crashing through the sliding glass doors on the far side of the room. As the sound shattered the stillness of the night, like ripples across the surface of a still pond, he sank back on the bed and took his head in his hands and held it tightly, as if it had become the fragile cracked vessel of his own sanity and he was struggling desperately to keep it, too, from shattering into a thousand fragments. Staring down at the glistening patterns of the broken glass that littered the carpet, he searched for the answer to his problems as if he might find it there in front of him. Finding no relief from his immense confusion, he sat with his face in his hands and wept softly to himself, wondering how it had all come to this.

Chapter One

VOICES IN
THE THICKET

The Big Thicket lies in the extreme southeastern portion of Texas, not far from the Louisiana border. It is bounded on the east and west, respectively, by the southern-flowing Neches and Trinity rivers, not far from where their waters commingle with the brackish tidewaters of the Gulf of Mexico.

Unlike the rest of the Lone Star State, which is known for its vast horizontal expanses of flat, open land and big sky, the Thicket—though it encompasses little more than five hundred square miles all told—is very much a world unto itself. It is a world of shadows and darkness, where the thick forests of tall longleaf pines shut out the sunlight; where the natural boundaries and escarpments created by the towering trees, misty bayous and dense, shadowy undergrowth of canebrakes, palmetto and wild honeysuckle conspire to separate neighbor from neighbor and breed an eerie and abiding sense of isolation.

The people who inhabit this solitary region are, to this day, a breed apart. They do not, for the most part, sport the ten-gallon hats or affect the expansive braggadocio so often associated, in the popular imagination, with the citizenry of the rest of Texas. The denizens of the Big Thicket have about them, instead, a brooding clannishness and the taciturn wariness of the dispossessed—as if, over the generations, they have been overwhelmed and turned inward by the unyielding loneliness and claustrophobia of their natural surroundings.

The sixteenth- and seventeenth-century Spanish explorers who were the first white men to venture along the fringes of the Big Thicket discovered a primeval rain forest so dense as to be impenetrable, and so foreboding that it was shunned even by the cannibalistic Atakapan Indians who dwelt on the coastal plains to the south. These explorers returned to their homeland wide-eyed with tales of a vast woodland infested with wolves, panthers, alligators, poisonous serpents, man-eating mosquitoes, evil spirits, malarial swamps and saw briers so huge that they would grab hold of a man and never turn him loose.

In 1806, after the Louisiana Purchase, the region of Southeast Texas encompassing the Big Thicket was declared "neutral ground," and no settlers were allowed there. Soon, the thick uncharted and unclaimed wilderness became a refuge for what one historian disdainfully referred to as "the cur dogs of the human race": renegades, horse thieves, brigands, deserters and fugitives of all manner and degree of sordidness. As the nineteenth century wore on, an increasing number of unserved arrest warrants issued in states all across the Old South began to bear the stamp "GTT" ("Gone to Texas"). When the United States acquired the area, the Thicket had already earned the reputation that persists even today, which was summed up best by one of the region's elder statesmen: "They's a whole lot of bad blood in there that ain't never been bred out."

Texas became the twenty-eighth state of the Union in 1845. A steady stream of settlers had begun trickling into the Thicket from the older Southern states to the north and east. They were, for the most part, the poor, the landless and the dispossessed, largely of Irish, English, Scotch and Welsh stock. Looking for their own land there on the fringes of the wilderness, they came in search of the God-given right to be left the hell alone, safely out of the reach of

politicians, tax collectors, sheriffs, education-mongers, religious or-
ganizers and other useless scourges of the civilized world. With
them they brought their Old World folk ballads—"Barbara Allen,"
"The Hangman's Rope," "The Farmer's Curst Wife"—and their
Sacred Harp songs: eighteenth-century English hymns, as well as
newer American camp-meeting spirituals.

They also carried with them to the Big Thicket their harsh fundamentalist beliefs and their unflinching fear and trembling for the
edicts of their wrathful Old Testament God. Their God was a God
whom they honored with their guilt and fear on Sunday mornings,
and whom they defiled with their inventive assortment of peckerwood transgressions the other six and a half days of the week.

These early settlers brought with them, as well, a dark temperament that was rooted in the uncompromising brutality of the times
and the haunting, omnipresent threat of sudden death by disease or
disaster. Yet there was something else that seemed to be already
waiting for these renegade pilgrims there in the Thicket. Perhaps it
was the primeval pneuma and evil vapors of the foul swamps or the
"ghosty" spell of those strange apparitions which were said to stalk
the depths of the huge pine forests by night. Whatever it was, it
seemed to take hold and weigh upon the already somber dispositions and bad blood of the settlers—tainted as it was already by
inbreeding—until it festered into a perverse essence of the pioneer
spirit. For these crude pilgrims grew to have an abiding fondness for
the bounteous array of earthly temptations laid before them there in
the wilderness: temptations like incest, wife beating, knife fighting,
drunkenness, hog and cattle rustling, poaching, bootlegging, gambling and cockfighting—temptations which their fierce God seemed
to have laid before them as if to satisfy himself with proof of the
weakness and corruptibility of their flesh.

It was to this untamed land that there came, in 1843, two decades
before the Great Confederate War, a Baptist farmer named Aaron
Franklin Jones, the great-grandfather of the prodigal singer. He was
born in Alabama in 1837, the son of a farmer of the same name
whose Irish and English bloodlines had commingled more recently
with the blood of the Cherokee Indian. After setting off down the
Natchez Trace to seek his fortune, Frank Jones settled in Nacogdoches, a town just to the north of the Big Thicket that had once been

an old Spanish settlement. On September 9, 1860, he took as his wife Sarah Woods, who was also from Alabama.

In 1862, the year after Texas seceded from the Union and prepared to fight for the God-given right to hold slaves, Frank Jones joined Company A of the 17th Regiment of the Texas Cavalry. It was against the tragic backdrop of the Lost Cause of the Confederacy that Frank Jones, patriarch of the Texas lineage of the Jones family, was said to have distinguished himself with his own small act of valor. Family legend has it that old Frank's moment of glory came at what has come to be referred to as the Hogpen Incident. It is said that while serving under the flag of the Old Confederacy, Frank was leading a small patrol of men through the wilderness just across the Sabine River from Union-infested territory in Louisiana. He and his platoon were caught far from their headquarters in a sudden spell of bitterly cold weather that caused at least one man to die from exposure. As they struggled to survive a second night of this crippling weather, Frank and his men came across a sizable pen full of hogs. Realizing that gross bodily indignation was, indeed, a small price to pay as an alternative to severe frostbite, Frank Jones saved the day by persuading the soldiers to lie down in the muck and bed themselves with the hogs, thereby conserving enough of their precious bodily heat to sustain them through the night. Due to Frank's decisiveness, not a single life was lost that second night. In due time, he was praised for his valor and decorated with medals and ribbons.

Frank's bravery at the Hogpen Incident would be the Jones family's finest hour for nearly a century. Such a glorious moment would, in fact, not come again for another three generations, long after old Frank's progeny had come to be scattered far and wide across East Texas like thistledowns floating in a spring wind. It would not come until a wayward son would rise from his issue, one who would raise his voice and be heard far beyond the boundaries of the Old Confederacy; and whose voice would resonate with a pain and anguish that was not only his own but that of all those rough-hewn Thicket pilgrims who had come before.

In 1865, after the death knell of the Confederacy had been sounded, Frank Jones turned back to the soil for his sustenance. His wife, Sarah, bore him seven children. His third son, David Rollie Jones, was born July 18, 1872, in Nacogdoches. He grew to be a short, stocky, taciturn man, and around 1894 he turned to dirt farming like his father, shortly after marrying a high-spirited Mississippi-born girl named Mary Ferris.

Rollie's marriage to Mary Ferris was destined to be a bad one, and it lasted little longer than it took him to plant his seed in his fourteen-year-old bride.

Mary was a small, feisty young woman, also of part-Indian extraction—a woman who, as some of her grandchildren still recalled years after her death, had a strong taste for hard liquor, and could "outcuss most men." And on the day that she had her final round of acrimony with Rollie Jones across the log that straddled the creek in front of their humble house that led to the rest of the world, that's just what she did. With a string of loud execrations trailing off behind her, she simply strolled out of Rollie's world, never to return. She was already great with Rollie's child, like a tree ready to drop its fruit; however, the unborn son that she carried within her that day was destined to be the black sheep of his generation of Joneses and would not lay eyes upon his real father until he was a full six years of age.

Toward the end of the century, Rollie Jones married again. This time, he took for his wife a devout Christian woman named Jennie Frances Boykin, who was born in Leon County, Texas, on February 21, 1881. For a short time after his marriage, Rollie tried his hand at farming the blackland dirt of Leon County, in east-central Texas. Pretty soon, though, he drifted back to Southeast Texas, where he knew a man could always coax enough peas, potatoes and sugarcane out of the hard earth to squeeze by on. Rollie eventually settled in the small town of Lufkin, where he turned his hand to commerce. In the years before World War I, he prospered. As time passed, his holdings grew to include a grocery store, a furniture store and a small restaurant. Rollie built himself a nice big home, bought one of the first Model T touring cars in Lufkin and even became a deacon in the Baptist Church. He also bought himself an old Victrola, which he delighted in playing while he fixed himself a drink and danced around the parlor with one of his many daughters.

By the early 1920s, however, Rollie's fortunes had fallen into a state of disarray. Due to the combined forces of his immense generosity and his weakness for strong drink, his businesses had all slipped through his hands. With his finances and his health in a state of near ruination, he sought refuge on a farm near Crockett, Texas.

There, he nursed the wounds of his failure and once again turned back to the soil in order to eke out a meager living for himself and his family.

When his many daughters would gather around the piano in the parlor and sing in their own little impromptu gospel quartet, Rollie would often wander silently through the house, alone. He would sadly reflect on the fate that had befallen him, and his thoughts would turn back to the tales he'd heard of the Hogpen Incident, of the valor of his father, old Frank Jones, who'd passed away on March 3, 1918, in the Old Confederate Soldiers' Home in Austin. He wondered to himself if such glorious times would ever roll around for the Jones family again.

Around the same time that Frank Jones was collecting his medals for his bravery in the Civil War, another unvanquished son of the Old Confederacy made his way westward, drawn by the prospect of free land and the allurement of the tall tales of Texas. His name was Jepton "Litt" Patterson, and he was born of Irish and Dutch stock near Jacksonville, Florida, on March 15, 1847. "Uncle Litt," as his kinfolk came to call him, was still a small boy when his father, Joseph, fell in battle while serving in General Robert E. Lee's great gray-coated army. His family's meager holdings were irretrievably lost in the rubble of Reconstruction.

Uncle Litt was a man cut from stern Christian cloth. As he settled there amidst the rampant violence and lawlessness of the Big Thicket, he wasted little time in carving out his own small realm, upon which he conferred the unflinching dictates of his strict, teetotaling Calvinistic beliefs. It was in the Thicket that Uncle Litt met and married Martha Ann Loftin, who was born in Mississippi in January 1867.

Uncle Litt could neither read nor write. He was the kind of fervent believer, though, who could quote the Holy Scriptures from one end to the other, and go on and on until he was blue in the face. Each year, he raised himself a good crop of corn, cotton, peanuts and sugarcane there on the patch of land that he'd cleared. And as the years went quietly by, he also raised a huge flock of fourteen children to help him harvest these crops. It was of little consequence that twelve of Uncle Litt's fourteen offspring were girls, for they all grew to be sturdy, upright young women, cut from the same stern cloth as their daddy. As they came of age one by one, he taught them to chop cotton, clear timber and do the work of men.

Uncle Litt's seventh child was Clara, born on March 10, 1896. She grew to be the strongest of all the Patterson sisters. She was full of the same high-principled Christian devotion and unflinching moral fiber that caused her father to cast such a long and imposing shadow there in that primitive land, the Thicket. Clara soon outstripped her other sisters in her love for hard work, and when she learned to plow with a mule, it liked to tickled Uncle Litt to death. From that moment on, Clara was his "pick of the litter."

Like her father, Clara had an easygoing and comical side to her often stern disposition. Also like her father, she had an Irish temper. (Many years later, at a sedate gathering of the Patterson sisters, who were, by then, gray-haired matriarchs of the large clan, Clara shocked her aged siblings with that temper of hers: in a fit of pique, after losing at a game of dominoes, she picked up a handful of the carved wooden pieces and flung them at her sister Dessel, the tormentor at whose hands she had suffered humiliation and defeat.)

As if he meant to ensure that his strict belief would continue to be observed within the Patterson family in the years after he was gone, Uncle Litt built a small, crude backwoods chapel near his homestead. He served as the deacon of this humble church, which stood near the Little Pine Island Creek, not far from the small sawmill settlement of Thicket. The little chapel came to be called the White Oak Baptist Church.

Uncle Litt—reverent old man that he came to be in his later days —had a way of startling the old-timey "sit-down" Baptists who worshipped there at the White Oak Baptist Church. This was in the years long before the freethinking "Pentecosts" would come sweeping down through the Thicket turning people everywhere to their fast singing, hand waving and speaking in strange, unintelligible, clucking tongues, expressing the powers which were visited upon them by the Holy Ghost. Uncle Litt would often burst forth and shatter the hushed reverence of the traditional Baptist services by shouting up and down the aisles, chanting in those ancient unfathomable dialects and singing the praises of the Lord at the top of his lungs in an uninhibited manner, the likes of which most folks in that part of the country had never seen before. Sometimes, he would even be overwhelmed completely by the power of the Holy Spirit. He'd fall plumb out on the church floor, breathing heavily, in the throes of a religious seizure. Sometimes, he'd lie there for a good five or ten minutes before he even got back up again.

At home, Uncle Litt could be just as fervent and high-strung in his worship. Often, in the early evening, he would gather his many children together and command them all to kneel in prayer. Almost as if he were in a trance, he himself would fall to his knees and pray for hours on end, until dusk's last light had slowly faded and turned into the deep darkness of the late night—until his children's cramped knees and tired eyes burned and ached desperately for sleep.

Just as Uncle Litt taught his children to work hard, he also raised them to do something else—something which had been expected of the Pattersons since time immemorial. He taught them to raise their voices and sing the praises of the Holy Gospel. "Most of them Pattersons just seemed like they came into this world a-singin'," recalled one elderly in-law of the huge family. "A lot of 'em could sing those old gospel songs so good it'd raise the hair on your head."

As Uncle Litt's older daughters grew to early womanhood, he bought an old pump organ and placed it in the sitting room of the modest wood frame house he'd built on his patch of good, dark earth. With his favorite daughter, Clara, playing the organ, the Patterson sisters would often gather round, and there, in that remote corner of the world, they would bring their hauntingly beautiful voices together and raise them heavenward. The mellifluous sound would soar skyward, high above the tops of the towering pines, reaching out to appease their harsh Protestant God.

The decades passed. Uncle Litt's fourteen children bore him dozens and dozens of grandchildren, many of whom would be blessed with the beautiful gospel baritone and tenor voices on which the family had so long prided itself. The Thicket would ring with the heavenly sound of these voices, which were as beautiful, in their own way, as the diurnal trills and cries of the mockingbirds, cardinals and other songbirds of that piney forest.

Of all these Pattersons yet to come, there would be one who, though ordinary in most every other way, would be particularly blessed in this respect, one who would grow to sing with preternatural power and clarity. This wayward son would sing not only of the great beauty and wonder of God's promise to those in the wilderness; he would also sing of all the pain of the here and now, and of the sorrow of the world, such as it is.

When young Mary Ferris was crossing the log and leaving Rollie Jones behind for the last time, Uncle Litt was still falling out with the spirit in the church aisles. The long arm of progress and change was beginning to reach even into the remoteness of the Big Thicket in 1895.

As late as 1870, the region's only commodity deemed to be of any value whatsoever by outsiders had been its sulphurous springs and bogs, which were said to have healing properties. In the early 1860s, Sam Houston, founding father of the Texas Republic, even visited one of them, seeking treatment for an old leg wound. (But, as one of his servants later recorded, "when he came back home, he was in worse shape than when he left.")

It was in the mid-1870s, though, that all hell finally broke loose there in the piney woods. New York bankers and Houston business-men had come to realize that there were great fortunes to be made in cutting the majestic pines for timber. The Santa Fe and other railroads were soon hacking rights-of-way through the dense for-ests. Huge sawmills were hastily erected; tiny settlements quickly sprung up around them, and crude horse trails were cleared away to connect one of them to the next. Between 1880 and 1905, in East Texas, more than 18 million acres of virgin pine were felled to appease the growing pains of a hungry, rapidly expanding young nation.

Bringing down the majestic trees was backbreaking work. During the sweltering heat of the summer months, it often required a man to work waist deep in the bayous while fending off the cottonmouth moccasins, "stingin' lizards" and bloodsucking malarial saltwater mosquitoes that floated in on the hot Gulf breezes.

The woodsmen of the Thicket fell to the sordid task of deflow-ering their magnificent wilderness demesne with a vengeance and glee that was above and beyond the call of duty. First they chopped down practically all of the regal stands of virgin timber. Then they hunted down the bears that roamed the Thicket until they'd shot and killed the very last one. (Years later, when there was talk of creating a national forest there, where the world's largest magnolia tree stood, a handful of these indignant woodsmen snuck out by night and chopped it down. There was a similar reaction when a pioneering Hardin County newspaper publisher, Archer Fullingim, had the gall to run a column in his paper, the Kountze *News*, urging the preservation of the nearly extinct ivory-billed woodpecker. A few days later, a shotgun-toting woodsman came into his office and flung a dead woodpecker on his desk. "Is this," he asked with a wide grin that revealed several missing teeth, "what you been lookin' for?")

These rude men, working with their axes and teams of oxen, hacking away so perniciously at the vast woodland sanctuary that they called home, continued to harbor among themselves an abiding disdain for those ignorant enough to believe that the Big Thicket could ever really be conquered. The loggers still returned from the forest's depths with tales not much different from those carried home by the earliest Spanish explorers: tales of phantom ghost lights and strange creatures with the bodies of horses and the heads of lions. Never, these men reassured each other, could a road be built that would span this great rain forest. For surely, before any mortal could ever hack his way clear through, from one end to the other, the foul pneuma of the swamp would rise from the misty depths and reach out with its long, green tentacles of honeysuckle and saw brier and render the narrow man-made passageway as impenetrable as it had been before he began.

On Saturday afternoons, when these dour hard-bitten woodsmen took leave of their unremittingly hard labor long enough to piss away their week's wages on beer and raw whiskey, Uncle Litt would drive his mule-drawn wagon through tiny sawmill settlements like Thicket, Honey Island and Sour Lake. There, much to his disgust, he would behold these gross specimens of unsanctified humanity indulging in their unrepentant cursing, gambling, whoring and hell raising, as they leered out at him from the grimy slab-board cafés and ramshackle saloons. He drove further down the muddy streets and came across the more dissolute of their numbers sprawled out, dog drunk, in the mud and the filth left by the cows and horses. A few of the more unmanageable of this vile lot would be tied to the thick tree trunks with log chains, left there until they sobered up and regained their senses. Surveying this scene of such shameless iniquity, he would scowl and look away in disdain. He would then sit upright in his wagon and prod his mules and ride on.

It was in Lufkin, Texas, the small county seat of Angelina County, that Mary Ferris briefly settled after she gave old Rollie Jones his final cursing out and took her final leave of him. On January 10, 1895, the lone child of her first, ill-fated marriage was born. He was given the name George Washington Jones. It had also been the name of one of Frank Jones's comrades-in-arms (most likely a brother or cousin) in the 17th Texas Cavalry.

In later years, after this black-sheep son had grown into a tall, strapping youth and was eventually reunited with his father, Rollie Jones would attempt to enlighten him as to the valor of his grandfather Frank Jones at the Hogpen Incident during the Confederate War. (It is, indeed, a rare father who does not pour such tales of family glory into his oldest son's ears, in hopes of spurring him on to some valiant gesture of his own that will bring further distinction to the family name.) George Washington Jones would listen to his daddy's remembrances of the now misty past as if he understood what he was talking about. After his father had spoken at great length and with much deliberation, the black-sheep son would then grin that great, lopsided grin of his and leave Rollie wondering if all his words and admonishments weren't merely going in one of his big ears and out the other.

George Washington Jones was still an infant when Mary Ferris moved with him back into the home of her parents, George and Margaret Ferris, at Thicket, the small shanty town within walking distance of Uncle Litt's White Oak Baptist Church. George Washington Jones was still less than a year old when Mary Ferris married again, on December 23, 1896. Her new husband was Robert Lee Killingsworth. When she moved to set up housekeeping with her new husband, her oldest son, George Washington Jones, was left to be raised by his maternal grandparents.

As the years went by and he slowly came of age, George Washington Jones took to the untamed meanness of the Big Thicket just as easily and naturally as the wild root hogs of the piney woods took to acorns. When he was eleven, he was already out making his own way in the world, toting water for the workers at a nearby sawmill and learning to indulge in the idle-hours wildness that was so rampant in those crude lumber settlements.

George Washington Jones grew to be a strong, handsome young man, well over six feet tall, better than two hundred pounds and lean and tough as hickory wood. With a thick head of black hair, high cheekbones, a dark complexion and rugged backwoods features, he often put people in mind of—as one family member recalled—"a big ole Indian."

George Washington Jones was also a man who knew how to have himself a good time. He could play the french (mouth) harp and strum a few chords on the guitar at the same time; with his wheezy, uneven voice, he would even make a stab at singing now and then.

He could dance up a storm—or, as the old-timers were fond of saying, he could really "out-two-step a nigger." Tall, lean and limber, he could really turn the girls' heads when he got a few drinks under his belt. He won first place in the dance contests that they had many a Saturday night up at Sour Lake.

Perhaps it was the Indian blood that coursed through his veins—from both his mother's and father's lineage—that was the source of George Washington Jones's fatal flaw: his weakness for strong drink. "He was born with that on him," one of his dozen and a half or so half-siblings—a Killingsworth—recalled many years later. "I never seen a Ferris, including his mama Mary, that didn't like a good drink of whiskey. A lot of 'em drinked like a fish."

It almost seemed as if George Washington Jones had breathed in all the foul vapors of the swamp and it had festered there in his soul at times. When he drank it was almost as if he became a lightning rod for all the anger and outrage of his dispossessed ancestors that had been handed down to him through the years. The alcohol lit a raging fire of meanness in his veins that would send him reeling off on furious, violent rampages. Often, when drunk, he would fight. When he fought, no matter how drunk he was, he fought like a cornered animal. He fought with his fists, with a knife, with a hatchet or with whatever else he could lay his hands on in the heat of the moment.

Nevertheless, George Washington Jones could also be a gentle and generous man when whiskey was not percolating through his bloodstream. Even as he grew older and came to be more and more of a stranger to sobriety, his excesses could never fully conceal the basic goodness of his heart.

Clara Patterson and her sisters would often ride the three miles between their homestead and the small settlement of Thicket, on mules, to collect the mail and run other household errands. Clara first laid eyes upon George Washington Jones on one of these errands. He seemed to have a wildness about him, like the wildness of the creatures of the Thicket. That wildness was softened and subdued by his easy grin and his even easier disposition. Surely, Clara must have seen in George Washington Jones not only many of the things that her father, Uncle Litt, preached against, but also many of the things that the old man, with his harsh stoicism and Calvinistic piousness, could never be. Clara became drawn to this lean, muscular sawmill worker who seemed to merely joke, drink and fast-dance his way through life, without so much as a care in the world.

On August 14, 1915, Clara and her sister Dessel rode their mules into Thicket to get the mail, just as they so often did. Before they reached the settlement, Clara let her sister in on her secret: that she planned to elope with George Washington Jones that very night. At first, Dessel was horrified and frightened for her sister, who she knew was about to bring the awful wrath of Uncle Litt down upon her head. She pleaded with her to reconsider the recklessness of what she was about to do. Clara had made up her mind and could not be swayed. After they had arrived in Thicket, Clara sent Dessel home with both mules. She and George were married that night in a simple ceremony at the home of her older sister Elizabeth.

When Uncle Litt saw Dessel riding up the lane that evening, leading Clara's riderless mule behind her, it puzzled him. After much persuasion he succeeded in prying the truth out of Dessel. When he heard her story, it knocked the wind out of his sails so badly that he had to just stand there, numb and silent, letting his mind wrassle around with the whole thing for a long while. In the process he felt the anger slowly beginning to rise within him, and he wondered how could it have ever come to this. His favorite daughter, his pride and joy, had run off and gotten married without his blessing. Nothing like this had ever happened to him before. That, in itself, was bad enough, not to mention the fact that she'd run off with a Ferris. Uncle Litt knew the Ferrises to be a wild dancing and drinking bunch of people—not church people like the Pattersons, and surely not the kind of people he cared to get tangled up with bloodwise.

The more Uncle Litt thought about the whole mess, the more the anger boiled within him. For a long time, he swore to his other children that he would disown Clara and never let her set foot in his house again. The old man seemed so disturbed by his favorite daughter's abnegation of his stern Calvinistic realm that his other children feared that he might lose his religion altogether.

Uncle Litt had no way of knowing that the worst was yet to come. In the years yet to pass, this unsanctified marital alliance of such dramatically opposing temperaments would produce a son. And that son's own life would be riven asunder—as if by a bolt of lightning—as he, too, struggled to reconcile these opposing temperaments, both of which would come to be passed down to him through the bloodlines. This son's struggle would be far more anguished and painful than anything Uncle Litt could even imagine as he lingered that day at sunset to gaze across his fields.

After their elopement, George and Clara Jones set up housekeeping in a small rent house there in Thicket. It was one of a dozen or so such dwellings that they would call home in the following years; George would be forced to pick up stakes, time and time again, and temporarily relocate to Saratoga, "Depot Town," Daisetta, Sour Lake, Honey Island, Votaw, Rye or wherever else in the Thicket region there was logging, sawmill or oil-field work to be found.

On March 9, 1918, George and Clara's first child was born. She was a daughter and they named her Ethel. She quickly grew into a lovely child whose presence in the household seemed to bring great joy and assuage the rough beast within George Washington Jones.

Their second child, a boy named Herman, was born on February 10, 1921. On May 26, 1922, a second daughter, Helen, was born, and she would grow to possess a strength of character and stoic wisdom much like that of her mother. A few years later Clara gave birth to a set of twins, Joyce and Loyce. Soon the Jones household was overflowing of the sound of the five children's voices and laughter.

It was Ethel, the firstborn, who remained the object of George's most devout affection. He practically worshipped his oldest daughter, and worried and fretted constantly over her well-being.

For some time, Uncle Litt remained unreconciled to his daughter Clara's untimely marriage, and some of the other Pattersons still persisted in looking down their noses at George Washington Jones. Nonetheless, George, Clara and their five small children really made a go of it—for a while. The family eventually settled in Saratoga, a small sawmill town about ten miles south of the community of Thicket. George landed a good job, peddling ice for a Mr. Pickerall, who owned icehouses in Saratoga and nearby "Depot Town," where the spur of the Santa Fe Railroad stopped.

Every day, George would load Mr. Pickerall's old flatbed truck with the large blocks of ice and deliver them to sawmills, oil fields and homes from one end of Hardin County to the other. The hours were long—sometimes from three in the morning until nine at night. George Washington Jones, when sober, was a hell of a worker and a natural-born handyman and salesman to boot. He built Mr. Pickerall's ice trade up to where he was bringing enough money home himself to put a decent meal on the table for his entire family.

Ethel, the oldest daughter, was an intelligent and obedient child. At an early age, she learned to help her mama with the housework, and even to embroider her own dresses. Her father continued to dote on her. He showered her with small gifts—candy and knick-knacks. When it rained, he refused to let her walk in the dampness and would wait at the school gate to drive her home in the ice truck. Whenever he got a little bit ahead, moneywise (which was not often), he would buy her little dolls.

Good fortune continued to smile on the Jones household. Sickness, though, was an occasional visitor. Herman and Helen both suffered through bouts of malaria—a common ailment there in the swampy woodland. Once little Herman fell bedfast with a fever, and Uncle Litt came around. With the laying on of his hands, he allowed the spirit of the Holy Ghost to enter the body of his young grandson and heal him in a manner that no man-made medicine could. Standing over the boy with his eyes closed, praying fervently for quite a long time, Uncle Litt suddenly jerked his hands away from the child. "He's healed now," he quietly informed his daughter Clara. And indeed, Herman got right up from the bed and went out in the yard to play.

In the dead of winter in 1926, a dark shadow fell across the household—a shadow that would not lift for a long time. The first tendrils of its darkness were felt one day as Ethel sat quietly in the kitchen by the wood stove. Suddenly she shivered and looked up at her mother. She told her that she had a chill.

Clara, knowing that this was a danger sign, quickly wrapped her young daughter up in blankets and put her to bed. But it was already too late to turn back the darkness. Ethel developed a fever that quickly deepened into congestive chills. George Washington Jones desperately called upon the expertise of what few physicians there were in that remote region, but already his favorite daughter's condition had deteriorated to the point where no earthly power could save her. Even Uncle Litt, with the laying on of his hands, could not fend off the dark shades of death. Ethel lingered near death's door for several more days and on a Sunday afternoon, February 28, 1926, just a few days short of her ninth birthday, she quietly passed away.

Ethel's death struck such a blow against George Washington Jones that he never fully recovered. His daughter was dressed in one of the beautiful dresses that she'd embroidered herself and was carried to Phelps Cemetery, a small clearing on the edge of the thick pine forest just north of Saratoga. George and Clara placed the dolls that she loved so much in the wooden coffin of their firstborn. And as the ghost winds whispered through the branches of the tall trees, she was lowered into the cold earth, only a few yards from the grave of her maternal grandmother, Martha Ann Patterson, who'd died just three years earlier.

There was something about the sorrow of the wind in the pines and the chill of the dark earth that claimed his daughter that cold winter day that seemed also to drain the strength and hope right out of George Washington Jones. It was as if a contagion of the spirit had entered his own soul—one which, no matter how long he cried or how deeply he drank, he could not shake. It was not until years later, after the wind and the rain had begun to turn Ethel's small marble headstone gray, that he could even bring himself to return to his young daughter's grave.

From that moment forth, things seemed to go from bad to worse in the Jones household. George often would fall into dark moods. His unpredictable fits of raging intemperance seemed to seize him more and more often. Even the arrival of a second set of twin girls, Doris and Ruth, on April 10, 1928, did not lift him very long from the darkness that pulled him down.

Around this time, Hoover's Great Depression also began to cast its somber hues across the remote settlements of the Big Thicket. The timber business slacked off, along with the production in the small oil fields that had been discovered around Saratoga near the turn of the century. As the lumber and oil industry gradually played out, so did George Washington Jones's steady job with the ice company. He found himself unable to put a square meal on the table for his six surviving children, and was forced to turn his hand back to long hours of foraging in the mosquito- and snake-infested forest in order to eke out a meager living.

The Thicket was all but covered by the darkness of the Depression by 1931. The Joneses were now living in a crude log-and-slab-board shack on timber company land that George had bought from one of his uncles for next to nothing. The family had a couple of Rhode Island Red laying hens that foraged in the rough dirt yard, and George started a small garden of butter beans, okra and tomatoes on his patch of low land. A hard rain would usually come and wash it all away before the seedlings even had a chance to take root.

Some months it seemed that there was no way to keep the houseful of small children from going hungry. Clara Jones, being no stranger to hard times, knew how to get ahold of some flour and work around with it and make enough egg gravy or tomato gravy and corn bread to stave off hunger for a few more days.

As times went from bad to worse, the only means that George had to scratch up a few dollars to keep his family from starving was to take his ax and crosscut saw and sneak into the vast timberland. Most of it was now owned by outside corporations like the Kirby Lumber Company, the Houston Oil Company and the Southwest Lumber Company. In the forests, he would cut and section the tall white oak trees and sell them at the lumberyard in Saratoga, where the Slavonian artisans made barrel staves out of them.

The timber companies at first turned a blind eye to the hardwood foraging that they knew was going on in their holdings. But as more and more men turned to cutting stave wood as their only way of making ends meet, the timber companies began to crack down with a vengeance. They hired other, equally desperate woodsmen as watchmen, and they were not particularly lenient with those that they caught.

One winter night, George and a cousin-in-law, Arnold Marcontell, were a couple of miles back in the woods on Menard Creek. Working by firelight to avoid detection, they had felled and sectioned a huge white oak. Nearby on a large tarpaulin lay their uneaten dinners, along with their tools and a .22 rifle which they'd brought along to take care of any small game or snakes that they might happen across. As the two of them worked into the night, they suddenly heard, moving in their direction, the sound of men running and dogs barking in the darkness just beyond the creek bank. Realizing that the timber company's guardians had gotten wind of their nocturnal activities, they dropped their axes, plunged into the ice-cold water of the creek bed and took off running. Though they did manage to make their escape, in their haste they left everything behind, including the .22 rifle, which was worth more, in those fallow years, than a man could earn in a whole summer's wages.

At such times, George Washington Jones's household would go hungry. The younger children would cry, and Ruth would occasionally fall ill with the spasms. Fighting back tears of desperation, Clara would lie across the iron bedstead and pray. Old George, weary from his profitless endeavors, would pull out the bottle of home-brewed corn whiskey that he kept at hand. Raising it to his lips, he would drink long and hard from it, hoping to stave off the darkness which had lingered in his spirit since the death of his firstborn. The despair seemed to settle in still deeper as he watched his living children go hungry.

It was late in 1931, in the unmitigated bleakness of these times, that Clara Jones, now thirty-five years old, with the first gray harbingers of impending middle age gathering in her hair, much like the first harbingers of autumn that were beginning to gather on the East Texas landscape, fell into labor with what would be her second son and eighth and last child. On September 12, Old George took the children down the road to wait at a cousin's house, and he sent for Dr. A. W. Roark, who had delivered most all of the Jones children.

The birth of Clara's last child turned out not to be an easy birth. The baby boy was a big one, twelve pounds, and by the time the doctor finally coaxed him unwillingly from his mother's womb, his arm was broken.

As the doctor handed Clara her newborn son, to whom she would give the name George Glenn Jones, she couldn't help but notice that the first cries the child made were unusually clear and resonant —even for a Patterson, so many of whom seemed to come into this world singing. When this boy child drew his first breath and wailed in the age-old protest of the newborn, it was as if he already possessed some ancient, wordless prescience, not only of the harshness of life in this isolated corner of the world into which he'd been born, but also of all the travail that awaited him there in years to come.

As the months passed, little Glenn Jones—as the family came to call its newest addition—grew into a small but healthy child. "He had such soft brown eyes and such a big wide grin, he'd just break your heart!" recalled Katie Hodges, a neighbor lady who often babysat Clara's young brood.

Little Glenn Jones was a shy child, and his mother and his five sisters saw to it that he was pampered just a little more than most children his age. Katie Hodges would scoop him out of his mother's arms, and he would cry and cry. But directly he would calm down and she would take him and the other children down the path to the little bayou in the shadows beneath the pines. There she would hold him, and he would smile as he dangled his feet in the water and watched the older children pick mayhaws and wild blueberries and frolic in the tall canebrakes and palmettos.

Young Glenn Jones was an ordinary child in many ways except one. It soon became clear to his mama that, unlike her other six surviving children, he had within him an extraordinary measure of the soulful musical gift that had been handed down through the Patterson bloodline for so many generations. ("The little feller could carry a tune before he could even talk good," one his cousins recalled.) Clara noticed that, to her youngest son, music was like some ancient truth that he was born already knowing and that needed merely to be reawakened. When he was little more than a year old, his mama would take him on her lap on the porch swing and softly sing the old folk song "Billy Boy" to him. He amazed everyone when he learned, at his mama's command, to sing the song back to her, all the way through. As young Glenn grew a little older, he would stand up close and sway his body as he listened to the mournful old ballads, like the 1933 Carter Family song, "Give Me the Roses While I Live," which they played on their old Victrola:

> Kind words are useless when folks lie
> Cold in a narrow bed
> Don't wait till death to speak kind words
> Now should the words be said
>
> Give me the roses while I live
> Don't wait until I die
> To spread the flowers o'er my grave
> You see as you pass by . . .

And before long, he knew all the words to these songs, too. Clara still attended the White Oak Baptist Church as often as she could. On warm Sundays in the springtime, when her large brood of children often grew restless and were apt to squawk out with some ill-timed hallelujahs of their own amidst the preacher's hushed intonations, she, little Glenn and the other children would stand just outside the window, where the cry of the mockingbirds, the buzz of the mosquitoes and the smell of jasmine, honeysuckle and green pine needles filled the air. They listened and smiled warmly as Uncle Litt and the dozens of other Pattersons who now made up the congregation lifted their voices in heavenly praise.

On stiflingly hot summer nights, when it became necessary to burn pine knots and rags in the yard to hold the thick clouds of mosquitoes at bay, Uncle Litt often came by to visit his daughter Clara and her family. The old man was now gray and feeble and slow-moving in his ninth decade. He would gather the small children around and have them kneel and bow their heads in supplication as he prayed up a blue streak. It went on for hours. He quoted the Old Testament up one side and down the other deep into many a night.

Old George's mother, Mary Killingsworth would sometimes come around to visit too. She now had half a dozen grown children of her own, from her second marriage to Robert Killingsworth. She still favored her firstborn, Rollie's black-sheep son George, and she was one of the few people who could make him walk the straight line when he got off on one of his wild, drunken tears, as he so often did. Old Mary Ferris scared her little grandchildren halfway to death, because they knew if you got on her wrong side, she could be one rough old customer. She had a fierce temper; when she got started, she cussed up a blue streak and could go on just as long and fervently as Uncle Litt when he got to praying.

The Patterson sisters—who, like Clara, all had large families of their own now—would often gather on the porch of Clara's small house in "Depot Town," the small settlement just north of Saratoga where the family had moved while Glenn was still a baby. The sisters would raise their voices in a gospel fervor, just as they'd done in their younger days. They'd sing "Going Life's Way," "A Beautiful Life," "Just a Little Talk with Jesus" and the other Sacred Harp songs that Uncle Litt had taught them or they'd learned from their songbooks. Their mellifluous praises soared heavenward, over the tall pines and into the dark sky.

Little Glenn Jones, sitting there on his mother's lap, would smile as he listened to the beautiful music that the older folks made, and he would move his lips and make music of his own. Eventually, he'd fidget and climb down from his mama's lap and wander out into the yard and yank all his clothes off and go running gleefully across the road to their neighbors the Edwardses' house. Lenora or one of the other Edwards girls would later hear the telltale rattling of the latch on the garden gate. When they opened it, there would be the younger Jones boy, standing there just as naked as the day he was born, wearing nothing but that big jack-o'-lantern grin of his. The Edwards girls would smile and blush, then they'd scoop the naked little baby up in their arms and carry him back across the road to his mama.

Though there was still little work for a man like George Washington Jones to do there in the Thicket, there was no shortage of trouble for him to get himself into. The Southeast Texas oil boom had also reached its long arm back into the Big Thicket by now, and had transformed many sleepy little sawmill settlements like Saratoga into wild and woolly oil-patch boom towns.

The presence of oil around Saratoga had been common knowledge since 1867, when a farmer named Fletcher Cotton had first noticed that his hogs always returned from certain parts of the Thicket all slick and glossy. One day, he followed them to a dark, fetid bog. Some of the more enterprising local geezers, in hopes of turning a quick dollar, bottled this dark swamp extract on which their hogs seemed to grow fat. With limited success, it might be noted—they attempted to market it, to the rare tourist who strayed by, as a curative balm for everything from digestive disorders to rheumatism. But as far as these old geezers could tell, there was no other practical use for the vile black liquid.

In 1901, Spindletop, Texas's first great oil gusher, blew in near Beaumont, some thirty-five miles to the south. The codgers in the Thicket were amazed to learn of all the various uses that the New York bankers and big-city businessmen had come up with for this seemingly worthless black swamp effluvium which their hogs loved to wallow in. As word of the oil discoveries around Saratoga and in other parts of the Big Thicket spread, a whole new generation of "bad blood"—gamblers, whores, oil diviners, speculators, rough-necks, drunkards and other forms of human excrement—quickly descended upon the region. The quiet fields where the hogs had once peacefully wallowed were soon lined with tall wooden oil derricks, and the muddy streets of Saratoga were sweet with the smell of pine sawdust, horseshit and crude petroleum, as temporary houses, slab-board saloons and fleabag hotels were hastily erected to accommodate this new wave of oil-field scum.

For this oil-field rabble, and for the woodsmen like George Washington Jones, the freedom to get drunk and raise hell and get in a fight on a Saturday night, down at joints like the Woodsmen's Dance Hall or Arthur Mormon's Tavern, was considered almost a God-given right—right up there with wife beating and rooster fighting. On many a weekend, after he'd laid in some groceries for his family, that's just what Old George did: raise hell.

If George Washington Jones didn't get too drunk before he got around to fighting, he could usually give his opponents a pretty good run for their money with his fists. Sometimes his antagonists— other woodsmen who frequented those shabby dance halls and beer joints, and who were fired by their own whiskey meanness—would merely bide their time. They knew Old George's fatal flaw only too well. They knew if they waited long enough, he'd end up dog drunk, staggering and reeling around in the muddy street, making a spectacle of himself. It was then and only then that they could jump him and give him a hell of a whaling.

One bastard that Old George got in a tangle with once tricked him by making him think he wanted to shake hands and bury the hatchet. They shook hands all right, but once the bastard had ahold of Old George's right hand, he used his free hand to break his nose.

Another time, some loudmouth oil-field roughneck got into it with Old George and popped him over the head with a claw hammer so hard he had to get stitches. But what goes round, comes round: later the same loudmouth got into it with another feller and ended up getting his head laid open with a fatal blow from an ax blade.

When Old George just got too hard to handle, what little law there was around Saratoga would see to it that he was chained to one of the telegraph poles in the middle of town along with the other wild and unmanageable drunks. Most nights he would stagger down the side streets, hoping to make it back home after a long night of hell raising. One very cold night, he didn't make it that far. A friend found him passed out, covered with bruises, lying in a ditch full of filthy, freezing water. The man who found him knew George to be a good man, despite the demons in him, so he threw him over his shoulder like a sack of potatoes and carried him home to Clara and his family.

There were other times when George Washington Jones, having drunk up the whole week's worth of grocery money, would make it home on his feet still full of whiskey and meanness. The children would shiver in their iron bedsteads as he came down the road singing "More Pretty Girls Than One" (a song, popularized by the Arthur Smith Trio in 1936, which was one of his favorites) at the top of his raspy, whiskey-soaked voice. Ranting and raving like a crazy man, he would violently throw open the front door, nearly tearing it from its rusty hinges. Cursing, hollering and blaspheming, he would break furniture and throw things around. He'd roust his wife and small children up out of their beds and raise his hand against them and sometimes slap them.

The next morning, with the first sunlight beginning to show wanly through the windows, little Glenn Jones and the other children would gather quietly around the kitchen table while Clara would hurriedly deliver a hushed blessing over the meager breakfast of cabbage, corn bread and egg gravy that she'd prepared for them. Directly, Old George would stir from bed and, holding his aching head in his hands, make his way wearily into the kitchen to warm his ravaged and bruised body by the kitchen stove. As they slowly lifted their forks to their mouths, little Glenn and his sisters and brother would warily follow his movements with their baleful eyes. Old George would blink his own tired, bloodshot eyes in the harshness of the morning light; and yawn and smile wanly at his little children. Only then would they know that, for a while at least, the storm had passed.

There were also happier times in the Jones household. In 1938 the family got its first radio, a big, crude-looking battery-operated machine. To the Jones children, this was a wondrous invention—one that brought all sorts of new music to this remote corner of the world. It brought in Cajun music from KVOL in Lafayette and from stations just across the Sabine River in southern Louisiana. It brought in the traditional mountain folk and gospel songs of the Carter Family ("Keep on the Sunny Side," "Wildwood Flower" and "Maple on the Hill"), who were then performing regularly on XERA, the powerful 100,000-watt border station in Villa Acuña, Mexico.

The most special occasion of all, though, was on Saturday night, when the Grand Ole Opry, the world-famous country music radio show, was broadcast live from Nashville. In thousands of isolated settlements like Saratoga, all across the Depression-torn South, the Opry was like a ray of bright light that rode through the night skies on a 50,000-watt clear-channel beam, and—even if only for a few fleeting hours—lifted away the harsh dreariness of the lives of those backwoods people who listened.

It was a rare Saturday night, indeed, when the Jones family did not gather around their radio to listen to this popular show. "We'd go out and water the [radio] antenna real good, and then I'd crawl in bed between Mama and Daddy, and we'd hear the Opry on that old radio we had," Glenn Jones recalled years later. "I'd tell Mama, 'If I fall asleep before Roy Acuff or Bill Monroe comes on, be sure an' wake me up!'"

The music that little Glenn Jones and his family heard on the Grand Ole Opry, though new to them, had a familiar ring to it. Much of it was the eerie, lonesome fiddle, guitar and mandolin music of the Appalachian hill people, the people of old Frank Jones: the Scotch, Irish and English settlers who the century before had stayed behind in the hills and hollows of the Carolinas, Virginias and other states of the Old South while their more restless kinfolk had rolled westward in their wagons to the newly opened territories, like East Texas. This was the strident, "high lonesome" music of the Kentucky-born Monroe Brothers, Charlie and Bill (the latter of whom, with his innovative mandolin and vocal stylizations, would in the mid-1940s forge a new music of his own, called bluegrass).

It was the music of Roy Acuff that really stirred something special in Glenn Jones and would come to have the most abiding influence on him. Acuff, who hailed from the mountains of eastern Tennessee, would, in the 1940s, become the first major national singing star to launch a career from the stage of the Grand Ole Opry. Backed by the Smoky Mountain Boys, a traditional mountain string band, Acuff sang songs that echoed the haunting melodies and dark moods of the old sacred hymns and Elizabethan and mountain-style ballads: songs like "The Great Speckled Bird" (a metaphysical sort of song, written by the Reverend Guy Smith, which quickly became a favorite in the Pentecostal Holiness churches after it was released in 1936), "The Great Judgment Morning" and "The Wabash Cannonball."

Young Glenn Jones could tell that when Roy Acuff—a man he would soon grow to idolize—sang a song, he was really sold on it. In the midst of singing a particularly mournful ballad, Acuff's gruff voice would occasionally break into a sob and he would shed tears right there on the Opry stage, in the middle of a live broadcast. It was as if some deep pain was festering in his soul, and this was the only way he could get it out. Such a heartfelt display of conviction and raw emotion impressed little George Glenn no end. Sometimes he would stand on the porches of the various small slab-board shacks that his family called home and he'd pretend those porches were the stage of the Grand Ole Opry, and that his mama's broom was a guitar, and that he was Roy Acuff.

Glenn Jones grew into a solitary child, small for his age, and slightly spoiled, due to the abundance of female attention that was lavished on him by his five older sisters. "It seemed like he was in a dream world," his oldest sister, Helen, recalled years later. "He'd sit by himself for hours. He didn't have much to do with nobody."

His formal education began at a small brick schoolhouse in Saratoga. From the beginning, he did not take particularly well to book learning. "My first year in school earned me a report card with an F in every single subject, and an F in conduct, which was as bad as you can get," he recalled with gleeful laughter some years later. "We didn't care much for learning."

Whenever he could get away with it, George Glenn preferred to play hooky from school and sneak off into the pine forest, where the birds and the squirrels were his only companions. One of his uncles or cousins would occasionally come riding on a mule through some secluded spot in the Thicket, and there he'd find the small boy standing alone, atop a huge log, singing his heart out in the wilderness.

Within the four frail walls of the various small rent houses that the Jones family called home there, within spitting distance of the decadent and mean streets of Saratoga, Clara Jones always did her best to maintain her own small bastion of Uncle Litt's stern Calvinism. Uncle Litt was gone now, having passed on to his final reward on December 18, 1935. He had been laid to rest up in Phelps Cemetery, beside his wife and his long-dead granddaughter, Ethel.

The old man's death merely seemed to inspire Clara to work that much harder to keep his religion alive. Through the years, rouge or eye paint had never defiled her face and strong drink had never touched her lips. Faithfully, she taught her own children all the

Holiness songs and prayers that her father and his father before him had taught to their children.

Since the timber companies had cracked down on the stave-wood cutting, Old George had found himself a new means of livelihood; it was of a kind that made it increasingly difficult for his wife to maintain a sanctified household. Old George had begun bootlegging—making corn whiskey and homemade beer—which was a common enough occupation there in the Thicket. He first launched this new enterprise merely as a means of assuaging his own considerable thirst, but soon his whiskey making had blossomed into a healthy cottage industry with a steady supply of regular customers.

During the long winter nights, while George Washington Jones was bottling his home brew, his children would build a bonfire in the backyard and gather around it to sing Uncle Litt's Holiness songs or play hide-'n'-seek in the dark. Sometimes, when the moon went behind the clouds, they'd fall to telling "ghosty" stories about the phantoms and unapprehended murderers who were said to stalk the depths of the Thicket by night, and about the mysterious lights on the old "Ghost Road" that ran up to Bragg, which were believed to be the anguished souls of murdered slaves.

After the children had been tucked into bed and the dim coal-oil lamps had been extinguished, other "ghosty" things would go on, right there in the Jones household. ("Growin' up back there in Hardin County, we didn't need to go to no scary movies, honey!" George's older sister Ruth recalled. "Because back in them days, we *lived* through it!") The children would see eerie shadows steal across the moonlit yard late at night. They'd hear strange voices, loud, angry, accusatory, the sounds of which came floating through the open windows stirred them from their slumber. These were the voices of men coming to steal Old George's liquor. Such dark nights, the door latch would rattle violently, and the children would scurry from the window where they'd been standing with their noses pressed against the glass. Then they'd jump back into bed and pull the covers over their heads and shiver with fear until the strange voices were heard no more.

Such goings-on would induce what little law there was there in Hardin County to undertake a feeble campaign to restrain the illicit whiskey trade. It was then that George Washington Jones would be forced to hide out in the Thicket for days at a time. But sooner or later things would cool down, and he'd be back in Saratoga and in business again.

Even with that little bit of spare change that was coming in from the corn liquor, the hard times persisted in the Jones household. What little money George did make from selling his whiskey he usually ended up taking down to Saratoga, where he pissed it away, buying himself some good store-bought whiskey. Having drunk all that up, he would once again jump feet first into the boom-town frenzy of the crude cafés and saloons along the muddy main street of the rude settlement.

At harvest time, George Washington Jones would often load his large family into his old truck and drive some ninety miles north to visit his father, Rollie, on his farm near Crockett. George and his older children would help Rollie bring in his cotton crop and tend his cattle. In the evening, they all would gather around in the parlor, and Jennie Frances Jones, Rollie's second wife, would speak at great length of the wondrous change that had come into her and her husband's lives. She recalled how, in 1926, the Reverend Scott E. Sharp, with his "Oneness" movement of the free Pentecostal faith, came through town, preaching of the sinfulness of slow dancing, cigarette smoking, hard liquor and moving-picture shows. Jennie recalled for her stepson's family how she had fallen under the spell of the Oneness. She had been a devout Christian woman even before that, but she had also been a sickly woman, with a whole cabinetful of medicine. After going to the altar at Brother Sharp's revival and receiving the Spirit of the Holy Ghost, she went back home and threw away all her medicine and let the Lord heal her body, as no earthly medicine could.

Jennie—or "Mother Jones," as her friends and fellow parishioners were fond of calling her—had, with Rollie's taciturn approval, begun devoting her life to the Oneness crusade. Each Sunday, she would walk three miles to church and three miles back home again, and she traveled throughout East Texas, praying for people through the power of the Holy Spirit. "Mother Jones" knew her place, and she knew that a woman should never profane the altar by calling herself a preacher. Even so, people got hungry to hear the Word of God, and when the Spirit moved her, she would not hesitate to go before the congregation, testifying in strange tongues and singing her praises to the Lord.

Rollie Jones was an old man now; age was beginning to gather in his face. He seemed to dwell more and more in the past, deeper in his own thoughts. He repeatedly talked about the misty past, about his father, Frank Jones, and his valor during the great Confederate War at the Hogpen Incident.

Rollie knew that his black-sheep son, George, worked hard when he worked, just as he knew that he drank hard when he drank, which, perhaps, was as it should be. He also knew that the drinking part of his oldest son's life was slowly but surely taking over the working part. Rollie knew, firsthand, that strong drink could be a net that even a sturdy man—let alone a weak man, like his oldest son—could get himself tangled up in to the point where he could never get loose again. Not only had he been tangled up in it himself in his younger days, but he'd also seen at least one of his other sons—from his second marriage—get pretty tangled up in it, too. Rollie talked to George Washington Jones about this, about this weakness in the bloodline; and Old George, as he scratched his head and blinked and grinned that wide, lopsided grin of his, seemed to listen. He'd go home to Saratoga and straighten himself up for a while, but then, sooner or later, he'd go out and get him some more whiskey and get himself all messed up again.

In 1941, George Washington Jones moved his large family to Kountze, another small, rugged sawmill community, some twenty miles west of Saratoga. He found steady work nearby, helping to cut down and haul away some of the last stands of virgin pine left in the Thicket.

The county seat of Hardin County, Kountze was named after two New York bankers who enriched themselves by reducing the thousands of surrounding acres of majestic trees to pulpwood and two-by-fours. It is a place so far-flung from the centers of world affairs that, even in more recent years, the lawn of the county courthouse was adorned with barbed wire to keep stray hogs and cattle from grazing there. The town's only paper, the Kountze *News,* even proclaimed with perverse pride on its masthead: "We're not the gateway to anything."

In Kountze, as the storm clouds of World War II gathered on distant horizons, the Jones family took up residence in another small rent house, near Williford Road, in the sawmill section of the small town.

George Glenn Jones had, by now, developed into a handsome, towheaded ten-year-old boy whose preternatural musical talent and remarkably clear tenor voice seemed to grow more pronounced with each passing day. He now knew all the words to those Roy Acuff and Bill Monroe songs that he heard so often on the Grand Ole Opry radio show each Saturday night, and he walked around his yard and up and down the dirt roads singing them at the top of his lungs. He produced his own accompaniments by beating loudly on one of his mama's tin cake pans.

One quiet evening, his older brother, Herman, who'd recently married, brought his new bride, Evalina, home to visit the family. As they were walking toward the house, they saw little Glenn playing out in the dusty road. When the boy saw them, he smiled and waved and came running over to where they stood.

"Guess what!" he told Evalina, with that wide-eyed jack-o'-lantern grin of his glowing beneath the dust and dirt that was caked on his face.

"What, child?" Evalina smiled softly as she humored the boy's guileless but endearing enthusiasm.

"I'm gonna be on the Grand Ole Opry someday!"

"Oh my! Well, that's wonderful, child!" She smiled again as she sighed gently to herself, knowing as she did that in hard times like these, dreaming came easy for a small boy, especially since dreams were about all there really was to hold on to.

In addition to his burgeoning musical talents, George Glenn Jones was also beginning to display more than his fair share of boyish orneriness. On the trips that he made with his family to the big city of Beaumont, some twenty miles to the south, he delighted in pointing at the strange ladies that they passed on the downtown sidewalks, leading them to believe that their petticoats were showing or that something else in their physical presence was in disarray. He laughed outrageously at his own antics and embarrassed the fire out of his older sisters.

The countryside there in Hardin County—like the rest of the nation—had still not shaken itself loose from the throes of the Great Depression. George Glenn knew that when Herman was away at work, his wife, Evalina, was frightened half to death by the hoboes who jumped off the trains that came down the Santa Fe main line that ran through Kountze just behind her house. They would come and knock on her door in search of handouts. George Glenn would sneak around back and beat on her door and rattle the latch until Evalina, who was standing inside, would nearly pass out from fear. Then he would let loose with that mischievous laugh of his, and she'd figure out who it was, and it would make her so mad she'd want to strangle him.

It was in Kountze that George Glenn met Brother Burl and Sister Annie Stephens, a husband and wife whose Christian evangelism and love for Holiness music became a pillar of strength in his life for years to come. The Joneses first met the Stephenses when they began attending the small nondenominational church that the couple had founded in Kountze. The Stephenses took to the Joneses the first time the family walked into their humble wooden chapel. Brother Burl and Sister Annie grew to love Clara, with her quiet Christian devotion, and they could also see the basic goodness in Old George's spirit, despite the man's weaknesses, which were many.

It was George Glenn, with that marvelous voice of his, that wide-eyed grin and his easygoing ways, who really seemed to capture their hearts, though. With Old George and Clara's encouragement, the boy began joining Brother Burl and Sister Annie at the singing revivals that they held every Saturday in front of the H&H Store, there in Kountze. The Stephenses, along with George Glenn and a handful of other neighborhood children, would sometimes sing all day. Traveling in Brother Burl's station wagon, they carried their street revival from one end of Hardin County to the other. On the sidewalks and in store fronts of hamlets like Votaw, Sour Lake, Silsbee and Honey Island, George Glenn and the other children sang for all those who gathered to listen and pray.

"Glenn just sang lovely," Sister Annie recalled with a warm smile. "The child was such a novelty: so little, with such a great big, wonderful voice. People sometimes blocked the sidewalks to hear him. We had some other children who were good, but really, there was no one compared to him."

George Glenn was still small for his age. Much of the shyness he'd shown as a small boy had given way to a more gregarious and fun-loving nature. Sister Annie noticed that wherever the crowd was gathered was where he loved to be. She also noticed that even though he wasn't book-smart, he was sharp in a much more practical sense. There didn't seem to be any kind of a jam that, once he'd gotten himself into, he couldn't figure out some way to work himself back out of again.

It took George Glenn no time at all to pick up anything that had to do with music: you could sing a song to him, and even if he'd never heard it before, he could practically turn around and sing it right back to you. One day, George Glenn came by the Stephenses' house after he'd been to a tent revival show where the preacher had played familiar Holiness tunes by tapping out their tunes on various-sized bottles full of water, which sounded similar to a piano. The preacher's performance had intrigued George Glenn. He gathered up a bunch of different-sized bottles of his own and filled them with water and fiddled around with them there in the backyard until he got to where he could halfway play a tune on them himself.

Once, George Glenn accompanied the Stephenses to a gospel singing at the Methodist church there in Hardin County, where the preacher was trying to encourage the children to join his music classes and learn to read "shape notes." The preacher, who had heard Glenn Jones sing, figured that he would use the little boy as a sort of example to make his case. He pointed out, for all those gathered, just what a good singer the boy was, but how useless it was for him to have such a talent when he didn't develop it with some formal musical training. Naturally, it upset George Glenn to be called to the attention of the congregation in such an underhanded way. It made Brother Burl and Sister Annie pretty hot under the collar, too. Later that day, they gave the boy a pep talk, and told him how it really didn't matter what that preacher had said. They believed that by the time those folks back at the Methodist church had gotten around to learning all their silly shape notes, George Glenn would already be on his way with his singing: on his way to places that they never even dreamed about.

When Grandma Mary Killingsworth came and stayed with her oldest son's family there in Kountze, Clara always welcomed her. She was about the only person left alive who could talk to Old George and straighten him out when he got on one of his wild drinking binges. There seemed to be little else that could restrain the rough beasts that strong drink unleashed in him, except perhaps for the pleasing sound of his youngest son's singing.

Many a moonlit night, as the frogs croaked in the bayous out beneath the tall pines and the mosquitoes buzzed in the darkness,

George Glenn and his sisters would be shaken from their deep slumber in the iron bedsteads by a familiar sound: the sound of Old George coming up the lane from a long night of drinking and hell raising, singing a loud, slightly off-key rendition of Bob Wills's "Corinna, Corinna" or one of his other favorite songs off the radio. The haunting sound floated through the window on the still night air, causing the children to tremble beneath the sheets. Directly, they'd hear the front door slam like a clap of thunder, and Old George, with malevolence in his eyes and whiskey on his breath, would come storming and cursing into the room. Waving his thick leather belt, he would yank his youngest son out of bed and push him outside onto the porch. With a sharp slap of the belt to his son's backside, he'd then holler at him: "Goddamnit, *sing!*"

Tears flowed down the boy's sleep-swollen eyes, bewildered and saddened as he was by this sudden and harsh incursion into the peaceful world of dreams. He would hesitate, thinking, perhaps, with slight embarrassment of the neighbors who slept nearby, in the darkness just behind their own open windows. As if he were seeking some heavenly reprieve from his mortal confusion, he would look up at the cloudless night sky where Orion the Hunter and all the other stars and constellations of the southern skies shone above him, like unblinking eyes. The belt would again land on his backside: "I said *sing*, goddamnit!"

With tears streaming down his face, the boy would sing. His voice would soar and tremble with the gospel fervor of Uncle Litt's prayers and Holiness music as he sang the mournful secular songs of Roy Acuff and Bill Monroe, which Old George particularly loved to hear. But there was yet a new edge in his voice as he sang these songs: the fiercely repressed yet clearly discernible timbre of tearful outrage and anger over the helplessness of his predicament—outrage and anger which he could not otherwise vent. Old George would sit down on the porch and eventually nod out in an alcoholic stupor. When he did, his son tried to ease away from him. But then, his father would stir and begin applying his belt again. Deep into the night, the terrible caterwauling—the confused troubled sound of Old George's hollering and his son's tearful singing—would continue. The frogs would fall silent in the bayous, the neighbors would toss and turn fitfully in their beds, and the stars above would shine on, like cold, all-seeing eyes, silent and unblinking.

Chapter Two

COIN OF THE REALM

The port city of Beaumont (which is connected to the Gulf of Mexico by the thirty-mile-long Neches Ship Channel) was, until the dawn of World War II, little more than a rowdy, backwater lumber and oil-boom town. (The name means "Beautiful Mountain"; the city's average elevation above sea level is twenty-four feet.) Until the turn of the century, special horse-drawn "mud sleds" were, in the rainy seasons, the only effective means of navigating the otherwise impassable streets, and until the mid-1950s, the Ku Klux Klan ticket routinely swept local elections.

In 1941, Franklin D. Roosevelt signed the Lend-Lease Act into law, and the wheels of the nation's war machine began to turn anew. In the course of the next two years, hordes of Depression-ravaged outlanders began flocking haphazardly seaward to fill the thousands of jobs that opened up in Beaumont's shipbuilding and petrochemical industries. The city's population soon burgeoned from 59,000 to 80,000. Soon, the narrow oak- and magnolia-shaded streets were filled to overflowing, and the town's primitive public facilities were stretched far beyond the breaking point.

In 1942, George Washington Jones gathered his family together and left the quiet Hardin County countryside behind and joined in this massive urban migration. In Beaumont, Old George found work as a $1.20-an-hour pipefitter among the 10,000 men and women who now toiled at the Pennsylvania Shipyard, on the Neches Ship Channel. He moved Clara and his children into a small, cramped living unit at Multimax Village, a large one-story, wooden government housing project that had been hastily erected in downtown Beaumont to accommodate the vast influx of uprooted and homeless day laborers. (Beaumont's more well-heeled citizenry had already begun referring to it disdainfully as "Multiply Village.")

The four frail walls of the Jones family's small apartment at Multimax did little to shield them from the noise, strife and unrest of the six hundred other poor-white families who'd also found temporary shelter there. Nor did these thin walls shut out the maelstrom of change that was now swirling like a cyclone through the entire city. Almost overnight, dozens of rowdy dance halls, beer joints and gambling houses had sprung up around the downtown area—establishments that offered a wide array of earthly delights on which men like George Washington Jones could gleefully squander their hard-earned wages while assuaging their cultural shock, here in the midst of this overcrowded and teeming urban environment. The city's whorehouses (one of which operated for a long time just across the street from the Chamber of Commerce) began doing a thriving "white envelope" business with City Hall.

As Beaumont's population continued to grow by such haphazard leaps and bounds, tension in the housing projects and crowded downtown streets continued to mount. In June 1943, they finally exploded. The result was a massive wave of race riots, and before the city was finally shut down by martial law imposed by the 18th Battalion of the Texas State Guard, there were at least three (reported) killings (of blacks) and 206 arrests.

Amidst this seething urban cauldron, a world away from the familiar wilds of the Big Thicket, the Jones family quickly settled into a predictable, if somewhat uneasy routine, as Old George worked hard and put in his hours in behalf of the war effort.

On March 2, 1943, his mother, Mary, passed away in her sleep. Later, when Old George showed up at his mama's funeral at the

Pace Funeral Home in Livingston, Texas, he was so paralyzed with grief and hard liquor that he could hardly walk. He infuriated the rest of the family when, in the midst of the services, he struggled to his feet and interrupted the preacher's eulogy with a few drunken, off-the-cuff remembrances of his own. After the services, as her drink-benumbed son looked on, Mary was laid to rest in the Saratoga City Cemetery, a rough clearing in the undergrowth within the shadows of the oil derricks, where the Thicket's swampy soil quickly reclaimed its dead.

Mary Killingsworth's death seemed to knock all the strength out of her black-sheep son, and sent him reeling still further down the pathway of dissolution that he was already so steadfastly on. On Friday nights now, he would be drawn, like a moth to a flame, to the seedy beer joints and red-light establishments down near the waterfront on Sabine Pass Avenue, or closer to the center of town, along Crockett and Calder streets. Before many a night was over, all the money from his freshly cashed paycheck would be pissed away and he would be found sprawled unconscious on some sidewalk in a wayward part of town. The police would haul him off to the drunk tank at the city jail until he sobered up. Then, they would turn him loose the next day and see no more of him, until the next time he got stumble-down drunk and they would have to haul him back yet again.

Some nights, though, Old George would make it home after the beer joints closed at 2 A.M. There, a familiar scene would be reenacted. He'd explode with uncontrollable anger, as if he were railing against the very firmament above him and the very ravelments of destiny which had ordained him to such a sorry lot in life. After rousting his family out of bed, he'd apply his belt to his youngest son's backside, calling for a song.

If and when George's older sisters heard the old man coming in time, they would hurriedly rush their baby brother out through the back door or help him wriggle through the bedroom window and out of harm's way. They finally came to realize that when the old man was drinking, his youngest son was better off out of his sight.

When Old George and some of his friends or co-workers gathered in the small living room, laughing and drinking, such an escape would not be possible. Without warning, Old George would suddenly have a hankering for some entertainment. Towering over his small eleven-year-old son, he would clap his hands and stomp out a rough beat with his foot and order the boy to tap-dance for him. Glenn Jones would look shyly into the cold, jeering faces of the strangers and he would turn away and cry. Old George's eyes would narrow with anger, and he would once again command his son to dance. The boy would finally comply, sadly jerking and flailing his small body around in the middle of the floor, like an organ grinder's trained monkey. It was then that Old George and the drunks would raise their glasses and laugh with glee.

Drunk or sober, George Washington Jones was, by now, fully aware of the prodigious musical abilities that his youngest son possessed, and in his own backhanded way, he encouraged the boy with his singing as much as anybody did. When his youngest son celebrated his eleventh birthday, he'd even managed to set aside enough money to buy him something that he'd been aching for for a long time: a small, three-quarter-sized Gene Autry guitar. When George Glenn held the guitar in his hands for the very first time, he gingerly plucked the strings and felt the pleasant sounds they made resonate and tingle through his body and the familiar wide grin spread across his face, bigger than ever before.

On one of the family's frequent visits back to Kountze, George Glenn took the guitar with him, and Sister Annie showed him the few chords that she knew how to play on the instrument. Later, back at Multimax, one of his older cousins, Arnold Marcontell, who also worked at the shipyard, began stopping by the house and teaching him more chords. Before long, the boy got to where he could accompany himself while singing the old 1929 Carter Family song "I Am Thinking Tonight of My Blue Eyes."

From then on, there was no stopping the boy. The guitar seldom left his hands. Before long, he'd learned to accompany himself when he sang the Roy Acuff and Bill Monroe songs that he loved so much. When Sister Annie saw him again, only a few weeks later, she was amazed to see that he could already play the small instrument better than she could.

One overcast morning, when the stench of the oil refineries hung heavy in the saltwater breezes, George Washington Jones awoke after a typically long, drunken night. Though his head and body still ached from the previous night's revelry, he could already feel the demons in his blood screaming out for renewed sustenance. Turning his pockets inside out, he came to the hazy conclusion that he'd spent all his money the night before, though he could not really remember. He tried, for a while, to fall back to sleep, but the demons would not let him. He gazed listlessly out the window at the people who passed by in the courtyard beneath the cloudy skies. Through the dimness and fog of his consciousness, he saw George Glenn's little guitar lying there in the corner of the room, and felt the germ of an idea beginning to take shape. He took a small tin cup from the kitchen and called for his son.

"Git your gih-tar and come with me," he ordered him.

The boy, dressed in a cheap cotton shirt and baggy hand-me-down blue jeans with the legs rolled up, picked up the little guitar and sheepishly followed his father out into the streets. They walked southward for several blocks, and stopped when they got to the crowded bus stop on Lucas Avenue. Old George nudged the boy gently in the direction of the crowd.

"Go on, now," he muttered softly, "sing!"

George Glenn's mouth fell open. He looked with frightened eyes at the cold faces of the strangers. Then he looked down fearfully at his own scuffed shoe tops, as if waiting to see if the feet inside them might suddenly take off running of their own accord. Old George nudged him again, more insistently this time. He tentatively strummed a chord on his guitar and began singing a familiar Roy Acuff song. As he listened to himself sing, through the thick, veiled numbness of his own fear, his own voice sounded weak and faraway, and its frail timbres seemed destined to fade to nothingness in the vacuum of the strangers' cold indifference. Still, he continued to sing, and much to his surprise, he could feel a stir of recognition and silent approval rustle through the crowd like a soft breeze. People who'd been reading their newspapers or talking with their friends paused and looked in his direction. As they listened, the boy could see the coldness in their faces starting to melt into warm pleasance. One smiled, then so did another. For the truth was that many of these people there at the bus stop, though they were now in city clothes, were really backcountry people, just like the Joneses. They recognized in the soulful resonances of this little boy's great big voice all the feelings that they knew to be true in their own hearts. They heard the Holiness fervor of the Pattersons echoing down across the generations; they heard traces of the eerie Christian mysticism of Uncle Litt's laying on of hands, and of the dark ghostiness of the Thicket; they heard the anguished mountain soulfulness of Roy Acuff, mixed as it was with the cutting edge of outrage and pain of the child thrust far too early into a world of strangers. Moreover, they heard the abiding mournfulness and the sadness— the sadness for which they had no name. The people smiled and patted the boy's head and they tossed more coins into the tin cup.

From the sidelines, George Washington Jones silently took all this in. He listened to each clatter of metal against metal until he calculated that the sum of the coins in the cup was equal to the cost—plus tariffs—of a bottle of cheap wine. Leaving a few stray coins for his son, he scooped the money up and headed down the street, with a shit-eating grin on his face, toward the liquor store. George Glenn shyly took his own leave and headed back up the street toward home. He felt peculiar. He felt elated, yet, at the same time, strangely sad—just as he would feel many, many more times later in his life, after he'd poured out his raw emotions for a crowd of strangers, like he'd done that day on the street corner.

But these coins in his pocket . . . He knew that there had been reward, palpable enough, in the smiles on the faces of the strangers . . . But these coins . . . They brought a whole new dimension of satisfaction to his efforts that he could not put into words.

A few days later, George Glenn picked up the tin cup and his guitar again, leaving the house alone this time, and made his way, with uncertainty, back toward the crowded downtown streets. He was nervous and rather unsure that such a marvelous scene as that which had unfolded a few days before at the bus stop could really ever come to pass again.

He stopped near a shoeshine stand this time, put out his cup and started singing. Once again, he was amazed at how soon the strangers' cold faces lit into smiles, and how quickly the coins began hitting the cup, like the steady sound of rain on a tin roof. With each clatter of the silver, little George Glenn reached deeper into his heart and sang louder, sang for all he was worth. He sang the familiar Roy Acuff songs, like "The Precious Jewel" and "The Wabash Cannonball." He sang all the Bill Monroe songs that he knew. He sang "You Are My Sunshine" (a song that was popularized in the 1940s by both Bing Crosby and Louisiana's singing governor, Jimmie Davis), and he sang "My Wild Irish Rose" (an old pre-World War I Tin Pan Alley song). He sang and sang, until his throat was hoarse and he could sing no more. Only then did he stop to count the coins. He was amazed to find twenty-four dollars—not only more money than he'd ever held in his hand before, but more money than he thought there was in the whole world. Triumphant, he headed back down the street with his pockets bulging and an ear-to-ear grin spread across his face. He stopped off at Fuller's Café and bought himself a lunch for thirty-five cents, and played the pinball machine there until they finally ran him off for being under-age. He headed down the street and bought ice-cream cones, candy bars and sodas for himself, whiling away the rest of the afternoon in the penny arcade. His pockets were once again empty by the end of the day. He reasoned, better to spend it this way than to take it home and have Old George get his hands on it; besides, it really didn't matter: he knew now that there was more where that came from.

Now that he understood that his music was his cachet—his key to the coin of the realm—George Glenn Jones, with his little guitar and his baggy, rolled-up blue jeans, became a familiar sight on the Beaumont streets. When he wasn't playing for money, he'd hang around the house and cut up and sing until his mama ran him off. He'd go down to the fire hall sometimes and sing and cut up and carry on for the firemen until they finally chased him away, too. It seemed a carefree life. Every now and then, though, some of his cousins from the Big Thicket—many of whom had also come to the city in heed of the call of the Great War Machine—would see him in his baggy blue jeans, all alone on the street corners. They couldn't help but notice how sad and lonesome he sometimes looked, sing-ing his heart out for the nickels and dimes of the strangers.

With this new dimension in his life, George Glenn now realized he had no further use for the needless abstractions of book learning. Once in a while, he would be coerced into putting in a full day at Dick Dowling Junior High School, but most mornings, even if he did bother to put in a brief appearance in the classroom, he'd merely wander off at lunchtime to sing, pick his guitar, play pinball or while away the hours at the picture shows down on Calder Avenue.

Another new game of George Glenn's was to climb aboard one of the many crosstown buses that passed through the downtown area. Most of the lady bus drivers knew him by sight, and they no longer demanded any fare of him, other than the privilege of hearing his marvelous voice. Standing in the back of the bus, he gladly obliged them, and he would ride back and forth, from one end of the line to the other, singing at the top of his lungs for the drivers and their passengers.

After the young prodigal singer had spent two years in the seventh grade without passing, he had no further trouble convincing his mama of the futility of requiring him to continue with the profitless formalities of higher education.

The year 1947 found George Glenn Jones come of age. He had now grown to his full size of five feet seven inches and 140 pounds, and no longer was he willing to suffer the brunt of his daddy's drunken whims and erratic cantankerous moods. Safe in the knowledge that he could always find a square meal and a sofa to sleep on at one of his older sisters' households, he began spending less and less time at home.

One day he was back at George Washington Jones and Clara's house; the old man, who was pretty deep into the juice that afternoon, started raising hell and heaving lengths of stove wood at him. In the face of this affront, the prodigal singer hurried out the door, without looking back; he did not stop until he'd arrived in Jasper, a small town about sixty miles north of Beaumont. He knew a boy in Jasper named Clyde Stephens, whose family owned a sawmill out on Highway 63, and he also knew that the Stephenses were usually good for a free meal and a place to stay.

It was Clyde Stephens who told George about Dalton Henderson, another local boy, about George's own age, who sang and played guitar. Dalton (who in later years would work with the Bailes Brothers and other country bands on the Louisiana Hayride up in Shreveport) and his sister, Wanda, sometimes sang on an early morning radio show on the local station, KTXJ, which broadcast from the second floor of the Texas Theatre there in Jasper. George Glenn was impressed by this, and decided it was high time that he got himself on the radio as well. At lunchtime one day he got Clyde to take him down to the schoolhouse and introduce him to Dalton.

Young Dalton soon had a chance to hear George Glenn sing, and though he was loath to admit it, he knew that this new kid in town could sing circles around him. He also saw that George Glenn could play some pretty remarkable lead runs on the guitar as well. George Glenn explained to Dalton as to how he also was a big fan of Harry Choates, the Louisiana Cajun fiddler who'd become a regional celebrity the year before with his original version of "Jole Blon." (After a short and wildly ill-starred life, Choates was laid to rest at the age of twenty-eight in a pauper's grave in Port Arthur. He had allegedly been beaten to death in an Austin jail while being held on charges of wife and child desertion.) Dalton could see that this was true from the way his new friend could saw out "Jole Blon" and other Cajun standards on a fiddle.

George Glenn explained to Dalton a few days later that the few possessions he'd brought with him from Beaumont in a cardboard box were now being held under lock and key at a local rooming house there in Jasper. The prodigal singer had stayed a couple of nights and failed to pay his rent and needed some money. Hearing this, Dalton quickly went home to his father and borrowed some money to ransom his friend's belongings. Then he invited George Glenn to move in with his own family.

For the next few months, George Glenn became a familiar fixture in the Henderson household. He'd stay for a few days or a few weeks, then he'd head off somewhere else—though he seldom said where. Then, sooner or later, he'd turn up on their doorstep again, with a big grin on his face and a big hug for "Ma Henderson," as he came to call Dalton's mother. Mrs. Henderson soon grew fond of the wayward boy, who—she couldn't help but notice—seemed as though he no longer had a home of his own.

George began singing with Dalton on KTXJ for a few dollars a week. The two of them would hitchhike the forty miles or so down to Silsbee, back in Hardin County, and play for tips in beer joints like the Log Cabin and Richard Reeves's Redtop Drive-In down along Highway 96. On Sunday evenings, they would perform at the little talent show that was held down at Lockhart's Café in Jasper.

Though the Hendersons were poor folks caught up in the same hard times as everyone in that part of the country, Myrtie Henderson, Dalton's mother, looked after George just like he was one of her own. She fed him, and while he lay in bed every morning with the covers pulled tightly around him, she would wash and iron the one cotton shirt and one pair of blue jeans that he had to his name. For these services, she'd put him to work in the garden digging her potatoes.

"Maw Henderson," he'd complain to her in his deep-voiced East Texas brogue, as he paused to brush away the sweat and push the long strands of brown hair back from his brow, "I sure don't like this here dirt under my fingernails!"

"You can wash that dirt off later, boy!" she'd scold him good-naturedly. "Just get after them 'taters."

Those in the Henderson household gradually began to notice that beneath the still surface of his easygoing demeanor, George Glenn could sometimes, without warning, be subject to moods and spells that could be as changing and unpredictable as the patterns of thick cumulus clouds that drifted northward from the Gulf across the wide Texas skies. For little or no reason at all, the fiery glint of anger would blaze in those close-set eyes of his, and it would take forever to get him calmed down again.

"He always seemed to be doin' somethin' to aggravate some-body," Myrtie Henderson recalled, laughing with warm affection at the antics of the wayward singer. "One time Dalton had this electric guitar with an amplifier, and George had done something to it, and Dalton slapped him over the head with another guitar he had. I had to take the broom to both of them to break 'em up.

"We had this real old woman stayin' with us that we called Aunt Maude—though she wasn't kin to us," Mrs. Henderson added, "and George was always pickin' at her. She was in her seventies and in real bad health, and she'd lost most of her hair. But he'd throw his arms around her and say, 'Let's dance, Aunt Maude!' or 'C'mon, Aunt Maude, let me curl your hair!'

"My husband, Bronson, would tell George to sit down and behave himself when he got like that," Mrs. Henderson continued, "and George would get mad then and go in the bedroom and pout. One time, I followed him in there and turned the light on, and he was just poundin' the bed with his fists and buttin' his head against the pillers. He was tryin' his best to get rid of that temper, because he knew he couldn't let it explode in our house."

Up until now, George Glenn had managed to stick pretty close to the teetotaling dictates handed down by Clara and Uncle Litt. He could see the mess that hard drink had already made out of his daddy's life. In those taverns, though, where he and Dalton played for tips, free drinks were often part of the payoff, and he could keep turning them down only for so long. For two high-strung teenagers like George and Dalton, beer and the occasional snort of whiskey were of course considered the forbidden fruits. They were just as alluring as the pool tables and the bright lights on the pinball machines.

"Sometimes, George would have a few drinks in one of those beer joints, and it would change his personality so much that it scared me," Dalton remembered. "All it took was for somebody to say something he didn't like, and he'd be ready to fight. Then he'd just fly off the handle and give everybody a good cussin' and leave."

George Glenn finally took his leave of the Henderson household. He did so with as little ceremony as he'd entered. One evening, after the family had been to the talent show down at Lockhart's Café, and George and Dalton had sung, they were all walking out to the car, to drive back home, when George abruptly told them, "Well, uh, I'm gonna be movin' along. Y'all have done helped me too much already."

"Where you gonna stay, boy?" Bronson Henderson asked the prodigal singer.

"Oh, I don't know." George Glenn shrugged and managed a weak smile. "I reckon I'll get in some back alley somewheres or somethin'."

Mr. Henderson pulled a couple of dollars from his pocket and handed them to the boy. "Don't you be layin' down in no back alley," he told him sternly. "Get yourself a room for the night."

George Glenn thanked the Hendersons and said goodbye. Then, with the little cardboard box that contained all his worldly possessions, he headed off, by himself, down the dark street. It was the last that Mrs. Henderson ever saw of him.

Among the vast multitude of backcountry folk who'd been uprooted and swept seaward like grains of sand in the great wartime urban migration were Rollie Jones and his wife, Jennie. It was in the port area of Houston, in one of the poorest and roughest sections of that great Southeast Texas city, just a few blocks from the piers along the Turning Basin, that the elder Joneses finally settled.

Rollie, whose earlier commercial ventures in Lufkin near the turn of the century had collapsed into ruin, had since prospered anew in Houston—this time, in real estate.

His wife, "Mother Jones," as always, continued to throw herself tirelessly into the never-ending business of eternal salvation. She helped found a small congregation, and as it grew, she became its cornerstone. Rollie donated a piece of the land that he owned there at 809 Daugherty Street and built his wife a small wooden church, which they called the Gospel Assembly.

During the late 1940s, George Glenn Jones often came down the highway from Beaumont, some ninety miles to the east, to visit his paternal grandfather. He would sit quietly in their small church and listen as members of the congregation became seized with the Holy Spirit and went forward to the altar to testify in tongues. He sang gospel favorites with them like "Camping in Canaan's Land" and "I Am Determined to Hold Out." During altar call, George Glenn would often be among those who fell under conviction and made their way forward to receive the Holy Ghost. He would even go before the congregation alone and share his own praises to the Lord, singing Uncle Litt's Holiness songs, which his mother Clara had taught him.

Rollie Jones, who lived with his wife in their small house, not far from the Gospel Assembly Church, was in his eighth decade now: white-haired and feeble. When he tried to speak of those faraway times—of the great Confederate War and of his father, Frank Jones, and his valor at the Hogpen Incident, he found that his memories were no longer clear, but frail and fleeting, like visions from a dream within a dream. As George Glenn listened to the old man reminiscing, he would nod his head and grin the jack-o'-lantern grin which he'd inherited from his father. He would act as if he understood the old man's confused feeble ramblings, though, in truth, to his callow, uncaring ears, they seemed of a place remote and alien: of another world, no more real than the foreign fields and battlegrounds told of in storybooks.

Having listened to old Rollie, George Glenn would once again go down the street to the Gospel Assembly Church and raise his voice in praise with the congregation and be anointed by the Spirit. He took his guitar later that evening and walked a few blocks to a little beer joint owned by his hard-drinking uncle Aaron Jones. Here and at the other little dives along McCarty Street, near the Turning Basin, he would sing and play while the burly longshoremen from the piers and the swarthy knife-wielding foreign sailors off the ships drank and cursed and threw him their coins.

Back in Beaumont around this same time George Glenn first crossed paths with Eddie and Pearl Stephens, a husband-and-wife musical team who proved to be the stepping-stone that the still underage singer needed to gain entry into the teeming world of Beaumont bars and dance halls, where the music and alcohol commingled so freely. He first met the couple when they were all set to perform one night at Playground Park, a popular open-air recreational park out on the west side of town on old Highway 90 that

George Glenn often frequented. Eddie and Pearl needed a backup guitarist. Seizing the opportunity, George Glenn offered to sit in as a substitute.

It wasn't long afterward that his duties with Eddie and Pearl were expanded into a full-time job. It not only paid fifteen dollars a week, but also afforded him free room and board in the couple's small trailer home. He was soon traveling with Eddie and Pearl to shows throughout East Texas and Louisiana, often sharing the back seat of Eddie's old car with the huge stand-up "bull" (bass) fiddle that Pearl played. He also backed the couple on the 4 P.M. radio show they had on KRIC, a small Beaumont station. He was paid an additional two dollars a week for these services.

After a long night of singing, George Glenn would often lie in bed alone in the cramped darkness of the couple's one-room trailer, trying futilely to sleep as he listened to the sounds of Eddie and Pearl tossing and turning restlessly in their own bed.

Acquaintances who knew Eddie and Pearl sometimes referred to them as an "odd couple," Eddie being smooth and good-looking and considerably younger than Pearl, who was beginning to show the wear and tear of middle age. Eddie played an acoustic Martin guitar to the accompaniment of a harmonica that he kept attached to it with a special holder, and he sang in a growling country voice that put people in mind of Ernest Tubb (a popular Texas singer who'd hit the big time when he landed a spot on Nashville's Grand Ole Opry in 1943). Pearl, with her big bull fiddle, seemed content, for the most part, to stick to the background, only occasionally coming forward to sing something like the old Wiley Walker–Gene Sullivan hit "Make Room in Your Heart for a Friend."

Eddie's own tastes were deeply rooted in the country music of the 1930s and early 1940s. He still knew how to sway a crowd with popular war-movement songs like "There's a Star-Spangled Banner Waving Somewhere" or Ernest Tubb's "Rainbow at Midnight." Just as often, he'd reach further back in time and sing a number like "Johnson's Old Gray Mule" (a folk-derived song, popularized by J. E. Mainer's Mountaineers in 1936), and he'd even make a bunch of crazy mule noises to go along with it. Every so often, he'd bring his new guitarist—"Little Glennie Boy," he called him—up to the microphone and let him warble out a tune or two of his own.

As George Glenn frequented the various and sundry Beaumont beer parlors and dance halls, he constantly kept his ears open. He could not help but notice that many different strains of music, both old and new, could now be heard in these rude establishments.

During this uneasy postwar era, Beaumont and the greater "Golden Triangle" (which the extreme southeastern Gulf Coast region, which also encompassed the nearby cities of Orange and Port Arthur, had come to be called) had gradually become a melting pot of all sorts of itinerant musicians. People of disparate tastes and dispositions were beginning to collide, interact and leave their indelible marks and fingerprints all over each other's music.

Among the dozens of singers and instrumentalists who'd gravitated to the area (in search of paying work, like everyone else) were Cajun ("Coonass") artists like Harry Choates ("Jole Blon"), Link Davis ("Big Mamou") and Huey Meaux (who would later gain notoriety as the producer of singers Freddy Fender and Doug Sahm)—all of whom had crossed the Sabine River from southern Louisiana, bringing with them their lively French-Acadian fiddle and accordion music. Numerous veterans from the groups that had earlier forged the big-band sound of Texas swing (a unique hybrid of Dixieland jazz, blues, pop, cowboy music and 1930s dance-band music) had also begun to filter into the area. Two of them were fiddle player Cliff Bruner (who played with Milton Brown and his Musical Brownies before forming his own influential Texas swing ensemble, the Texas Wanderers) and Rusty McDonald (who later, in 1950, would sing the lead vocal on Bob Wills's original recording of "Faded Love").

There were other stylists at work as well: men whose music spanned various categories without fitting neatly into any of them. There was Moon Mullican ("I'll Sail My Ship Alone"), a cantankerous old piano player whose bluesy bawdy-house style foreshadowed the work of Jerry Lee Lewis and other rockabilly artists. There was Floyd Tillman and Arlie Duff and rock-'n'-rollers like J. P. ("the Big Bopper") Richardson and many many more. They were then, most all of them (with the exception of a few, like Mullican), merely bit players in the huge transfusion of broke and hungry musicians who'd come streaming out of the hinterlands and into teeming coastal cities like Beaumont, where they proceeded to bounce haphazardly from one makeshift band to the next in rough-and-tumble sawdust-floored clubs like the Railroad Café, Shorty's on Voth Road and Yvonne's out on the Port Arthur highway.

The music that these men played had begun to echo with ever-clearer expressions of the general insecurity and turmoil which abided within them and swirled around them in this new, ever-changing environment. It was a music that spoke of the collective fears and restlessness of thousands of displaced men like George Washington Jones, men who found themselves unwillingly trapped in these new urban settings for which they cared so little. Such men had been robbed of the strong sense of place that they'd known back in the boondocks like the Big Thicket, where life—even though harsh—was at least slower, more predictable and, most important, their own. These men knew that, back up there in the country, if the thoughts swirling round in a man's brain got too dark or twisted, he could always wander back into the forests and fields, away from other men, and let these thoughts soften, until they were not thoughts anymore, but just feelings and colors that blended and flowed sweetly with the soothing sound of the water in the creeks and the wind in the trees. Here in the city, far from the fast-flowing streams and the tall pines, a man's dark confusion was merely rendered darker by the constant assault of man-made obstructions like traffic lights, time clocks and car horns. Here, the streets were filled with a multitude of strangers whose cold eyes merely confirmed and multiplied a man's solitary fears and confusion and reflected them back at him. The labor of a man's hands was no longer his own anymore, but merely an insignificant and largely expendable part of the huge centrifuge of activity around him.

There were other things for a man to worry about now, too, like black people, alcoholism and divorce, and there were wives and children who, every day, seemed to pay less and less attention to the old-time religion and country ways, while becoming increasingly obsessed with fast cars and fast dancing. All in all, it was just too much for a man to think about. Many a good man merely ended up seeking refuge on the barstools in the dives along Sabine Pass Avenue or Crockett Avenue, trying his best *not* to think about it; trying to squeeze a few hours of reckless, drunken euphoria out of the fleeting bit of freedom that existed between the Friday-after-noon punch of the time clock and the cold, nauseous hammerblows of the painful Sunday-morning hangover.

A new kind of music was born that spoke directly about the fears and worries that these men harbored silently in their hearts. This new music, which had come to be called honky-tonk, was a far cry indeed from the wholesome, otherworldly mountain-style music of

Roy Acuff or the Carter Family. Instead, this was a freshly mongrel-
ized music, bred and whelped in the sawdust and grime of the dingy
oil field, shipyard and factoryside cafés. It was hard-core, gutbucket
hillbilly music devoid of romanticism and full of bitterness, betrayal,
guilt and disillusionment; it was songs with titles like "Born to
Lose," "The Wild Side of Life," "Slippin' Around" and "Headin'
down the Wrong Highway." It was music that was played to the
raucous accompaniment of electric guitars, fiddles, steel guitars and
drums, which, when sounded in unison, created an insistent beat
that cut through the din of drunken laughter, fistfights and flying
bottles. A patron at Yvonne's Club (which today still stands, like a
forlorn ghost relic of this wild area, out in the shadows of the
elevated interstates, on the Port Arthur highway near the edge of
the salt marshes where the huge oil refineries belch fire into the
night sky) committed the faux pas of asking piano plucker Moon
Mullican to play one of the old Carter Family songs.

"Hell, no!" the mean-assed old piano player replied, looking at
the patron as if he had mild brain damage. "We gotta play music
that'll make them goddamn bottles bounce on the tables!"

George Glenn continued to perform under the wing of Eddie and
Pearl, but he was now beginning to branch out on his own occasion-
ally, testing the waters in this turbulent sea of honky-tonk music and
good times. He met another young and hungry musician named
Luther Nalley, who in later years would achieve considerable notoriety as a member of the distinguished Western singing group the
Sons of the Pioneers. Realizing that there was strength in numbers,
George and Luther soon struck an uneasy musical alliance. With
George Glenn singing and playing lead guitar and Luther contribut-
ing rhythm guitar and background vocals, they were soon earning
four or five dollars a night, plus all the free beers they could cadge,
at joints like Playground Park and the Teacup Inn on Sabine Pass
Avenue and Lola and Shorty's near the waterfront.

Luther couldn't help but notice what a formidable repertoire of
songs his new sidekick had. He saw that George Glenn could reach
back and play the old Holiness songs and other music from his
childhood, like "Maple on the Hill" (a folk-derived tune that first
appeared in sheet music in the late 1800s and was popularized by
the Carter Family in the 1920s). With equal ease, he could reach
forward in time and reel off hits of the day like Bill Monroe's "Little

Cabin on the Hill" or Merle Travis's "Divorce Me C.O.D." He could grab ahold of a fiddle and saw out ragged versions of a few popular Cajun standards. After belting out another hit of the day by Ernest Tubb (who'd come to be known as "the Texas Troubadour" and was at the center of this honky-tonk movement), he'd reach way back and deliver a serviceable rendition of an old country-blues standard from Jimmie Rodgers (an immensely influential Mississippi-born singer who died from tuberculosis in 1933 at age thirty-five).

"George was a hell of a showman back then," Luther recalled. "He'd laugh and cut up and pull monkey shines, jumping all around the stage and he'd just pick the fire outa that guitar.

"And no matter how long we played, George never held back," Luther added. "He'd always sing his heart out. A lot of times, we'd go down on the old Houston highway and play at this place called Miller's Café from noon till six. Then, when we finished there, we'd go down the road to this dancing-type place called Glenn Vista, and we'd play there till midnight. By the end of the night, George would be almost completely hoarse from singing so hard. He always kept a little bottle of cough syrup around, and every now and then he'd take a slug of that and get his voice going again, and sing some more."

As time passed, Luther and George grew to be close friends. When the weather was warm, they'd while away the hours fishing on the Neches River. The only major disagreement that the two of them seemed to have was one that arose over the music itself.

"We had fun when we played, but we did have quite a few arguments," Luther said, laughing. "See, I was not much of a country fan back then. I was into jazz, and every chance I'd get, I'd throw in some oddball chords on the rhythm guitar. Well, George just did not go for that. He liked those straight old 'vanilla' country chords, and that was it. Every time I'd start to play something else, he'd kinda turn around and look at me funny, like 'What the hell are you playin' there, anyway? Just keep it country!'"

In the years following the war, George Glenn returned to Richard Reeves's Redtop Drive-In, near Silsbee, where he and Dalton Henderson had played. He started going there regularly with V. L. Lewis, a big old Indian who sold used cars in Beaumont, and who loved to hear the boy sing while he sat there, night after night, getting drunk on the tall, long-necked twenty-five cent bottles of Falstaff beer.

Richard Reeves and his wife, Evelyn, who helped him run the bar, came to be moved by the ghostiness, the outrage and the sadness with no name which they could hear in George Glenn's voice. On a more practical level, they also could not help but notice that when George Glenn sang for the men who drank there each night in their tavern, these men seemed to drink their drinks even faster than usual and ordered more often. So they gave George Glenn a regular job, playing for tips.

George was a well-mannered-enough boy—who, despite his threadbare clothes, always kept himself fastidiously neat and clean in appearance. He would sometimes give Richard Reeves a bit of trouble, insisting on sawing on the fiddle and playing those Cajun songs, when Richard knew damn well that it was that lonesome honky-tonk music and the guitar-picking sound that made the men drink faster. When he tried to impress this fact upon George Glenn, the fire would flash in those dangerously close-set eyes of his, and he would fly off the handle and just be hell-bent on playing the fiddle that much more.

On many Sunday afternoons, George Glenn returned to Richard Reeves's Redtop Drive-In to perform with Eddie and Pearl. In warm weather, they would set up their microphones just outside the tavern, and the backcountry folks from the nearby Thicket would park their cars out along Highway 96 and sit in them and drink beer and eat barbecue and hamburgers and listen to the music.

It was becoming obvious by now, to those who bothered to notice such things, that young "Glennie Boy" was gradually beginning to eclipse the somewhat limited musical talents of his two older mentors, "the odd couple." More and more now, when the drunks waved their dollar bills and threw their quarters, it was the little "gih-tar-pickin' feller" with the great big voice that they hollered for. In the face of such popular demand, Eddie and Pearl would reluctantly bring their young guitar player forward to the microphone and let him warble out a Roy Acuff tune or an old Holiness song. Upon hearing the boy's marvelous countrified voice, some of the drunks, with their rough hands and thick whiskey breath, would come forward, and instead of putting their money in the kitty that Eddie and Pearl had set out, they would stuff their quarters and dollar bills into the boy's pockets. Eddie would watch this and say nothing—a look of dark displeasure would spread across his face.

After such performances, when the three of them had finished singing and were all gathered back in the kitchen behind the tavern, Eddie would look greedily at the money bulging in the boy's pockets. "Put that there money you got in the kitty with the rest of it, Glennie Boy," he'd order him.

A look of helpless outrage would then flicker across the boy's face and the anger in his eyes would swirl with renewed dizziness. "Hell, no!" he'd protest. "It's mine! They give this money to me, to hear *me* sing!" Then he would appeal frantically to the bar owner's wife, whom he knew to be close by: "Evelyn!" he'd holler. "You seen 'em give me that money, didn't you!?"

"Yep, I seen 'em." Evelyn would quietly address herself to Eddie, amidst the loud bickering and the sizzle of frying hamburgers: "If they'da wanted that money in the kitty, then they wouldn't have stuck it in his pockets. Let the boy keep it."

Around this same time another poor white boy, this one from rural Alabama, was beginning to rise like a dark phoenix out of the rubble of the dispossessed, and cast a long shadow across the face of country music. The boy's name was Hank Williams, and though he was just seven years older than George Glenn, he was already well on his way to becoming a legend as the first major national singing star since Roy Acuff to launch a career from the stage of Nashville's Grand Ole Opry (where he made his debut on June 11, 1949).

From the time Williams first hit the national charts, in February 1949, with a song called "Lovesick Blues," his music left an impression on George Glenn that was as profound as it was enduring. "He's my only hero but God," the prodigal singer would confess some thirty years later, long after his doomed idol was dead and buried.

George Glenn had no way of knowing it at the time, but the parallels between Williams's life and his own were uncanny. Both men had been born into the relative poverty of remote lumber settlements (where both of their fathers had, at various times, driven log trams). Both men had shaped their raw talents singing in primitive hard-shell Baptist churches and on city street corners, and both had, in their early years, fallen heavily under the musical influence of Roy Acuff. Both had fathers who were—each in his own way—

rather weak and shiftless figures. (Williams's father's "disability" was said to have resulted from shell shock he'd sustained in World War I, whereas George Washington Jones's "shell shock" seemed to come in quart and pint bottles.)

One thing that George Glenn did know for certain, though, was that those things that he heard in that troubled, plaintive voice of Williams's rang painfully true to him. In songs like "Long-Gone Lonesome Blues" and "Lost Highway," he could hear the anguish of the defeated and the dispossessed, and he could hear the abiding sadness for which he had no name—tempered as it was by the harsh realities of early death and hard times. He could hear also the dark echoes of mortal confusion, and he could hear the painful conflict of the footloose balladeer caught up in the fast-turning wheels of a worldly success which he could not come to terms with and which would eventually mangle him to death. He could hear the horrible conflict of a tortured soul caught in the act of being torn to pieces in the struggle between the corruptibility of the flesh and the harsh demands of an unappeasable Old Testament God.

Though he could not put all this into words, these things that he heard in Hank's voice moved him to no end. Still, he had no way of knowing, just then, that the seeds of this same mortal conflict were already beginning to take root in his own soul.

George Glenn's introduction to the music of Hank Williams was propitious in yet another way. Now that he was approaching his late teens, he found that his voice had dropped and that it was increasingly more difficult for him to sing comfortably in the high tenor range that was so often affected by his idols, Roy Acuff and Bill Monroe. He discovered that these new songs of Hank Williams's fit almost perfectly into his new vocal range, almost like a hand in a glove.

He had also come to realize by this time that he could save considerable wear and tear on his voice during a long night of singing in a smoke-filled bar if he occasionally backed off from his usual all-out "full throat" delivery and changed things up by singing, instead, with his mouth partially closed or even with his teeth slightly clenched. He discovered that this allowed him to dramatically bend, twist and otherwise embellish individual notes, with all the power and precision of a woodwind player. Even more important, he found that this also enabled him to hold back the full power of a melody and let it resonate eerily in his throat, giving the impression of barely controllable emotions swirling wildly around inside of him, held in fragile, temporary abeyance. When he did this, he also noticed that it not only tingled his own spine but seemed to send cold chills through all those who listened as well.

With these newfound discoveries, George Glenn set about learning every one of Hank Williams's songs just as fast as they were released. When he performed in the dingy bars and taverns, it was often these lonesome songs of Williams's that he sang all night long.

Not long after May 13, 1949, when "Wedding Bells," Hank Williams's second chart single on M-G-M Records, was released, the doomed singer himself came through Beaumont to promote his new record. It was at station KRIC, where George was doing his usual 4 P.M. show with Eddie and Pearl, that he met Williams—who, though only twenty-five years old, would be dead in just three and a half more years, leaving behind him the dark legacy of the sacrificial lamb offered up on the altar of country music.

Williams, who happened to be a friend of Neville Powell, KRIC's program director, had agreed to come by and sing his latest hit song over the air to help promote a personal appearance he was making that night out at the Blue Jean Club on the Port Arthur highway. Eddie and Pearl, along with "Glennie Boy" Jones, were called upon to serve as Williams's impromptu backup band.

As George stood behind his idol and heard the music begin, his reverence and awe faded to cold fear. "He made me mad!" he later recalled. "I wanted to kick it [the song] off [with the guitar], but he didn't let me. He just started singin' it cold. And as soon as he started singin', I was so dumbfounded that my fingers just froze to the neck of my guitar. I never even hit a lick."

After the song was over, the doomed country idol and the awestruck prodigal singer actually had a few fleeting moments to talk with one another. ("It seemed impossible," George Glenn later remembered, "like a miracle.") In his deep-voiced East Texas brogue, with his words tumbling nervously out on top of one another (as if racing to keep up with his jumbled thoughts), George Glenn quickly owned up as to how much he thought of Hank and how he sometimes played his songs all night long. Hank smiled at him, and George was amazed when he found that his idol did not talk down to him ("like some of them will do when they've had a little success"), but instead spoke to him man to man. Speaking softly, Hank explained to the boy how, when he was scratching around, trying to get his own career started, he had idolized Roy Acuff and gone around trying to sound just like him and trying to be just like him, until finally one day somebody had sat him down and pointed out to him that the people who bought records and went to shows done had one Roy Acuff, and it was doubtful that they was gonna spend their money on another one when they could have the real thing for the same price. After all this had sunk in, Hank had finally gotten wise and started concentrating on sounding more like Hank Williams.

This made sense to George Glenn, who had no way of knowing that his hero—even as he spoke to him—was already moving much too fast down a lost highway of alcohol and drugs, from which he would not return. As George Glenn shyly said his goodbyes and stood there, nervously fidgeting and shifting his weight jerkily from one foot to the other, at the end of this brief encounter (which would be their first and last), he promised that he would keep Hank's advice in mind. What he could not have fathomed, even as he stood there so awestruck that dreary afternoon, was that it was already too late: that he was already caught up in the dark Hank Williams legend, far deeper than he could ever imagine.

George Glenn was finally out on his own by late 1949. Having come out from under the wing of Eddie and Pearl, he was now a familiar face in the revolving door of the Beaumont honky-tonk scene. He'd sit in with Slim Watts, a tall, lean, pistol-toting singer who headed a jazz-influenced dance band called the Hillbilly Allstars, which headlined at the Blue Jean Club and other dance halls around the city. "It was a pretty rough atmosphere," recalled Gordon Baxter, another journeyman musician who was caught up in this same scene. "There was plenty of women and plenty of whiskey, and there were fights most every night. Guns were something that all of us had grown up with, and if anybody gave you any trouble, you just grabbed your pistol."

Among this informal and slightly bedraggled cadre of semi-starving musicians was Huey Meaux, who for a while served in a makeshift backup band for the hard-ass old piano player Moon Mullican. Mullican's band at that time also included Texas swing veteran Cliff Bruner, Bennie Barnes (another talented young singer from Beaumont who was destined to enjoy fleeting fame as a recording artist) and the prodigal singer himself.

"We played down at th coast at a little place in Gilchrist called the Gulf Inn," Meaux remembered. "It was strictly one of them 'chicken wire across the fuckin' bandstand, travel at your own risk' type of joints. George picked a little rhythm guitar and sang a little bit in that high, wailin' voice of his. Back then, he was just a happy-go-lucky cat who was just in it for the music, the beer and the broads, just like the rest of us."

It was at Playground Park, where George also played frequently, that he met the Bonvillion family, and soon found his life taking an unexpectedly serious turn. Willie Bonvillion was a French Cajun who had "crossed the river" and done well for himself there in Beaumont as a superintendent for Sargl's, a commercial paint contracting company. Willie Bonvillion was also an enthusiastic music fan, and often he brought his attractive, dark-haired daughter Dorothy along with him when he went to Playground Park to listen to the bands that performed there most nights.

Never one to be shy when it came to women, George had been captivated by Dorothy Bonvillion's good looks almost from the first time he spotted her in the crowd, and he'd wasted little time in introducing himself. As the two of them began seeing more and more of each other, they quickly fell in love, and after a brief courtship, they were united in holy matrimony. The simple ceremony was performed on June 1, 1950, by George's close family friend Brother Burl Stephens at a small guest cottage in Port Arthur, where Brother Burl and Sister Annie were holding a series of revival meetings. Since George Glenn was only eighteen, his mother Clara had to sign for him.

George Glenn's marriage to Dorothy was destined to be a bad marriage. And (like Rollie's first marriage to Mary Ferris) it lasted only about as long as it took for Dorothy to complicate matters by becoming pregnant with George Glenn's first child.

Things seemed to go smoothly enough for the two of them for a while. The young couple moved in with Dorothy's parents and set up housekeeping. Willie Bonvillion, who enjoyed his son-in-law's music immensely, bought him a fancy guitar and even made the down payment on a portable Bogen amplifier and p.a. system for him to use when he played at dances. With paternal friendliness, he encouraged him to further develop his talents—but only as a hobby.

Willie Bonvillion was much more concerned about his daughter than George's career. She had grown used to the comforts of the middle-class prosperity which he'd worked so hard to attain ever since he'd first crossed the river from Louisiana quite a few years earlier. He was rather doubtful as to whether his new son-in-law, with his honky-tonk music, could provide for her in the manner to which she'd grown accustomed. After considerable persuasion, he convinced George Glenn that he should go to work as a $1.25-an-hour apprentice for the Sargl Paint Company.

This was the first serious introduction to the somewhat grim realities of the workaday world that the prodigal singer had ever had; and he stayed with it only long enough to realize that he did not care for it at all. The painting job was dreary work—a world away from the dancing and drinking and fleshly delights of the beer halls and taverns that he'd grown to love so much. If he wasn't scraping paint off walls all day long in some dark, filthy hallway, getting dirt and plaster all in his hair and down his neck, then he was hanging off the side of the Gulf State Building or some other tall downtown edifice, dangling on a scaffold like a spider on a fragile strand of web, being buffeted by the cold coastal winds.

Affairs at home in the Bonvillion household weren't getting any more pleasurable either. His new in-laws seemed intent upon taking over every aspect of his life and transforming him into some paragon of nine-to-five, middle-class respectability that he knew he could never be. When he came home at night, it was not Dorothy, but her mother who greeted him at the door. And Mrs. Bonvillion never tired of reminding her son-in-law that she did not care to have her daughter, who was a teetotaler, hanging around those seamy Port Arthur highway beer joints that he still frequented by night.

In a futile attempt to escape this grinding and insistent familial pressure, George Glenn moved Dorothy into a small apartment nearby. They weren't there long before Dorothy informed him that, seeing as how she had never done any cooking or dishwashing before she married him, she didn't intend to start now. It wasn't long before the young couple ended up back at her parents' house again.

There was also a certain unease between the rest of the Jones family and the Bonvillions. The Joneses, being the proud backcountry people that they were, did not care a whit for the Bonvillions' "highfalutin" middle-class ways. One day, George Glenn's sister

Ruth was talking with her brother and his new bride. Ruth said something smart to Dorothy, and Dorothy said something smart back to Ruth. By dint of the Jones blood flowing so wildly through his veins, George was filled suddenly with the unappeased ancestral fury of the dispossessed and unvanquished. The anger swam dizzily in his close-set eyes, and he raised his hand and slapped his insolent young wife.

It wasn't long before George had had about all he could stand of the painter's apprentice job, and he gladly left it behind. For a short time he had a job driving a 7-Up truck, and then for a little while he even had a job in a funeral parlor. But one day, when he went with his boss to pick up a dead woman, and the man told him to pull the dead lady's drawers off, he knew he'd had as much of that job as he could take, too. From here on out, if he could arrange it, it would be music all the way.

By May, 1951, less than a year after their wedding day, George and Dorothy had separated. Soon, Willie Bonvillion and his daughter went to court and brought their wrath down upon George, and for the first of what would prove to be many times, he came to realize that the long arm of the law could reach farther and hit harder than George Washington Jones ever could. On July 23, 1951, Dorothy, now six months pregnant, filed for divorce in the District Court of Jefferson County, charging that her husband was "a man of violent temper and is addicted to the drinking of alcoholic beverages, and has threatened [his wife] with physical violence and harm."

Dorothy's petition was eventually granted, and her ex-husband was ordered to pay her $35 a week in support money, along with an additional $466 in medical expenses relating to the impending birth of their child. On July 27, George Glenn was further enjoined by the court to refrain from "bothering, molesting or in any way interfering with" his ex-wife.

On August 24, the estranged father-to-be, having failed to pay these sums levied against him, was held in contempt of court and ordered to jail, where he languished for five long and hot days before his family was able to bail him out. Having again fallen woefully behind in his payments, on September 28 he was imprisoned once more. On October 28, amidst all this acrimony and litigation, his first child, a daughter, Susan, was born.

George Glenn's family was soon able to regain his freedom. But even so, even he could see that this most unpleasant series of events was merely bound to repeat itself if he did not find some means of escape from this terrible mess he'd unwittingly gotten himself into. Acting upon the District Court judge's recommendation that it was perhaps as opportune a time as any for patriotism, the prodigal singer headed for the local armed forces recruiting station. On November 16, 1951, George Glenn Jones marched off as U.S. Marine Corps Private #1223231 to serve his country, which was now entrenched in mortal combat in the far-flung fields of Korea.

After the prodigal singer, now twenty years old, arrived in California to serve out his two-year tour of duty Stateside, he wasted little time in throwing himself into the small but thriving country music scene that had, by then, sprung up on the West Coast.

He completed his basic training at the San Diego Marine Corps Recruit Depot, and was then assigned to the Moffett Field Naval Air Station in San Jose. Like many of the other crew-cut "jarhead" enlistees, George Glenn would occasionally return from weekend liberties all hung over and skinned and bruised from his impromptu, off-duty efforts at defending the honor of the Marine Corps. His patriotic efforts also pulled him a few stretches in the brig.

Usually, though, when he went AWOL ("over the hill") or committed some other minor infraction, it was for the higher cause of country music. He occasionally appeared on Cliffie Stone's "Hometown Jamboree," a live music and entertainment show broadcast on station KXLA in Los Angeles, which featured other up-and-coming young artists of the day, like Buck Owens.

While in California, George Glenn also hooked up with two influential West Coast disk jockeys, "Cottonseed" Clark and Cliff "Cactus Jack" Johnson. These two local impresarios soon put him to work singing at dances, auctions, grocery-store openings and other low-key events (where he usually performed in his brown Marine uniform), billing him as "Little Georgie Jones, the Forrester Hill Flash."

When George Glenn returned home on leave, to Vidor, he brought with him a robust, smiling, dark-haired young woman whom he introduced to his family as "my wife." After he returned to the West Coast, George Glenn spoke of her no more, and the Jones family never saw or heard of her again.

On the national music scene at the time, yet another ill-starred phoenix had risen up from obscurity and come to dominate the country record charts. His name was William Orville ("Lefty") Frizzell, and he was a former amateur boxer only four years older than George. Like George, Frizzell had also emerged from the Texas oil fields and the rough-and-tumble Southeast Texas honky-tonk music scene. If there were any lingering doubts about whether the rest of the country could enjoy the hard-core strains of the modern honky-tonk sound, which was already so popular in Texas and the southwestern United States, Frizzell dispelled them: in October 1951, four of his single releases—"Always Late," "Mom and Dad's Waltz," "Travelin' Blues" and "I Want to Be with You Always"—landed simultaneously in the country top ten, a feat accomplished by no other country artist since. (And if there were any lingering doubts about the toll that such success could exact on a wayward Texas singer, Frizzell would help dispel that, too, when in 1975, after too many years of women problems and looking at the world through the bottom of a whiskey glass, he died of a massive stroke at age forty-seven.)

As this new phoenix was rising, in the early 1950s, another was about to fall. On New Year's Day, 1953, Hank Williams, who was not yet thirty years old, finally reached the end of his long, dark highway. He died lying comatose on the back seat of his Cadillac convertible—the victim of a fatal mixture of vodka and chloral hydrate—while being driven to a concert in Canton, Ohio. On January 4, 20,000 people gathered in Montgomery, Alabama, for his funeral (which was a bizarre mixture of grief, voyeurism and pageantry, the likes of which would not be seen in the South again until 1977, when Elvis Presley was laid to rest amidst truckloads of guitar-shaped wreaths, garish floral arrangements and legions of grieving fans, many of whom wore brightly colored T-shirts bearing "the King's" graven image).

Those who gathered at Williams's funeral not only mourned his return to the Alabama dirt from which he'd risen, but without knowing it, they were also celebrating the subsequent ascendance of his legacy as country music's dark archangel of despair. For Williams's influence, as a singer and songwriter and as a shadowy, mythic presence, was soon destined to unfurl, blossom and become far greater in death than it had been in life. (*Downbeat*, the prominent jazz magazine, in late 1953 named him "Most Popular Country

Artist of All Time.") For decades to come, his ill-starred legacy
would hover over George Glenn Jones and all of country music like
a dark apparition.

As George Glenn reflected on Hank's passing, he must have also
pondered the changing of the guard that had taken place in his own
family. On May 13, 1951, old Rollie Jones had passed on to his final
reward, and laid to rest with him were many of his tales of the Old
Confederacy and the Hogpen Incident.

It was only a short time later that George Washington Jones was
hurriedly summoned to Houston, where, in return for a small cash
settlement, he was asked to relinquish all further claims to his father's estate. Old George hastily signed the papers laid before him
and took the handful of cash money and ran with it. It was something that none of the Joneses gave much more thought to at the
time.

In November 1953, George Glenn once again returned to Beaumont and civilian life. He had already read many of the rags-to-
riches stories in the fan magazines about Hank and Lefty, and he
figured that it was about time for him to get on with making some
records of his own. Though Beaumont was, decidedly, not the recording capital of the Western world, he started looking around
there nonetheless. Surprisingly, as fate would have it, he did not
have to look very far at all, because a man named Jack Starnes, who
was familiar with his talents, was already looking for him.

Starnes was a local Southeast Texas wheeler-dealer who favored
diamond rings, long cigars and big shiny cars. Operating on the
assumption that if you can *spell* the word "manager," then you can
paint it on a sign and hang it out and become one, he had hustled his
way into the hurly-burly Beaumont music scene. For a short time,
before the two of them parted ways in a flurry of lawsuits and
accusations, he had even managed Lefty Frizzell's career.

Starnes, along with another Texas businessman, formed a
fledgling record label they called Starday in the spring of 1953. By
the time George was back in civilian duds, the label had already
released sixteen singles on various artists, some of which had even
garnered favorable write-ups in *Billboard,* the leading national music
trade magazine.

Since the founding of Starday Records, Starnes's home and the
café that he and his wife operated right next door to it, on Voth

Road, about a dozen miles north of Beaumont, had become a center for local music activity. Starnes had purchased a couple of portable Magnacorder recording machines and used them to fashion the back porch of his house into a small makeshift studio. He tacked egg crates to the walls to baffle the sound.

In Starnes's crude back-porch studio, in January 1954, George made his rather inauspicious debut as a recording artist. The backup musicians on these first sessions were from a group called the Western Cherokees, which, until his split from Starnes, had served as Lefty Frizzell's road band.

The five songs that George hurriedly recorded in Starnes's studio that first day included several that he'd written himself. One of them was called "No Money in This Deal," a lively tune with a slightly skewered set of lyrics and a jaunty but unmemorable melody. The song was more than a little reminiscent of Lefty Frizzell's 1950 hit, "If You've Got the Money, I've Got the Time," and the whimsical, almost gentle inflections that George brought to it echoed with a similarly heavy-handed Frizzell influence.

Also on hand that day on Starnes's back porch was another local musician, Gordon Baxter. Like George, Baxter was another fringe character from the local Beaumont music scene who had a fistful of original songs and vivid dreams of a big-time recording career.

"I had had a session at Starnes's earlier that day," Baxter remembered. "It was my first session, and as it turned out, it was also my last. It went very badly. See, I had never heard my own voice on tape before, and when Jack [Starnes] played it back, it sounded so awful I got mad and accused him of letting the tape drag. But it turned out it was me. I realized that day, for the first time, that I was completely tone-deaf. And that was the end of the line, as far as my dreams of being a singer were concerned.

"So I just kinda said, 'Aw shit!' and I leaned up against a wall, sort of in a somber mood," he continued. "There was this young, scrawny scrap of a kid who'd just been sitting back there all this time and hadn't said a word. He wore a flattop, and his eyes were so big and so close together that they kind of looked like you were looking into a big double-barreled shotgun—only when you did look into them, you kinda got the impression there was not much going on in there. But then he came up to the microphone and went up on his tiptoes and began to sing, and I was just amazed! I could hear a clarity and beauty in his voice that just gave me chill bumps."

As Baxter stood there listening to George, he couldn't help but figure that despite his obvious talents, this nothing kid who seemed to be from the backwoods probably didn't have a snowball's chance in hell of making it very far beyond the egg-crate walls of this little jerkwater upcountry studio. After all, the way Baxter looked at it, people already had all the singing stars they needed: they had Webb Pierce and Lefty Frizzell, Ernest Tubb, Roy Acuff, Eddie Arnold and Red Sovine . . . They didn't really need any more. Even so, this kid sure as hell could sing his ass off, though—no doubt about that. When Baxter looked down and saw the kid's name, George Jones, embroidered across the back of his belt, he made a point of remembering it. After all, you could never tell about these things . . .

For George himself, the mere fact that he'd even gotten as far as Jack Starnes's back porch was proof enough that he was now on the right track. It was not long after that when Luther Nalley ran into his former barroom singing partner in downtown Beaumont, and George enthusiastically related to him the events that had transpired out at Starnes's house. Then he proudly showed Luther his newest and most prized possession: a light blue 1949 Packard. All along one side of the big automobile, he'd had painted in bold yellow letters: GEORGE JONES, STARDAY RECORDING ARTIST. As George showed off his brand-new used car, Luther couldn't help but notice that that big, jack-o'-lantern grin of his was now spread wider across his face than he'd ever seen it before.

Chapter Three

HOUSTON AND NASHVILLE: UP THE LOST HIGHWAY

In Southeast Texas in the early 1950s, all roads led to Houston. The teeming port metropolis some ninety miles west of Beaumont was growing so rapidly from the spoils of the cattle, oil and shipping industries that it was practically bursting at the seams. If you came down the pike to Houston with music on your mind, the man you went to see was Harold W. ("Pappy") Daily. A droll, poker-faced, cigar-smoking entrepreneur from Yoakum, Texas, Daily had spent fourteen years working for the Southern Pacific Railroad before using $250 in borrowed capital to venture into the coin machine and jukebox business in 1933. As the years passed, he had slowly built himself a small empire by virtually cornering the market on juke-boxes, wholesale and retail record distribution and music publishing in the Houston area. (Willie Nelson's "Night Life" and "Family Bible" were merely two of the valuable copyrights he later managed to acquire.)

After an unsuccessful bid for a seat in the Texas legislature ("I got my ass kicked; it was the best thing that ever happened to me"), Daily expanded his enterprises and investments still further until they also included the Houston Jamboree, a Grand Ole Opry-style country music show that featured local talent and was broadcast over KNUZ every Saturday night from the stage of the downtown city auditorium. Having served as a regional distributor and producer for national record labels like M-G-M and Four Star, he had joined forces with Jack Starnes in 1952 and formed the fledgling Starday label. ("Star" for Starnes and "day" for Daily.)

A few weeks after George's first recording session in Beaumont, Starnes brought his new artist down the pike to meet Pappy Daily and to have him record some additional material in another make-shift studio (which also had egg crates on the wall) that Bill Quinn, an associate of Pappy's, had fashioned in the living room of his home at 5628 Brock Street in Houston.

Pappy Daily was a shrewd, hard-driving but honest businessman who was, at heart, as puritanical in his hard country tastes as George was. He was a man who knew how to exact his pound of flesh without drawing blood—and who ultimately won not only the respect but also the affection of the many artists with whom he worked.

The first time they met, Pappy and George stood for a long time there in Bill Quinn's living-room studio sizing each other up. Pappy had already listened to the tapes that his partner had made with the young singer earlier, back in Beaumont, and he was not—to say the least—overwhelmed. True, George did strike Pappy as one of the best *imitators* that he'd ever heard—he was like a damn parrot almost. He could mimic Acuff or Lefty or Hank or Jimmie Skinner or just about anybody you asked him to. Still, as Pappy listened to him record additional material there in Bill Quinn's studio, he couldn't help but wonder if, underneath all those layers of imitations and heavy-handed influences, the kid even had a singing style of his own.

Pappy stood there puffing his cigar. He mulled all this over with what, by appearances at least, seemed to be no more than a mild interest. "Well, kid," he droned in his disarmingly dry, nasal manner, "we've heard ya sing like Roy Acuff, we've heard ya sing like Lefty Frizzell and we've heard ya sing like Hank Williams. Now, can ya stand there and sing like George Jones for me?"

George scratched his head awkwardly, shifted his weight jerkily from one foot to the other and seemed to consider this for a moment. "I dunno." He shrugged uneasily as a shy, thin smile spread out beneath his short, upturned nose. "I don't reckon I ever tried too much. I don't reckon people would much care about hearin' it if I did, would they?"

"Hell," Pappy replied, unaware that he was echoing the advice that Hank Williams had given the boy just a few years earlier, "if you *can* sing like George Jones, then you better sure as hell do it! People sure as hell don't wanta pay to hear nobody that sounds like somebody else!"

Beneath his cold, stone-faced assessment of George's talents, Pappy—almost in spite of himself—could feel himself warming to this guileless, wide-eyed kid from the East Texas boondocks. "I eventually got to where I loved him like one of my own sons," Pappy later recalled. "He was just a damn good boy—the best kid I ever knew. He was the most generous person I ever met. Money didn't mean a damn thing to him. The only time he ever bothered anybody was when he was drinkin'."

Though neither Pappy nor George realized it that day, this first wary encounter between the two of them was the beginning of a friendship and professional association which would survive numerous trials by fire and endure for nineteen years.

In February 1954, "No Money in This Deal," one of the first songs that George had recorded in Starnes's Beaumont porch studio, was released as Starday #130 (the fledgling company's thirtieth single release). On the B side was "You're in My Heart," another original song that he'd recorded during that first rushed session in Beaumont. Like practically all of the twenty-nine Starday single releases that had preceded it, "No Money in This Deal" failed to make a showing in the national charts. Pappy, in fact, made little effort to promote the record beyond the rather limited south-central Texas domain where his own distribution network held sway (and through which he could usually unload enough copies of all his records to recoup the meager recording costs and eventually turn a modest profit). Nonetheless, George's first single did end up selling nearly

9,000 copies and even received passing mention in the review section of *Billboard*'s March 6 edition, which, without giving even scant mention of the vocal performance, called it "a lively country novelty" with "a good catch phrase."

During the next few months, Pappy and George made numerous return visits to Bill Quinn's small studio, where the cost of recording was minimal and the many technical limitations were overcome only by dint of the musicians' sheer enthusiasm. "The place was held together with chewing gum," laughed Don Pierce, Starday's promotion man, who became a partner in the label in 1954, after Jack Starnes decided to sell his one-third interest for the princely sum of $7,500. "There was egg cartons on the wall, just one microphone that hung down from the wooden ceiling beams, and usually Eddie Noack or some songwriter would be passed out on the front lawn. The control room was just another room in the house, and Bill couldn't see the musicians from in there. So he'd flip a light on, and that was their signal to start playing. The session musicians were paid about five dollars a side [song]—there were no unions down there in those days—and everything was pretty much done in one take."

Each time George emerged from the small studio, Pappy would listen intently to the new tapes. But try as he might, he still could hear nothing in George's voice that really set him apart from the dozens of other Acuff-Williams-Frizzell imitators who were now crawling out of the woodwork from every whichaway, trying to get a deal on his label. Pappy's uncertainty was not mollified by the fact that all their follow-up singles to "No Money in This Deal"— "Wrong About You," "Let Him Know," "You All Goodnight" (early records which prompted one *Billboard* reviewer, in late 1954, to categorize George as a singer "directly from the Hank Williams school")—had merely gotten lost in the shuffle, along with the dozen or so other singles Pappy was now releasing each month on Starday's various artists. "I didn't think too much of George back then," Pappy admitted. "We did have quite a bit of trouble establishing him as an artist."

Of the several dozen other struggling artists who were now signed to Starday, Pappy and Don Pierce considered their real ace in the hole to be Sonny Burns. Burns was a big, burly, frog-voiced singer from Nacogdoches, the land of old Frank Jones. It was Sonny's records that sold best on a regional level, and it was Sonny who—at six feet two inches, with his hair pomaded as dramatically as high tide at Waikiki—had the powerful stage presence and fine singing style that drew the loudest applause down on the Houston Jamboree each Saturday night. (Sonny further endeared himself to his local following when he took the vows of his first, short-lived marriage there on the stage of the City Auditorium during a Saturday-night broadcast on May 22, 1954.) "We really did consider Sonny to be our number one shot," Don Pierce recalled. "We always had advance orders on his records. In fact, they outsold George's by a mile."

When George had returned from the Marines, back in late 1953, Sonny had already begun recording, both for the small HJA label in Houston and also for Jack Starnes's back-porch Starday operation in Beaumont. It was at Starnes's house on Voth Road where the two of them met in early 1954. Sonny had also been booking live appearances through Starnes. On one particular occasion, Starnes had (inadvertently or otherwise) booked his house band, the Western Cherokees, into two different clubs in two different states on the same night. It was Sonny that Starnes called upon to pull together a makeshift band and fill in for the Cherokees at one of the two shows, in Lawton, Oklahoma. Among the ragged crew of local musicians that Starnes hurriedly rounded up for Sonny to take with him to Oklahoma was George, who was so fresh from the Marines he was still wearing his khaki uniform.

In Lawton that night, George, without even trying, greatly impressed Sonny with his talents. The two of them soon became constant companions, traveling together to the two-bit bookings that Starnes was able to set up for them all across East Texas and Louisiana.

Despite George's obvious musical gifts, Sonny could see that his new sidekick (who stood almost half a head shorter than he did) was, for the most part, carefree and really without much sense of direction: just pretty much willing to go along whichever way the wind blew strongest. Sonny began to gradually take him under his wing, doing his best to see that whenever he got twenty or twenty-five dollars a night as a front man, his little sidekick got at least ten or fifteen.

Sonny—who was himself as notoriously impulsive and hardheaded a young honky-tonk singer as you were likely to find in all of

East Texas—also began to impress upon his new friend one of the more deleterious pleasures of the flesh for which he'd developed a particular fondness: raw whiskey.

"Sad to say, I'm the one who got George started drinkin' hard," Sonny insisted (despite ample evidence to the contrary). "Though it sure ain't nothin' I'm proud of. Back then, I thought it was about half smart to get drunk and carry on, and I always hated like hell to drink alone."

In Sonny's big, beat-up old 1947 Buick, the two of them would go roaring out across the flat sun-drenched prairies, on their way to yet another nickel-and-dime club date. Directly, Sonny would pull out a bottle he always kept under the seat or in the glove compartment. After taking a healthy slug for himself, he would then thrust it in George's face. "C'mon, son!" he'd snarl. "If you're gonna ride with me, then you're sure as hell gonna drink with me!"

George, who was more accustomed to the smooth and subtle way beer snuck up and kicked him in the ass when he drank too many bottles of it, hesitated at first. Sonny would wave the bottle in his face one more time. Finally George gulped down a big mouthful of the 100-proof and shuddered. His close-set shotgun eyes danced dizzily in their wide sockets. Sonny, steering the car with one hand as they careened down the narrow ribbon of bumpy highway, would then grab the bottle back, take another snort and then thrust it under George's nose once again.

"Sometimes he'd get sick and I'd have to pull over to the side of the road and he'd throw up," Sonny recalled ruefully. "Then we'd get back in the car and we'd get rollin' again, and I'd hand him the bottle and make him take another drink. It ain't nothin' to brag about, but that's the way it was."

Under Sonny's seasoned guidance, George also began to find his way around the thriving country music club scene that then existed in Houston. George was more delighted than surprised to discover that Houston, too, was yet another wild-ass town in a wild-ass era, with a musical scene that was bigger but otherwise not really much different from the one in which he'd come of age back in Beaumont. Along with Sonny, he plunged feet first into the myriad of whiskey-drinking and skirt-chasing pleasures that the teeming port city had to offer. They soon were busy playing, for ten dollars a night and free drinks, in joints like the Plantation Club, Bob's Tavern or the NCO Club at Fort Polk. They could almost always pick up a few

dollars more singing at Magnolia Gardens, a big open-air place out
to the east of town. They even managed to grab a few minutes on the
bandstand at the Grand Prize Jamboree, which was broadcast from
Eagle Hall on station KPRC, or at Cook's Hoe-Down, a huge downtown dance hall where stars of the day like Ernest Tubb and Bob
Wills routinely drew crowds of several thousand.

George's and Sonny's real home away from home, though, was
Amma Dee's, a sawdust-on-the-floor dive on Canal Street, not far
from Sonny's small apartment, which he often shared with George.
"That was an awful place, just a hell of a place," Sonny recalled, his
voice full of warm nostalgia. "Every time you turned around, it was
gettin' closed up for some kinda fightin' or shootin' or codes viola-
tion, till finally the liquor control board shut it down for good.

"Ole Amma Dee. Bless her heart." Sonny smiled. "She was a
rough-lookin' ole customer, but she was as good as gold to us. We'd
drink there and play there sometimes. When we was busted—which
was most of the time—she'd always lend us some money. Back then,
we never sat still long enough to buy records, much less a record
player. We could always con one of the barmaids there into playin' a
single on the jukebox over and over for free, until we could scribble
down all the words and learn to sing it ourselves."

George continued to impress Sonny with his carefree and easygoing ways. ("He was kind of a meek little feller, really.") Occasionally
it would startle him to see how easily raw whiskey or emotional
tension could unleash a more malevolent side of his character—
such as it did one night when, after singing on the Houston Jamboree, the two of them, who'd been drinking heavily, rounded up a
couple of girls and headed out to a motel on the Beaumont highway,
not far from old Rollie's church and Uncle Aaron's beer joint. "We
had gotten adjoining rooms and me and the gal I was with were
fixin' to do our thing," Sonny remembered. "Then, all the sudden, I
heard this bloodcurdling scream through the wall. The girl that
George was with was comin' unglued. Turned out, he wanted to get
it on and she didn't, and he got all upset and wasn't going to take no
for an answer. I was afraid that if they didn't settle down, we'd have
the law on all of us. So I just called the whole thing off and we all
went on home."

In order to supplement his meager income from his music and also
to help promote the club appearances he continued to make in

Beaumont, where he was still living, George landed a spot as a disk jockey on KTRM, which was then Beaumont's leading country station. KTRM, which broadcast from the second floor of the downtown South Coast Life Building, was a place to which many local musicians gravitated; they were drawn there not only by a sense of camaraderie but also by the prospect of increased public exposure via the airwaves. Slim Watts, who headed the Hillbilly Allstars, had a show there, as did Gordon Baxter (who, after abandoning his dreams of a recording career, would later go on to distinguish himself as an author, daredevil pilot, Vietnam correspondent and local radio personality). Another regular there at KTRM, whom George would eventually befriend and even write a few songs with, was a young Southeast Texan named J. P. Richardson. Under the pseudonym of "the Big Bopper" (and also under the production and career guidance of Pappy Daily), Richardson would later achieve fleeting fame with the song "Chantilly Lace" before having his life and career cut tragically short by the same February 1959 air disaster that also claimed the life of singer Buddy Holly.

Despite the iron-handed reign of KTRM's station manager, Jack Neal (who once used the chrome-plated .357 magnum he kept in his desk to single-handedly veto a majority vote by the station's other stockholders to oust him), the atmosphere at KTRM was light-hearted, and often riotous. "We did all kinds of tricks on each other," Gordon Baxter recalled. "We'd set off alarm clocks during each other's newscasts, or maybe nineteen alarm clocks. We'd turn a cat loose in the studio, then turn loose a whole bunch of coon dogs. Somebody even brought a police motorcycle up the stairs one day and turned all the lights and sirens on in the middle of a newscast."

George more than enjoyed this aspect of life at the station. He even ran a contest over the air whereby listeners could win themselves a free record if they guessed his age correctly. (Few did, since on account of his deep voice and the chronic hoarseness that nagged him from his long hours of singing, he already sounded old beyond his years.) Overall, though, he did not particularly distinguish himself as an air personality. "I'd start one of them seventy-eight [rpm] records goin'," he later recalled, "and I would be so damn nervous I'd let the needle go plumb across the record and scratch it all up."

"He just couldn't seem to grasp the equipment," recalled Slim Watts, who helped break George in on a fifty-five-minute afternoon

The small log-and-slab-board cabin in Saratoga, Texas, where George Glenn Jones drew his first breath on September 12, 1931. The Jones family lived in many such humble dwellings but moved frequently, from one sawmill or oil-field settlement to the next, wherever George Washington Jones could find paying work. The cabin has since been moved a short distance from its original location and reassembled on a nearby farm. More recently, Jones has considered purchasing the cabin and having it reconstructed in Jones Country, his music and recreation park.

Jones's parents, George Washington Jones and Clara Patterson Jones, married in 1915, raised seven children and lived to celebrate their fiftieth wedding anniversary. Shown here during a peaceful moment in their long, strife-ridden marriage, they pose in front of one of their domiciles, near the Big Thicket in Southeast Texas.

(Circa 1945) George Glenn Jones, with rolled-up blue jeans and a minia-
ture guitar, sings for spare change on a Beaumont street. Once the
prodigal singer discovered that his music was the key to the coin of the
realm, he became a constant figure on Beaumont's downtown corners
and sidewalks. His surprising discovery that money could be made singing brought his formal education effectively to an end. He left school in
the seventh grade, never to return.

ABOVE A recent photo of Richard Reeves's Redtop Drive-In, now Evelyn's Tavern, an old haunt of George's located on old Highway 96 near Silsbee, Texas. In the first few years after World War II, George gave some of his earliest solo performances here. He would often sing, play his guitar and fiddle for tips from the beer-swilling woodsmen and farmers who frequented the tavern. He also performed here on many Sundays in the late 1940s as a guitarist and occasional backup vocalist for the husband-and-wife duet Eddie and Pearl.

RIGHT (Circa 1947) George playing for tips and free beers at Lola and Shorty's, a small honky-tonk club near the riverfront in downtown Beaumont. Luther Nalley, who would later distinguish himself as a member of the nationally famous Western vocal group the Sons of the Pioneers, is barely visible in the right background. (Photo courtesy of Luther Nalley)

ABOVE Yvonne's Club is now a deserted and faded ghost relic standing in the shadows of the oil refineries and elevated interstates on the outskirts of Beaumont. In the late 1940s and early 1950s, Yvonne's was a center of local music activity, and was also noted for its raw whiskey, wild women, fistfights and flying beer bottles. The club was the site of occasional performances by national country music stars such as Hank Williams and Ernest Tubb. It was also a gathering place for dozens of local musicians, including honky-tonk pianist Moon Mullican and George Jones himself. It was in such oil-field and factoryside taverns and clubs that the mongrel music known as honky-tonk was first spawned.

RIGHT (Circa 1950) George with his first wife, Dorothy Bonvillion (center), along with his mother-in-law (left) and his mama, Clara (right). Though George and the first of his four wives are smiling serenely in this photo, their marriage was destined to be a short-lived and acrimonious one.

(Circa 1952) George serving his country as U.S. Marine Corps Private #1223231. George served out his two-year stint during the Korean War era in good standing. He spent his entire service time in California, where he continued to advance his fledgling career by singing at dances, at shopping-center openings and on occasional radio shows. He performed under the name "Little Georgie Jones, the Forrester Hill Flash."

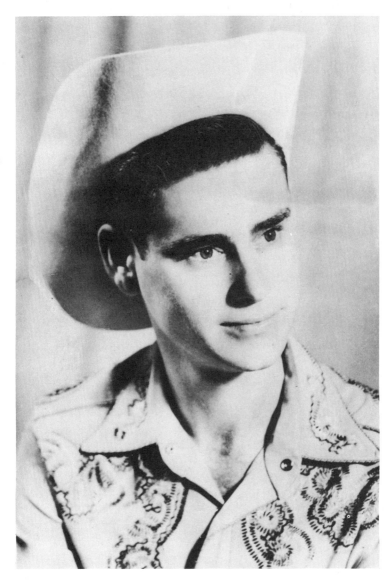

(Circa 1956) An early Starday Records publicity photo, probably taken in the wake of Jones's first national hit, "Why, Baby, Why." His standard-issue Marine Corps flattop temporarily abandoned, his hair is once again long. (Photo courtesy of Starday Records)

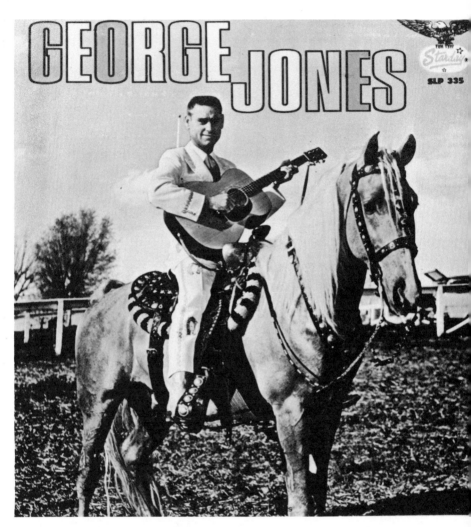

GEORGE JONES

Starday
SLP 335

(Circa 1954) This carefully posed album-cover photo casts George in the dubious role of the Texas cowboy troubadour. To his occasional chagrin, the dozens of songs that he hurriedly recorded during his brief stint on the Starday label were relentlessly repackaged and re-released in later years as he achieved national stardom on other record labels. (Photo courtesy of Starday Records)

(Circa 1963) George, with his flattop once again, clowns around backstage at a concert. During the early 1960s, touring schedules for country singers like Jones were often relentless, spent in less than first-class conditions and involving months at a time on the road. The specters of nervous tension and exhaustion were often constant companions, and whiskey and the occasional amphetamine tablet were the natural antidotes. (Photo by Keith Kolby)

"The Possum" grinds it out with his band, the Jones Boys, on the honky-tonk circuit in a dance hall in New Braunfels, Texas, in the early 1960s. (Photo courtesy of *The Music City News*)

LEFT Movie poster from the 1964 Marathon Pictures feature film *Country Music on Broadway,* in which Jones made an appearance. (Photo courtesy of Fred Goodwin)

ABOVE The newly affluent singer spent thousands of dollars having this spacious new home built on his ranch near Vidor, Texas, in the mid-1960s. He lived in his dream house, dubbed the Rhythm Ranch, for only a couple of years before it, too, slipped through his fingers.

RIGHT King of the Realm: Publicity shot of Jones with cowboy hat and bright Western shirt taken in the mid-1960s.

In the fall of 1963, George swept the music trade magazines' annual awards as the most popular male vocalist in the country field for the second year in a row. Standing directly behind him is his longtime producer and mentor Harold W. "Pappy" Daily. (Photo courtesy of the Country Music Foundation Library)

show that ran from 2:05 to 3:00. "He seemed to have a terror, deep within him, of that soundboard, like he was scared to death he was gonna hit the wrong knob or somethin'. He was also scared to death of Jack Neal, who was a big bear of a man, and who, if he didn't like what you were playing, would sometimes just walk right up in the middle of your show and take the record off the turntable and leave you to talk your way out of it. George just froze whenever he came around."

While George was on the air broadcasting at KTRM, Sonny passed through town one day and decided to stop by the station and pay his sidekick a visit. As he started up the stairs, he was caught off guard by what he saw there in the lobby of the South Coast Life Building. "There was this old man standin' there in old filthy khaki clothes, with a woman's corset kinda tied halfway around him, like a brace. He was all wined up, with tobacco juice runnin' down his mouth. He had his hand out and he was tellin' everybody: 'I'm George Jones's daddy, and I got back trouble. Can ya help me out a little bit?' "

George was once in the middle of his fifty-five-minute show when someone handed him an advertisement to read over the air. It pertained to an establishment on Laurel Street that had recently opened its doors there in Beaumont and which was going to be selling "antee-kews." Although George did not have the slightest idea what in the hell an "antee-kew" was, he did his damnedest to say the word right nonetheless. He told listeners that if they was looking for a huge selection of valuable, hard-to-find "antee-kews," then they best get themselves on down there for the best "antee-kew" bargains they would find anywhere in town.

After his broadcast was over, when Jack Neal or someone explained to him that what the store was really selling were *antiques*, George began realizing that his radio days were numbered. In fact, about the only thing that did stick from his brief stay at KTRM was the nickname that Slim Watts or somebody there at the station had offhandedly stuck him with one day: "Possum." Anybody who bothered to take a good look at those close-set eyes, that upturned nose and that shy, inscrutable, close-mouthed grin of his that never really let you in on what he was thinking, would agree that this new moniker fit him only too well.

Sonny and George rarely missed a Saturday-night performance at the Houston Jamboree down at the City Auditorium, where they shared the stage with many of the other local artists who were now recording for Pappy on Starday. A few of the regular faces among this ever-changing cast of characters were: Arlie Duff (whose 1953 single "Y'All Come" was then still the only Starday release to have made it into the national top ten), James O'Gwynn, Glenn Barber, Floyd Tillman (another honky-tonk player, who'd earlier hit the big time with the self-composed honky-tonk standard "Slippin' Around"), Country Johnny Mathis, Eddie Noack, Jerry Jericho, Sleepy LaBeef (one of the pioneers of the country/gospel/rhythm-and-blues-derived musical style known as rockabilly, which would soon sweep the nation) and Leon Payne (the blind singer and composer of "Lost Highway," which had been popularized by Hank Williams in 1949).

Pappy and Don Pierce really began to notice the strange electricity that seemed to run through the crowd whenever Sonny and George put their voices together on a duet. When they tore into a version of a honky-tonk number like "The Wild Side of Life" (popularized by Hank Thompson in 1952), it seemed like George's high wailing style perfectly complemented Sonny's somewhat deeper and huskier cadences. Together, they gave a song a peculiar penetrating effect that always drew the loudest applause. The almost comic "Mutt and Jeff" image of Sonny, with his gruff demeanor and pomaded hair, standing up there beside the much shorter and slighter George, with his flattop and wide-eyed look of innocence, really seemed to tear the hell out of the audience, too.

It quickly dawned upon Starday's two owners that since George's single releases were going nowhere fast, maybe they ought to team the two of them up together in the studio as well. They figured they might just be able to give George's career the boost it needed by letting him ride on Sonny's coattails for a while.

On some Saturday nights, toward the end of the informal three-hour show down at the City Auditorium, George and Sonny, along with Sleepy LaBeef and Hal Harris (an influential early rockabilly guitarist), would all gather on the stage and raise their voices as an impromptu gospel quartet. With deep conviction, they would sing the Southern Holiness songs that they all knew so well—"Jesus, Hold My Hand," "I'll Fly Away"—as well as the inspirational songs that had more recently been popularized by the archangel, Hank Williams: "I Saw the Light" and "When God Comes and Gathers His Jewels" (a Williams original which echoed with the haunting influence of Roy Acuff's 1944 hit "Precious Jewel").

At such times, friends like Sleepy LaBeef couldn't help but notice how George could really sing the hell out of those old Holiness songs. "Back then," Hal Harris recalled, "George was the kind of guy who, if you mentioned God, he'd take his hat off."

George's friends also noticed that on occasional nights his care-free demeanor would slip away and he would appear to become lost beneath the crushing weight of troubling thoughts. On such nights, when he was already on the verge of exhaustion from long hours of singing, he would drink even deeper than usual. In the vivid hours before dawn when one's speech is slurred, but one's thoughts often seem the most vivid, he would contemplate the tragic specter of Hank Williams, which now held sway over hundreds of struggling young country singers like himself. Sitting and drinking until the first morning light, he would listen intently to what little of himself Hank had left behind in threnodic laments like "I'll Never Get Out of This World Alive," "Lost Highway" and "Six More Miles to the Graveyard." To George, these songs now seemed to hint of a dark well of despair and loneliness: a well so deep and bottomless that a man could easily fall into it and drown—much as Hank himself had done.

After he'd spent a long night on stage, singing these songs of Hank's, laying out his raw emotions for a crowd of strangers, he found that it left him feeling all twisted up inside—happy and sad and angry, all at the same time: "It makes you sad because you're singin' all those sad words, about how a man can do a woman and a woman can do a man, until you're just like the people in the song, and you're living it and their problems become your problems, until you're *lost* in the songs and it just takes everything out of you. . . ." It almost seemed as if the music cast a spell of its own that turned his soul inside out and drained something out of him which he could never quite replenish. It would not be until years later that he could actually put these thoughts into words—it was almost as if "country music was a strange power over everybody that loves it, and is about the only thing in the world that you can curse and still love at the same time. . . ."

The crushing weight of mortal confusion that sometimes visited George in the deepest part of the night always seemed to melt magically away again in the light of day. It was particularly true in Houston, where there was really little time for such pointless introspection, but where there were always more songs to sing, more free drinks to drink and more loose women to chase.

At a Princess drive-in restaurant in the late summer of 1954, George, much to his own surprise, ran across a young woman who was able to hold his attention for more than the usual few fleeting hours. Her name was Shirley Ann Corley, and she was a pretty, slender, dark-haired eighteen-year-old from the small East Texas town of Center. She had come to Houston to spend the summer with a girlfriend and taken a job there at the drive-in as a carhop.

After George introduced himself to Shirley that first night, in his usual flirtatious way, she noticed that he kept dropping by the drive-in more and more often. And, to her surprise, she found herself developing more than a fleeting interest in the wide-eyed, easygoing young man from Beaumont, with his dark, swept-back hair (he was beginning to let it grow out a little bit now) and his countrified good looks. Shirley was certainly no country music fan, but when he showed up one day flashing around a brand-new copy of "No Money in This Deal," telling her that it was him singing on that record, she gladly believed him. A few days later, when he told her that he really needed someone to settle down with, someone to love him and take care of him, she believed him even more.

After a two-week courtship, Shirley and George were married in a simple ceremony there in Houston on September 14, 1954. "I was crazy about him," Shirley later told a girl from a Texas magazine. "I was smart enough to know that I shouldn't have married him. But I did."

With his new bride in tow, George proudly headed back up the highway to his home stomping grounds in Beaumont, where rents were cheaper. There, the two of them settled temporarily in a small apartment near the corner of Cable and Maple streets, just down the street from his sister Ruth.

Pappy and Don Pierce, following up on their original commercial instincts, had in the meantime begun recording Sonny and George together on several duet records, including "Heartbroken Me" and

"Tell Her." These duet records, it turned out, sold briskly through Pappy's local jukebox and wholesale and retail distribution network.

Don Pierce had also begun crisscrossing the rest of the country, visiting radio stations and other record distributors, more determined than ever to turn another one of Starday's many single releases into a bona fide national hit.

George's own solo singles continued to meet with resounding indifference on the part of the great record-buying public. However, his emerging talents as a songwriter were actually beginning to attract a little bit of attention. A few of the songs which he had originally written and recorded on Starday were now being "covered" (re-recorded) by Faron Young, Red Sovine, Hank Locklin, Roy Drusky and Tibbie Edwards—country artists who, though not yet famous, had managed to scramble a few rungs further up the precarious ladder of success than George had thus far.

Despite the commercial gold mine that they would eventually prove to be, George remained flagrantly careless with his nascent songwriting talents. "He could sit on a bed in a motel room and make up songs, one after the other," Pappy Daily explained. "But I could never get him to write 'em down. I bought him three recording machines so he could put 'em on tape when they came to him, but he never did. He ended up losin' all three of those damn machines, or gave 'em away or somethin'."

It was fortuitous indeed that someone from George's long-distant past, someone else who knew of such things as the loneliness and the ghostiness of the Big Thicket and who had often struggled to put these things into words, chose to emerge around this time. His name was Darrell Edwards, and he had grown up just across the road from the prodigal singer back in "Depot Town," near Saratoga. It was Darrell's sister Lenora, in fact, who used to scoop George up and carry him home when he was still just a naked little baby that had strayed from his mama.

When Darrell Edwards had come of age, he had moved away from the Thicket. He'd served as a career officer in the Coast Guard while pursuing his lifelong love for writing poetry. Darrell had not seen George in years, and even when he first heard his songs on the jukeboxes—and heard in his voice those same strains of loneliness and ghostiness that he'd so often struggled to capture in sonnets like "A Mockingbird's Song to a Sinner at Dawn"—he still did not put the singer's name together with that of the small boy he'd known back in Saratoga.

After someone in his family had pointed out the connection, he'd hesitantly tracked George down after a show in Beaumont. He'd showed him some poems he'd written which, he figured, if set to music, would make damn good country songs. George, in turn, played Darrell some bits and pieces of melodies and verses that he had not found the time or patience to work into finished songs. Soon the two of them were off and running.

One day Darrell was standing by himself in front of a corner grocery store near the grimy Golden Triangle city of Orange. He could not help but overhear the man and woman who were sitting in a car nearby, arguing loudly. Intrigued by the wild emotions in their voices, he watched as the woman pulled off her shoe and socked the man over the head with it. When Darrell heard the man implore the woman, with a voice full of sadness and self-pity: "Why, baby, why!?" it moved him. And the man's words stuck in his head and swirled around until, several days later, he sat down with George and started writing a song about it. When they finished, they'd come up with an upbeat honky-tonk lament of marital discord which, in the manner that its jaunty melody played off against the lovelorn sentiments expressed in the lyrics, was hauntingly reminiscent of Hank Williams's self-composed 1950 classic "Why Don't You Love Me (Like You Used to Do)."

George played "Why, Baby, Why" for Pappy later that week. The old man agreed, without changing his expression or taking the cigar from his mouth, that it would be a real good song for George and Sonny to record together.

In mid-1955, Bill Quinn, with Pappy's financial backing, had moved his recording operation out of his living room and into the brand-new Gold Star recording studio, which he'd built next door to his house on Brock Street. The new studio offered all sorts of state-of-the-art features such as separate microphones and sound booths for the drummer and the singer, and the capacity to overdub and produce intriguing effects like "slap echo." Pappy was anxious to take his most promising new duet team in there and try it out.

When the appointed day in June that they were to record "Why, Baby, Why" rolled around, George and Pappy sat waiting at the Gold Star studio for Sonny, who, unbeknownst to them, had gotten involved in a wild card game across town and gotten so drunk that he'd forgotten all about the session. Finally Pappy, who was notorious for keeping an eagle eye on the studio time clock, said to hell with Sonny. He told George to go on ahead and record the song by himself and then overdub himself in the chorus, singing a harmony part against his own lead vocal. That way, he figured, they could at least make the record *sound* like a duet, if nothing else.

When Pappy and George wrapped up the session that day at Gold Star, they had recorded four songs: "Why, Baby, Why"; "Ragged but Right" (a lively number that George had written on his own); and two more songs that George and Darrell had written together— "What Am I Worth" and a lyrically evocative ballad called "Seasons of the Heart."

Now that Sonny was temporarily out of the picture, Pappy had once again begun to pay closer attention to George's voice. He noticed how it seemed to ring with particular clarity when he sang those songs that he was now writing with Darrell, the muse from the Thicket. Pappy now, too, could faintly hear the same haunting echoes of ghostiness, outrage and the sadness with no name that had so moved those people on the Beaumont street corner more than a decade ago. Pappy called Don Pierce a few days later and was particularly excited about the four new sides they'd come up with in the new Gold Star studio. ("I think we've got the sound now," he told his partner.) Now Pappy figured that maybe, just maybe, they'd finally come up with something that they could run with—something that would put Starday on the map, and make them all a little bit of money for a change.

Every Saturday night down at the City Auditorium, George and Sonny continued to tear the crowd to pieces, and the accompanying weekly broadcast of the live show over KNUZ seemed to bring more notoriety their way all the time. Slowly but surely, it was all starting to go to Sonny's hard head. "Back then, I was just a country boy who'd come to town, and I thought I was about the greatest thing that ever was," Sonny laughed. "Pappy was payin' me twenty-five dollars a night down at the Jamboree, and he was payin' George about fifteen. I knew George had some lawyers or somethin' after him for child support from his first marriage, and that he and Shirley also had a baby on the way. So I told George that we should go to Pappy and tell him he needed a ten-dollar raise so that he'd be gettin' as much as I was. I figured that if Pappy didn't give it to us, we'd threaten to quit and that would really pop his cork."

When the two of them tracked Pappy down at his office on Eleventh Street, the old man was sitting behind his desk studying some invoices and puffing on a cigar. "Yeh, kid," he greeted Sonny without looking up from his papers or taking the cigar from his mouth. "What can I do for ya?"

"Pappy, you know me 'n' George are outdrawin' everybody else you're bringin' in down at the Jamboree," Sonny growled in his frog voice as he eased his six-foot-two frame menacingly over Pappy's desk. As he paused to let the weight of his words sink in, he shot a sly, self-assured conspiratorial grin over his shoulder at George, who was standing meekly behind him, with the jack-o'-lantern grin plastered across his face. "I think George here should be gettin' as much money as me."

Pappy continued shuffling the invoices and still did not bother to look up. "Well, kid," he droned through the clenched teeth which held his big cigar. "I think I know what I can afford to pay down there."

Sonny knew it was time to play his hand. "Well, Pappy, if ya can't see clear to givin' George a ten-dollar raise, then we're both gonna leave."

The old man shuffled his papers some more and moved his cigar from one side of his mouth to the other, never bothering to look up. "Well, then, kid, you just be careful. And don't call me unless you land in jail."

Having Pappy outgun him and call his bluff like that, without even blinking an eye, made Sonny madder than hell. He grabbed George and they rushed out the door. They jumped into Sonny's big old '47 Buick, and after stopping to purchase a couple fifths of whiskey, they roared eastward through Houston's crowded downtown streets and suburbs until they were once again careening past the grazing cattle, wooden fence posts and flat, sun-baked South Texas countryside. It was a long ride to Sonny's hometown of Nacogdoches, where they were headed, and every twenty minutes or so, the float on the carburetor of Sonny's old Buick would stick and he'd have to stop and get out the little .25 caliber pistol he carried in his guitar case and tap the carburetor to get it going again. Then the two of them would push their big white cowboy hats back on their heads, take another drink of whiskey and jump back in the car and roar off again.

As the miles flew by, the sun began to sink below the faraway horizon. As the shadows turned to a deeper darkness, they began to pipe-dream out loud, as they so often did, about all the girls, fancy Cadillacs, expensive guitars and embroidered and sequined stage outfits that they would have when they finally hit the big time and made it on the Grand Ole Opry up in Nashville. To hell with Pappy Daily, anyway, they laughed.

But what they did not know just then, as the vast darkness of the big sky began to swallow up the landscape, was that, for Sonny, it was already the beginning of the end. For George, though, the long ride down the lost highway was just starting.

Back in Houston, the more that Pappy Daily and Don Pierce listened to those four songs of George's from his first session at Gold Star, the more they liked them. They couldn't seem to agree as to which one should be the next single. "Pappy realized George's strength as a balladeer long before I did," Pierce explained. "He felt that 'Seasons of the Heart' [which, in later years, would be recorded by Willie Nelson, Johnny Cash, Jerry Lee Lewis, among others] was the big song. I knew that, in those days, it took much longer to sell a ballad, because it had to make it on the radio first. Back then, we had those old seventy-eight records. The breakage was terrible when we shipped them, and we only had money for postage to service a few radio stations anyway. I also knew that an upbeat song like 'Why, Baby, Why' would be easier to sell directly to the jukebox distributors for the beer-drinkin' trade."

Pierce's judgment prevailed, but meanwhile another complication had arisen. Webb Pierce, an artist on Decca, who had earlier recorded for Pappy on the Four Star label and who was now burning up the country charts with a string of number one singles, had gotten hold of "Why, Baby, Why." Pierce had recorded a duet version of the song with Red Sovine (who would later achieve modest success with maudlin hits like "Phantom 409" and "Teddy Bear") and planned to release it as a single.

"Webb had started his career with Pappy on Four Star, and then when he hit big, he had jumped over to Decca," Don Pierce (no relation to Webb) recalled. "Well, that made Pappy real mad. Webb knew that if he wanted his records to get any distribution in Texas, then he was going to have to get right with Pappy. So he talked to him and he agreed to hold off with his version of 'Why, Baby, Why' and give us a few weeks to see if we could do anything with George's version."

In late August 1955, Pappy and Don Pierce made another casual roll of the dice and released "Why, Baby, Why" (with "Seasons of the Heart" as the flip side) as their small label's 102nd single release. A few weeks later, Webb Pierce and Sovine's version was also released as a single on Decca Records, and due to Webb's overwhelming popularity, it quickly climbed to the number one spot. ("Webb sorta stole the bread right outa my mouth!" George later joked.) Initially, George's version of "Why, Baby, Why" was greeted with somewhat less enthusiasm by *Billboard* than even "No Money in This Deal" had been: "This and the flip [side]," a reviewer wrote in the magazine's August 27 edition, "both carry above-average material that could benefit from better projection than the cleffer provides" (which was a deferential way of saying: get another singer).

Despite such critical reservations and despite the heavy-handed competition from Pierce and Sovine's duet version on the much larger Decca label, George's rendition of "Why, Baby, Why" eventually climbed all the way to the number four position in *Billboard*'s national country charts—considerably higher than any previous Starday release had ever gone. Suddenly, the name George Jones was being whispered and bandied about on tongues that wagged far beyond the remote purlieus of the small corner of East Texas that he still called home.

After their arrival in Nacogdoches, Sonny and George stayed at Sonny's mother's house for a few days before drifting down to Beaumont, where they passed another week or so playing for five or ten dollars a night in some of George's old haunts. Then—though they still did not know that "Why, Baby, Why" was about to break loose—they decided to temporarily part ways. George figured on returning to Houston with his tail between his legs, struggling along on the fifteen dollars a night he was getting at the Jamboree, and making the best of a bad situation.

Sonny was of a different mind: "Bein' as hardheaded as I was, I decided I wasn't gonna give in. I was gettin' tired of bein' a puppet on a string, which, as a recording artist, I could see I was becoming. And I'd also decided I didn't want nothin' more to do with Pappy Daily. So I drifted down to Galveston, and then on back to Houston, and I mainly stayed drunk for about the next three or four years. But every now and then I'd keep runnin' into George. And with Pappy behind him like he was, he just kept gettin' bigger and bigger."

Fourteen weeks after its release, "Why, Baby, Why" fell back out of the charts. It would be many more months before one of George's single releases would again meet with such success. There was more than a little disappointment when his next chart single— "What Am I Worth"—climbed to the number fourteen position in late 1956 only to sputter back out of the charts one week later.

All the same, "Why, Baby, Why" had succeeded in drawing quite a bit of attention George's way and opening some doors which, before, had merely been slammed in his face. Most importantly, it had enabled him to land several guest appearances on the Louisiana Hayride in the fall of 1955.

The Hayride was a live country music show that was broadcast over station KWKH from the stage of the 3,800-seat Municipal Auditorium in Shreveport, Louisiana, every Saturday night. In terms of national prestige and popularity, it was second only to Nashville's Grand Ole Opry. By way of the "Hayride Radio Network," which had been established in 1950, its weekly broadcasts now went out over twenty-seven radio stations in four states: Louisiana, Texas, New Mexico and Colorado.

During the late 1940s and early 1950s, the Hayride had also earned a reputation as something of a "Triple-A" farm team for the Grand Ole Opry; dozens of singers, including Johnny Cash, Webb Pierce, Faron Young, Johnny Horton, Cajun Jimmy C. Newman and even Hank Williams, had used its stage as a stepping-stone from regional popularity to national stardom.

The only problem was that there was now a new wrinkle in the nature of things: a wrinkle that threatened to quench the flames not only of George's promising career but of the career of every other country singer as well. The wrinkle's name was Elvis Presley. And it was this sultry-eyed, twenty-one-year-old Lothario who was now starting to drive audiences wild with his new music, called rock 'n' roll. It was Presley (whom many hard-core country music lovers considered to be nothing less than an affront to all things civilized) with whom George and these other struggling-to-be-famous country artists were now forced to share the Louisiana Hayride stage with on many Saturday nights.

For an unreconstructed hard country singer like George, this could be an unnerving experience indeed: to go up against a semihysterical crowd of 3,500 young rock-'n'-roll neophytes who now moaned and screamed and wet their collective pants while waiting impatiently to witness Elvis's wild, bestial gyrations and to hear those indecipherably glottal utterances of his which passed for singing. To George's—and most every hard country singer's—horror, these audiences had, almost overnight, grown coldly indifferent toward the more down-home strains of country and honky-tonk music such as he played. In fact, it had gotten so damned bad here lately that, like it or not, you just about *had* to throw in a couple of those new fast-type rock-'n'-roll songs into your own set if you expected to get any kind of hand at all. "I guess everybody in the world tried to be a little bit like Elvis at the time," George later remembered. "There was no way you could compete with him if you were just doing country."

Deep down, George—as set in his hard country ways as he already was—cared not a whit for this new rock-'n'-roll pariah. On some Saturday nights in late 1955, when he was scheduled to precede Elvis on the Hayride, the prodigal singer would get out there onstage and shake a leg and sing some of Elvis's hit songs and do a ragged-ass imitation of "the King," trying his best to steal his thunder. "I just did it to aggravate old Elvis, and it worked!" he later explained to his friends with obvious glee. "Y'know, he was a good kid, but, man, was he *ugly* back then!"

One Saturday night, after he'd made his brief appearance on the Louisiana Hayride, George jumped into his old car and drove south, en route to yet another nickel-and-dime booking that he'd agreed to play the next night several hundred miles to the south. (The success of "Why, Baby, Why" as well as the additional exposure via the Hayride Radio Network was now beginning to earn him spots on a few national tours and "package" shows in far-flung cities with other, more popular country artists of the day.)

At times like these, George hated to be alone—just as he would all his life. He particularly hated those solitary hours between midnight and dawn, when a man's thoughts seemed to weigh heaviest on him. As he drove across the vast stretches of moonlit fields and pine forests on this dark night, he felt glad that he at least had a bottle of whiskey for company. The night wore on. He smoked one cigarette after another and restlessly flipped across the stations on his car radio.

He was tuned into XERF, one of the several powerful American-operated Mexican border stations. As he listened, a preacher came on the radio and began preaching up a storm, ranting and raving with perfervid righteousness about the sins of fornication, fast dancing, Communism, whisk~y, life insurance, fluoride and cigarettes. As George Glenn listened, the preacher's message moved him deeply. The first thin fingers of dawn began to reveal themselves in the eastern skies and he felt the presence of the Holy Ghost enter his body, and he felt the same rejoicing gladness that used to fill his soul when he would answer the altar call at old Rollie Jones's Gospel Assembly Church. As the light of the Holy Spirit entered him, he felt the taint of earthly corruption fall like a veil from his soul, and he tossed the whiskey bottle and the cigarettes out the window.

The hours passed ever so slowly. Dawn broke, and the sun rose higher until it was a bright angry globe whose all-consuming heat scorched the sagebrush and made George's eyes burn. The preacher was no longer preaching, and to his disappointment, he no longer felt the presence of the Holy Spirit within him. His inner glow of conviction had melted away with the morning mist, and he once again felt alone and empty.

Stopping the car by the deserted roadside, he licked his lips uneasily and listened to the eerie humming of the high-tension wires which glistened overhead in the harsh sunlight. With longing in his eyes, he looked back down the long ribbon of highway from whence he had come, and where the hot, dry air now shimmered against the stillness of the distant horizon. He started to turn the car around, but then he thought better and stopped himself. "No," he shook his head and muttered to himself, "I'd never find the spot where I threw them out anyway."

In Beaumont, where he was now living in a small apartment at 2650 Victoria Street with Shirley and their baby son, Jeffery Glenn Jones (who was born in October, 1955), George was now beginning to savor the taste of local fame. On June 3, 1956, his stature as a hometown hero (which was already solidified with his appearances on the Houston Jamboree and the Louisiana Hayride) was raised yet another notch when the Sunday edition of the Beaumont *Enterprise* carried one of the first feature articles ever written about him. The story was accompanied by a flattering line drawing of the prodigal singer and was written by Milton Turner. The headline read: HE

PLAYS HIS GUITAR ENTHUSIASTICALLY, BREAKING STRINGS AND
GAINING STARDOM.

"He plays his guitar like he sings—enthusiastically," Turner
wrote. "The result is he breaks about three or four guitar strings at
each performance. He is breaking other things too! . . . According
to his manager, another local boy, Bill Hall, 'Why, Baby, Why' has
sold over half a million records." (Actual sales figures were about a
tenth of that.)

"In recent weeks," the article continued, "he's plowed through
New Mexico, Montana, Idaho, Tennessee and Florida, to name a
few, and Canada. Most of the time, he performs (on package shows)
with such entertainers as Ray Price, Carl Smith, Johnny Cash, Carl
Perkins and others: . . . So—when you see a big, blue Cadillac
with Texas plates whisk past on the highway, take a good look: It
might be George Jones of Beaumont on his way to Timbuktu."

On weekend nights when he was at home in Beaumont, George
would often be among the half dozen or so country artists featured
on the Saturday-night shows that were held at the City Auditorium,
where he'd once stood in line with his sisters to see Hank Williams
perform. Other times he would perform down at the smaller Beaumont Sportatorium, where they featured country singers and
"wrassling" matches on the same stage.

The audiences would often include many of George's cousins and
in-laws who'd come flocking into town from the Big Thicket, which,
in the wake of the postwar boom, was slowly becoming crisscrossed
by paved roads and electric power lines.

George Washington Jones now idled away many of his waking
hours in the shabby beer joints down along Gladys Street. He was a
familiar sight at these concerts also. Grinning widely, he would
weave his way unsteadily through the crowd, with a flush of pride
written across his tobacco-stained face, just as thick and obvious as
the smell of wine on his breath. After the concerts, he sold the
records and souvenir photographs of his ever more famous son and
pocketed the proceeds.

"Y'know," he'd explain self-assuredly in his wheezing, wine-
soaked voice to whoever would listen, as his son played onstage, "I
wrote all them songs myself, and I give 'em to my boy, George
Glenn!"

George was at home with his wife and young son, on a rare night
off between shows, when he suddenly felt a deep restlessness settle

in upon him. He wandered down to a little beer joint on the river-front near Pine and Walnut streets. He had a few beers and then he got up to sing a few songs, and was having him a pretty good time when some smart-mouthed son of a bitch at one of the back tables started giving him a load of shit. George, who was never one to back down from a fight when alcohol had lit a fire in him, hollered back at the loudmouth. He told him that if he wanted trouble, then he could just wait until he finished singing, and then if he'd step outside, he'd be happy to oblige him. When George did finally step out the tavern door, the son of a bitch was, in fact, waiting for him. George swung and knocked him down, but then he came up with a switchblade knife in his hand. George felt the knife brush his leather jacket, then he swung at him again and the son of a bitch ran off.

Casually brushing himself off, George walked on down the street, unaware that the knife blade had touched him. As he walked on, he ran his hands over the tear in his jacket, and he felt wetness. Under a streetlamp, he held his hand to his face and saw that the wetness had color. After he realized how badly he'd actually been cut, he checked himself into the Hotel Dieu, a small hospital on the corner of Sabine and Emmett avenues, and had himself bandaged up. A few days later, when he again played down at the Saturday-night Jamboree in Houston and got to jumping around onstage, he still felt so weak he almost fainted.

Elvis Presley's "Heartbreak Hotel" reached the number one position in both the pop and country record charts in February 1956 (where it stayed for twenty-seven weeks). It temporarily sent the country music industry sprawling flat on its ass. Sales figures for country records plummeted dangerously, and soon even the most dedicated country artists—as a matter of sheer professional survival—were all rushing to pump some of Elvis's glottal bestiality into their own music. They, too, wanted to jump aboard the fast-moving bandwagon of rock 'n' roll, which now had Presley solidly in the driver's seat.

Though Pappy Daily sold rock-'n'-roll records in his stores and actually recorded more than his share of early rock-'n'-roll and rockabilly artists on his own Starday label, there was no one who had less comprehension or harbored more disdain for this newfangled music than he. "I don't even call it music." He'd shake his head and puff on his cigar. "It's just loud noise with words that don't make no sense. . . . Reminds me of a buncha people all on dope, jumpin' up and down and goin' crazy."

Nonetheless, Pappy could see the handwriting on the wall. He knew that this was what the people who bought records now seemed to want, and if it was the only way there was to get his artists back in the charts, then he'd damn sure grit his teeth and give it a try.

George was harboring similar mixed emotions as the two of them made their next trek over to the Gold Star studio in early 1956 to try and record some of this incomprehensible rockabilly music. To assuage their shared misgivings about the entire project, they agreed that the songs they recorded there that day—backed by a core of talented local session musicians who eventually came to be known as the Starday House Band—would be released under the pseudonym "Thumper Jones," which George had come up with after reading "Thumper Rabbit" in the newspaper comic strips.

George and the Starday House Band did manage to put together a surprisingly credible version of "Heartbreak Hotel." They also recorded two rather ragged Little Richard and Jerry Lee Lewis-inspired songs that George had written himself, called "Rock It" and "(Dadgummit) How Come It." George sang so hard that day at Gold Star that he hurt his throat and could not sing again for several days. He put everything he had into those "Thumper Jones" sides, but try as he might, when he sang them, all the hard country fervor and clenched-jaw restraint that he always knew how to bring to a honky-tonk ballad merely dissolved into a raw, full-throated cacophony. He yelped, screamed and squealed with abandon, as if he were trying desperately to rise above the pulsating accompaniment of the percussive "slap bass" and Hal Harris's heartily inspired and heavily vibratoed electric lead guitar lines.

"It don't sound like George Jones," Pappy muttered later as he and George listened to "Rock It" and "How Come It." After their release as flip sides of the same single, on May 5, 1956, the songs failed—to no one's surprise—to catapult George to rock-'n'-roll fame. "In fact, it sounds more like a nigger than a white boy!"

"Pappy," replied George (who in later years, when caught in the wrong frame of mind, would occasionally rip up and break copies of these "Thumper Jones" records when he found them in friends' collections), "I don't ever want you to try and cut me as anything but country again, all right?"

"Hell, George," replied Pappy, who would be deeply relieved

when the threat of rock 'n' roll had finally passed overhead like a Texas twister, leaving those in the country music business with the same clear skies and solid audiences that they'd known before. "I'm just an old hillbilly! How could I ever cut you anything *but* country?"

Hell, Pappy had been in the record business long enough to know that if you found a horse you could ride, then you damn well best *stay* on that horse.

Pappy, being the shrewd old music business wheeler-dealer that he was, knew that the real key to breaking George wide open in the hillbilly music field was—in addition to more hit records—a guest appearance on Nashville's Grand Ole Opry.

The Opry had changed little in the two decades since the Jones family had first listened to and been enthralled by it on their battery-powered radio back in the Big Thicket. It was still dominated by Roy Acuff, and it was still the most widely heard and most overwhelmingly popular of all the many live country music shows like it that had sprung up across the country. Its clear-channel and NBC network-syndicated Saturday-night broadcasts now reached an estimated 10 million listeners.

The Grand Ole Opry was also—as anyone like Pappy who attempted to wheedle a guest spot for a new artist on its hallowed stage soon found out—a closed shop. It was an organization that was quite openly governed by factors like jealousy, politics and favoritism and often paid homage to musical mediocrity. The Opry had booted Hank Williams's ass out in 1952, after rumors of drunkenness and womanizing began following him around like a bad smell. And those in power there had also snubbed Elvis Presley and suggested he go back to driving a truck, after he'd made his first and only appearance there in 1954. It had become a haven for Nashville's own Mount Rushmore of country egomaniacs: aging banty roosters like Acuff and Hank Snow—men who were fast becoming mere caricatures of their former greatness—men whose once immense musical talents had, in the course of passing years, become as ossified and lifeless as the full-sized statues of them that would later stand in the nearby Country Music Wax Museum.

Pappy persisted in his efforts, though. Every time he came through Nashville, he dutifully paid visits to members of the petty ruling *politburo* at WSM-Radio, the subsidiary company of the Nashville-based National Life and Accident Insurance Corporation, which owned and operated the Grand Ole Opry. He continued to pull all the strings he knew how to pull, but was repeatedly rebuffed.

"Pappy, why the hell don'cha just forget it," George would say with a grin when his mentor apprised him of these failed efforts. "They don't want me up there, and it really ain't worth the trouble."

"I dunno, George," Pappy would sigh as he leaned back in his chair, cigar in hand. "Seems like them people up there just don't wanta take a chance and see what somebody new can do."

In early 1956, Pappy finally pulled on the right string, and one Saturday night, he and George found themselves in downtown Nashville, waiting in the shadowy wings of the Ryman Auditorium, a musty old edifice that was originally built in 1892, and served as an evangelistic temple until 1943, when it had become the home of the Opry and become known as "the Mother Church of Country Music."

George was ready as he clutched his guitar and smoothed the lapels of the flashy new stage outfit that Pappy had bought him just for this occasion. On his finger was a brand-new diamond ring that glistened in the backstage shadows.

Pappy couldn't help but notice how subdued and casual George seemed as he prepared to walk out on the same hallowed stage where his idols, Roy Acuff, Bill Monroe and the late, great Hank Williams, had so often tread. "He didn't seem to know what it was all about," Pappy remembered. "By then, I think some of the ~rs had already started to go out of his eyes a little bit."

George and Pappy were angered when, at the last minute, one of WSM's dark-suited officials informed George that he could not take his guitar onstage with him. It was just like Pappy said, George thought as the anger swirled in his shotgun eyes, they really don't wanta see how good somebody new can do.

"Hell with it!" the prodigal singer barked loudly at Pappy. "If they won't let me take my guitar, then to hell with 'em! Let's go home!"

All of a sudden, singer George Morgan, an Opry regular, got wind of the jam that George was in. Appearing like a phantom out of the backstage darkness, he handed George a guitar owned by Little Jimmy Dickens, another Opry star of the day. "Go on! Get the hell out there," he told him.

Before anyone had time to object, George, with borrowed guitar in hand, hit the stage and launched into a song. It wasn't long before the applause was echoing loudly through the Ryman's old wooden rafters, and the prodigal singer smiled and looked out into the swirling crowd that packed the 3,500-seat auditorium. He could see now that these people here at the Grand Ole Opry were really not much different from those people back on the Beaumont street corners who, so many years ago, had smiled in warm recognition and tossed their coins when they heard those familiar strains of ghostiness, Christian mysticism, mortal outrage and the sadness with no name that echoed in his voice. He smiled again and strummed the guitar and sang another song and the applause echoed even louder. He kept on singing, because he knew it was too damn late for anyone to stop him now.

Slowly but surely, the portals of opportunity were beginning to spread themselves open for the prodigal Southeast Texas singer, just as widely and easily as the supple thighs of the fast and loose women he'd known back in Beaumont and Houston. Not only had the Grand Ole Opry invited him back for more guest appearances, but on August 25, 1956, the dark suits at WSM had even granted him permanent membership in their exclusive club. *Country & Western Jamboree* magazine had called him one of the best new country singers of 1956, and *Billboard,* in a nationwide end-of-the-year poll of disk jockeys, named him as one of the year's most promising new country vocalists. His photograph—usually accompanied by a brief write-up—was also beginning to appear with some regularity in the pages of *Country Song Round-Up,* the leading national country music fan magazine.

By early 1957, Pappy and Don Pierce had succeeded in engineering an arrangement with Mercury Records under which this larger national label would give wider marketing and distribution to Starday's country releases under the new logo, Mercury/Starday. Pierce bought a small office building on Dickerson Road, just outside Nashville, and opened Starday's first office in Music City in the spring of 1957.

No one was happier about these developments than George. Two years had now passed since the success of "Why, Baby, Why" and though he and Pappy had managed to hang a couple of his singles in the bottom of the country top twenty in the months since, they had still not come anywhere near repeating the success of that first hit. Pappy and George both believed that the presence of Nashville's top session musicians on his records would add that extra spark that would enable them to once again crack the country top ten.

The Nashville to which George came, around the same time that the Russkies were hanging Sputnik in the nighttime skies, was a small, nondescript Middle Tennessee city on the muddy banks of the Cumberland River. It was a city dominated by the old wealth of hillbilly blue bloods, some of whom had even taken to referring to their hometown as "the Athens of the South" (perhaps, some outsiders guessed, on account of the incongruous-looking full-scale plaster-and-wood replica of the Greek Parthenon that had been erected in one of their city parks).

Nashville remained vaguely uncomfortable with the thriving country music industry that had sprung up in its midst by the early 1950s. The town's more highbrow civic leaders perceived that the "new money" generated by this hillbilly music industry was less clean than their "old money" (much of which had been made by peddling expensive Bibles and excessively overpriced industrial life insurance policies door to door, throughout the rural South, to illiterate sharecroppers and impoverished widows). This image problem inspired some long-forgotten shill to write in a 1952 Tennessee Department of Tourism publication:

> Though the average singer of hillbilly music is in the high income brackets, he lives a modest personal life without ostentation or notoriety. Since [his stage] show never changes, he has no need for a press agent. Since he is never involved in divorce suits, wild parties, scandals, nightclub episodes or mystery deaths, there are no hillbilly gossip columns. Most of these singers live in happy homes in modern, comfortable, two-garage houses. Some of them are investing in real estate, since many of them came from farms and know what an acre of land is really worth.

Nashville's music scene in reality was a vital, wild-ass industry that thrived on equal measures of booze, biphetamines and bullshit; it was an industry in which George Glenn Jones felt right at home. There was certainly no shortage of wild-ass companionship for a new boy in town like himself. The studios along Sixteenth Avenue South and the sleazy beer joints along Lower Broad Street, near the Ryman Auditorium, were now bristling with the adrenalized energy

of dozens of horny young "live hard, die young" disciples of the
Hank Williams mystique, many of whom George already knew from
his days on the Louisiana Hayride: singers like Webb Pierce, Johnny
Cash, Lefty Frizzell, Stonewall Jackson, and Faron Young (a former
protégé of Hank Williams's who, in fact, did hit the country top-five
big time in 1955 with a rollicking song called "Live Hard, Die Young
and Leave a Beautiful Memory").

George's home away from home when in Nashville was the
Clarkston Hotel at 315 Seventh Avenue North, a cheap, singularly
unluxurious downtown establishment that was nonetheless within
easy walking distance of the Ryman Auditorium. The Clarkston was
the unofficial command headquarters for the round-the-clock singing, songwriting, whiskey drinking, pill popping and womanizing
that were so freely indulged in by this restless and ambitious new
generation of up-and-coming country stars.

With just the one hit record under his belt, George's new association with the Grand Ole Opry now kept him busier than ever before,
touring across the United States and Canada with other Opry members for as much as fifty or even a hundred dollars a night—far
better money than he'd ever earned before. Even so, George managed to come dragging home from these lengthy tours exhausted,
hung over, sometimes with a broken arm or cracked rib—souvenirs
of a scuffle with an enraged fan or club owner, but always with less
money in his pockets than he'd had when he'd left.

"I went out on a short tour with George in the late fifties that
started at Verona Park, an open-air place near Cincinnati," Don
Pierce recalled. "He'd been drinking some, so we got him onstage at
Verona Park as early as possible, and he tore the crowd up, as usual.
Then we took him to some downtown tavern, and he played a show
there and did the same thing, and then he got his money and kept
right on partying. The next day he was broke again. He left his hotel
in Cincinnati without paying the bill, and some women followed him
on down to his next show, in Elizabethtown, Kentucky. The party
continued there. He played his show there in a movie theater, and
just tore the hell out of everybody all over again."

After the Elizabethtown show, Pierce drove on back to Nashville
by himself. The next day, he got a call from the errant singer, who
was still in Kentucky.

"Hey, Don," George casually informed him. "I'm broke. C'mon
up here and get me, will ya?"

"I can't, George," Pierce told him. "I'm busy today. Why don'cha borrow some money and take a bus."

There was a moment of profound silence on the line before the wayward singer exploded with wounded indignation. "A *bus!*" he hollered into the phone. "What the hell are ya talkin' about, Don!? I can't get on no damn Greyhound carryin' my damn *gih*-tar! I'M A GRAND OLE OPRY STAR!"

Sooner or later, George did manage to catch a ride back down to Nashville, as he always did. There, he soon managed to borrow enough money to make his pockets jingle anew, as he always did.

Yet such scenes were repeated again and again. One morning, about nine o'clock, George was sitting in his room at the Clarkston Hotel after a long night of partying, and he was having himself a drink of whiskey. His pockets were once again empty, and as he downed his drink, all of a sudden, the idiocy and unfairness of this struck him like a bolt of lightning. Here he was, a damn *star* on the Opry with several chart records, his picture in all those damn magazines, and he was still *goddamn broke: broke* just about all the goddamn time!

George had him another drink and he decided that he was going to go out to Starday's offices on Dickerson Road and have him a talk with ole Don Pierce about this.

Through his office window, Pierce saw George coming. With George showing up this early in the morning he knew this meant trouble, surer than hell, and he tried his damnedest to hide from the enraged singer. George had already figured out that Pierce was in there. He came charging into his office, seething with anger.

"Don," he hissed as he paced the floor. "What the hell is goin' on? I've had four damn records in the charts now, and I'm on the Opry, and everybody is tellin' me how great I am, but I still ain't got no fuckin' money! Are you sure you ain't got money that belongs to me that you aren't turnin' loose?"

Pierce—who was sometimes looked upon with suspicion by many contemporaries for what he himself later referred to as his "unorthodox" business practices—was certainly no stranger to such accusations.

"Really, George," he replied calmly, throwing up his hands, "I've already advanced you everything you've got coming, and more. . . ."

As Pierce heard himself speak these words, he could see that

George had worked himself into such a frenzy that he might as well be talking out the window. He watched the wayward singer's close-set shotgun eyes dance dizzily, and he heard his words tumble out furiously on top of one another as his anger rose still higher. As he paced the floor faster and faster, his imprecations grew still more malefic. He finally picked up an ashtray off Pierce's desk and sent it crashing through the window.

"Goddamnit, Don, I need some money! I think you're holdin' out on me!"

The two of them went round and round for what seemed like hours. Pierce was able to divert George's attention long enough to make a phone call to the local police, who hauled the angry singer away and let him sleep his whiskey meanness off in jail.

The next day, when George was sober, he paid Pierce another visit. "He was just *contrite*," Pierce recalled. "He was just beside himself with apologies. That's how it always was, because when he was sober and in his right mind, he was just the nicest and most humble fella you could hope to meet. Really, you couldn't help but love him."

In 1958, George's version of "Treasure of Love," a honky-tonk-flavored love ballad, which he sang in a languid, drawling manner (that was more reminiscent of the diphthong-twisting style of Oklahoma honky-tonk king Hank Thompson than anything else he'd ever done), was released on Mercury Records. "Treasure of Love" was written by J. P. ("the Big Bopper") Richardson (whom Pappy Daily had succeeded in breaking into the big time that same year with the million-selling pop single "Chantilly Lace") and went all the way to the number six spot in the national country charts. After nearly a three-year absence, George was finally back in the top ten.

Pappy had also been fooling around with another song that he felt had hit potential, even though he could not seem to find anyone who shared his opinion. The song, called "White Lightning," was a rollicking, up-tempo novelty number about the joys of making and drinking moonshine whiskey. It also had been written by J. P. Richardson, and was included on *Chantilly Lace*, the one and only LP that the Big Bopper completed for Mercury before his untimely death in early 1959.

The next time George was back in Houston, Pappy played "White Lightning" for him, along with a couple of other songs that he'd already pitched to a number of other country artists without success. "Here's some songs that nobody else don't seem to like," Pappy told him. "See what you think about 'em."

After listening to "White Lightning," George quickly turned to Pappy. "Don't give this one to nobody else," he told him. "I wanta record it."

In September, in Nashville—around the same time Khrushchev was touring an Iowa dairy farm in his shiny shoes, stepping in what he was trying to sell us—George finally got his opportunity to put "White Lightning" down on tape. It was at a late-night session in a small basement studio on Sixteenth Avenue South that its owner, Owen Bradley, merely referred to as "Quonset Hut." Don Pierce, who was producing the session, rounded up a motley collection of hungry young musicians, including bass player Buddy Killen (who would later distinguish himself as an eminently successful Nashville publishing magnate), a blind piano player named Hargus ("Pig") Robbins (who later established a reputation as country music's leading session keyboard man) and a gifted lead guitarist named Floyd Jenkins.

George and the handful of studio players kicked "White Lightning" around in the studio for a few minutes, and then Pierce (who, like Pappy, was not one for wasting time in the studio) let the tapes roll. Buddy Killen started the song moving with a galloping riff on his stand-up bass, and Pig quickly fell in with some swirling rhythmic figures on his piano, while Jenkins threw in some driving, boogie-woogie patterns that he picked out on the bass strings of his electric guitar. George, spurred on by this frenzied rockabilly-flavored instrumental accompaniment, tore into the song with a quirky and slightly manic high-register vocal performance.

"Buddy Killen played bass so hard that he tore the skin right off his fingers!" Pierce laughed as he recalled the fever into which the young musicians worked themselves that night. "There's a place in the final verse of the song where George flubbed the lyrics and stuttered on the word 's-slug,' which he didn't mean to do. We tried doing the song again, but it never was as good as it was that first time. So we just released it that way."

On March 15, 1959, a little more than a month after the song's composer, J. P. Richardson, died in the February 3 plane crash, along with Buddy Holly and Richie Valens, "White Lightning" was released. It quickly climbed the ranks of the country charts, moving at a much faster rate than had any of George's previous singles. It reached the number four position, the previous high spot that George had hit with "Why, Baby, Why" three and a half years earlier, then kept right on moving and did not stop until it became his very first number _ne single. But it did not even stop there. In fact, it even crossed over and made a slight dent in the national pop charts, where it clocked in at the number seventy-three position.

In April of the same year, attempting to capitalize on the momentum created by "White Lightning," George recorded another rockabilly-tinged novelty song called "Who Shot Sam" which he and Darrell Edwards had written, along with a man named Ray Jackson. The song—a lyrically imaginative story about a wild Saturday-night shoot-out in New Orleans—rose to the number seven spot, and like "White Lightning," it also made a feeble stir in the bottom of the pop charts.

With these two new back-to-back hit records, the call of the road was now louder than it had ever been before. The pay—a couple of hundred dollars a night now—was still nothing much to write home about. Once George got finished paying for travel expenses, backup musicians, booking agents' fees, the guitars that he often smashed up and those garish, rhinestone-studded "Mr. White Lightning" stage outfits that he now favored, there still wasn't hardly anything left in his pockets at all.

Life out there on the road wasn't always the easiest row to hoe either. It was just a never-ending merry-go-round of exhausting one-nighters in two-bit beer joints, roadhouses, high school gymnasiums, VFW halls, amusement parks and rodeos all across the country. Far too much of George's waking life was now spent traveling in the back seats of Oldsmobile or Cadillac limousines, jammed five or six to a car with other Opry members and road musicians. Crisscrossing the United States and Canada in such a manner, it was not unusual for them to journey four or five hundred miles from one show to the next, and to hit as many as forty or fifty bumfuck towns and backwater villages in as many days and nights. Naturally, after several months of this regimen, acute nervous exhaustion would often set in—particularly with a high-strung character like George Jones.

One such tour took him, along with Ernest Tubb and a handful of other Opry members, on a swing through the northeastern United

States and Canada. "The tour was not going well at all," recalled
Keith Kolby, a road musician who was also along. "We were havin'
trouble gettin' our money out of some of the promoters. Then the
customs officials held us up at the Canadian border near Niagara
Falls because they just didn't like Opry people. It ended up takin' us
three days to get into Canada—but we did have one hell of a party at
Niagara Falls during those three days! On top of that, somebody
stole all of our stage costumes out of this U-Haul-type trailer we
were carryin' around with us.

"One day, about two thirds of the way through the tour, me and
George was sittin' in this club in Rochester, New York," Kolby
continued. "And we was just disgusted and madder than hell. He
just threw me the keys to his Cadillac and said, 'Fuck it! Let's go back
to Beaumont!' I calmed him down a little bit, but then this girl came
up and asked him to sing her a song, and he just stood up, waited till
the count of three, then threw his beer all over her.

"A few days later, we had another show in Athol, Massachusetts—
turned out there was quite a few 'athols' there too!—and we was
back at the motel with a coupla chicks we'd picked up. One was real
good-lookin' and the other was a dog. George got to talkin' to the
good-lookin' one and she said somethin' he didn't like. So he
popped her a good one and run her ass off. The ugly one stayed
around, and half the band ended up catchin' the clap offa her."

Another wild-ass "poor boy" turned Opry star with whom George
sometimes traveled was Stonewall Jackson. He rode to national
fame in the summer of 1959 with the popular hit "Waterloo." The
two of them also wrote several songs together, including "Life to
Go," a prison song patterned after Johnny Cash's "Folsom Prison
Blues" and which was a top-five country hit for Stonewall in 1958.

When the two of them first met at the Clarkston Hotel in Nashville, it always tickled Stonewall how George never seemed to show
up in the same car twice. "Seems like he had a different one every
weekend," Stonewall laughed. "And they was always these old sev-
enty-five-dollar junker types that would barely run.

"I loved George to death—still do, for that matter," Stonewall
remembered. "Back then, it was like the whole world was his motel
room, and life was just one great big party. We had some great times
together.

"Like, one time we were on tour in Texas," he added, "and we
stopped in this club near Lubbock to get us a six-pack. We was

walkin' back to the car when somebody threw a beer can and just nicked my ear. Well, ole George just turned around and said, 'Gawdam, who throwed that!?' And here come this big ole cowboy round the corner and said, 'I throwed the sumbitch!' Ole George took a swing at him and missed, and the cowboy hit ole George right between the eyes so hard it sounded like a shotgun goin' off. He went over upside down, squirmin', and ended up with his face in a mudhole. Then here come all these other cowboys round the corner and they all started kickin' him in the head and everything. I tried to beat 'em back, but he still had his face in that mudhole and liked to drown before I was able to pull him up. The police finally came, but by the time they did, my own head was all swole up like I'd got into a hornet's nest, from bein' hit so much.

"It just seemed like we were always gettin' in scrapes like that." Stonewall grimaced. "I usually got left holdin' the bag."

For all his recklessness and violence, another side of George would just as often emerge on these tours. "When he was straight, he was one of the finest men you'd ever hope to meet," recalled Georgie Riddle, a musician who began touring with George around 1960 and who grew to love him like a brother. "He'd give away anything he had: wristwatches, gold rings, expensive guitars, even, once in a while, the jacket right off his back. If you needed it more than he did, the boy would give you his last dollar, even if it meant he'd have to go hungry."

Now that times were a little better, George wasted little time in moving his wife, Shirley, and their two young sons (a second child, Bryan Daily Jones was born in July 1958) out of the little Beaumont apartment where they'd been living. The small family moved to Vidor, an amorphous "white flight" suburb just across the Neches River from Beaumont. Vidor had sprung up in the postwar era as more and more people began to flee from the double-edged urban threat of taxes and black people.

"Vidor has a certain charm of its own," waxed amateur historian Gordon Baxter (with only a slight bit of undue hyperbole). "For years, the town couldn't support a practicing attorney, because most potential courtroom disputes never got further than two people going at each other in their front yards with double-barreled shotguns. There were several thriving funeral parlors that specialized in gaping wounds and the 'Don't he look natural!' look."

Vidor is also a township where, even in the latter decades of the twentieth century, the Ku Klux Klan has reigned supreme. The Klan's rallies and civic involvements are announced in the social register of the local newspaper; and the more sinister dimensions of that secret organization are hinted at by the eerie klavern symbols that are often hand-painted by night on mailboxes and telephone poles.

In Vidor, George first bought a small house on the outskirts of town near Lakeview Drive. Then, when he could afford it, he had an even bigger house built on nearby Hulett Drive. He also moved Old George and Clara into another small house, not far from his own.

Age was beginning to settle into the face and bones of George Washington Jones, now in his seventh decade. He was now drinking harder than ever. His raving fits of intemperance and occasional violence had taken him over to the point where Clara could no longer live under the same roof with him. She sought refuge, instead, in the homes of her children, who all had families of their own.

Old George would find himself some work now and then, such as laying some copper pipe for one of the neighbors, and for a while, he would straighten up and do just fine. Sooner or later, the demons would seize him again, and he'd run off to town with a handful of that copper pipe he was supposed to be laying and sell it for the price of a bottle of cheap wine. He'd get himself all messed up and—as often as not—end up in jail again.

In spite of everything, George Glenn loved his daddy, even though he'd never forgotten those tears of bitterness and outrage that he'd choked on as a child—those long-ago nights on the front porch back at Kountze. He knew his daddy to be increasingly harmless in his advancing years. He also knew where in the Bible it said: "Honor thy father and thy mother, as the Lord thy God hath commanded thee that thy days may be prolonged and that it may go well with thee"—even though he figured that the feller who wrote those nice-sounding words probably didn't have a daddy like his daddy—Old George.

The prodigal son himself could see that, slowly but surely, George Washington Jones was eating his insides out and slowly wasting himself away with strong drink. He'd raise hell with the old man about that and tell his friends not to give him wine money when he came around panhandling for it, but Old George knew his way around his youngest son all too well. He'd sell his carpenter's tools or go out and pick up bottles along the public highway or otherwise shame his good-hearted son into giving him the handful of coins for another cheap drink.

Old George would occasionally show up on his younger son's doorstep, all full of whiskey, wine and meanness, cussing and raving and waving a flimsy little pocketknife in his son's face, telling him he was fixing to cut him up. The old man's drunken antics were no longer much of a threat to George Glenn, but merely a troubling annoyance to be wearily endured, like the buzzing of a horsefly around his head. When his daddy would push him too far, he'd get disgusted and holler at him to get the hell out of his house and not come back until he sobered up.

The next day, when Old George finally came back around, grinning and blinking his bloodshot eyes, not even remembering his transgressions of the previous day, it would then be his younger son who would now be on a crazy-drunk rampage. Having worked himself into a jealous frenzy, George Glenn would be running around the house with a loaded shotgun, looking for his wife, Shirley.

At such times, his wife would just run out the back door and seek refuge at her mother-in-law's house. She knew, like everyone else, that George Glenn knew better than to come around his mama when he was in such a state. She knew that Clara hated to see the poison of strong drink ruining her youngest son as much as she hated to see how it had destroyed her husband.

"George really loved his mama and respected her," recalled Georgie Riddle, who lived with George in Vidor for a time. "She was one of the very few people that I ever saw who, when he got on a binge, could handle him and calm him down. He would never do anything to hurt her, and when she told him to straighten up, he listened."

Clara Jones had continued to find abiding strength through the years in the harsh dictates of Uncle Litt's old-timey religion. Strong drink had still not passed her lips, and rouge or paint had still never defiled her face. Though she understood little of the business that her youngest son was in, she was nonetheless beside herself with pride that he had taken the sanctified musical gift of the Pattersons out into the world and done so well for himself. When he came home all bruised and bandaged from his latest scuffle, or when he complained to her of his chronic hoarseness brought on by long hours spent singing through the cigarette smoke and alcoholic din for the whiskey-swilling fornicators, foul-mouthed sodomites and unrepentant wastrels that she knew frequented the sordid establishments where he now earned his coin, she would take him aside and admonish him sternly: "Now, Glenn, you know you don't *have* to sing in them kinds of places!"

On Sundays, George Glenn returned with Clara to the little White Oak Church, back in the piney woods of the Big Thicket. There, along with the newest generation of Pattersons, they would raise their voices in a gospel way, just as they'd done so often back in the old days. On their way back home, they would occasionally stop to linger and lay flowers by the faded tombstones under the tall trees in Phelps Cemetery. George Glenn would fall silent on these occasions with thoughts and fears that he could not put into words. He would gaze down at the grave of Uncle Litt, who was now less than a shadow in his earliest childhood memories, and he would ponder over the grave of his long-dead sister Ethel, who'd slept in the cold, damp earth for all those long years, since before he was even born.

George Glenn also visited Brother Burl and Sister Annie Stephens whenever he could; together they'd laugh and sing, just like in the old days. Brother Burl would also show George Glenn some of the inspirational poems he'd written: "Please Take the Devil Out of Me," "Boat of Life," "Cup of Loneliness," "Taggin' Along" . . . George Glenn loved Burl's poems. He recognized in them the same abiding truths and simple messages of Christian devotion which he had heard preached so many times from the pulpits of those old Baptist and Pentecost churches. He even took some of those poems of Brother Burl's and made music to go with them and put them on his records.

Darrell Edwards and George were also writing songs together with continued success. The Muse from the Thicket had, by now, also become George's traveling companion, drinking partner and right-hand man. He would chauffeur George around in one of the brand-new Cadillacs that his boss now favored, and whenever the prodigal singer had finished doing a show in Florida or someplace, and had gotten himself too messed up to make it to the next stop on the tour, Darrell could always be counted on to go sober him up and get him out to the airport and on his way to yet another show in yet another strange city.

Darrell and his family were now living down near the Gulf Coast, in Galveston. Whenever George Washington Jones had temporarily worn out his welcome in Vidor or needed to get his hands on a little wine money, the Edwardses would bring him down to their house and put him to work, letting him stay on for a month or so. The old man, with his long-john underwear, his whiskey face and his wayward ways, would work pretty good as long as the Edwardses kept him sober. But sooner or later, he always managed to slip away from them and wander off. They would have to go hunt him up in whichever of the town's beer joints he ended up in.

One day, Darrell put Old George to work helping storm-sheet the house. Darrell's son Alfred was up on the ladder, calling out measurements and angles. He had Old George down on the ground, where he was grinning widely as he cut the various lengths of storm sheeting to Alfred's specifications. Unbeknownst to them, the old man had a bottle stashed in his back pocket, and before they found out, he'd cut just about every one of those tin sheets at a crooked angle. Sooner or later and somehow or another, they got all that storm siding hung up there just the same.

The Edwardses would also get surprise visits from young George. Once the prodigal singer was drunk at home in Vidor and came around just enough to realize he needed another drink. There was one little problem, though, in that he didn't have any wheels to get to the liquor store. Somehow or other, he managed to get himself a ride down to the local Buick dealership, where he quickly paid cash for a shiny new Buick limousine. When he pulled up in the Edwardses' driveway a little while later and honked the horn of the new Buick, his shotgun eyes were dancing dizzily and the jack-o'-lantern grin was spread widely across his face. "Hey, Darrell!" he hollered as he gloated with drunken yet sincere pride, stumbling out of his factory-fresh Buick. "How do y'all like my new *Oldsmobile!?*"

Laughing quietly to themselves, Darrell and Alfred carried the wayward singing star upstairs and put him to bed until he sobered up enough to drive the shiny Buick back to Vidor, and trade it in for yet another car.

At other times, though, George would come wandering home to Vidor full of terrible whiskey meanness, just like his daddy used to do back in Saratoga. He'd get to hollering and cursing and blaspheming and smashing windows and breaking furniture and busting the TV and tearing down curtains in his house and slapping his wife around, just like a crazy man. Shirley—who was more or less a teetotaler like old Clara—would rush out the door with their two young sons and hide from her husband's wrath. The next day, when he'd come to his senses again, the prodigal singer would take his head in his heads, and with tearful remorse he would grimly survey the destruction that he'd left in his path the night before.

Sometimes it seemed to George Glenn that there was a deep tension that abided within him always, like the sadness with no name. Part of it, he knew, was the price exacted by his ever-increasing fame: it was a state of chronic nervous exhaustion that had accumulated from a thousand nights of pouring out his raw emotions to a thousand audiences of bleary-eyed patrons in sleazy beer joints, and from a thousand wild, disjointed memories of the faces of a thousand strange women at whiskey-drenched motel-room parties. There was the pure hell of a thousand hangovers with nowhere to sleep them off, except in the crowded back seat of a moving car on the way to the next show. All in all, it sometimes left him feeling as if there were snakes loose in his head.

There were other old skeletons that kept popping up, too: like Willie Bonvillion, who would soon have the law back on his ass again, claiming that he was eleven months in arrears in support payments from his first marriage.

One day, when George had just returned home from yet another lengthy whiskey- and amphetamine-soaked road trip, he sat quietly in the living room that Shirley always seemed to keep so neat and orderly in his absence. He found that the deep restlessness that abided within him would not leave him alone; instead, it grew in intensity, until it filled his head like the buzzing of a legion of angry insects. At that moment, it struck him just how calm Shirley always seemed to be, how well she always managed to hold things together, whether he was there or not . . . *whether he was there or not . . .*

Without thinking, he picked up his guitar. Fragments of a melody and bits of verses started popping out of his head, coming at him, falling together, line after line. Before long, he had written a song unlike any other he'd ever written before. Its troubling lyrics were fraught with portents of violence, jealous anger and a deep, irreconcilable sense of betrayal. When he finally recorded the song, "The Window Up Above," in 1960, he sang it in a taut, almost offhanded manner that called to mind the style of one of his heroes, Lefty Frizzell. He sang it in a manner which merely insinuated the presence of wild, barely suppressed emotions seething just under the

surface, like poisonous serpents writhing beneath the waters of a
still pond:

> *I've been living a new way*
> *of life that I love so*
> *but I can see the clouds are gathering*
> *and the storm will wreck our home*
>
> *For last night he hugged you tightly*
> *and you didn't even shove*
> *This is true because I was watching*
> *from the window up above*
>
> *You must have thought that I was sleeping*
> *and I wish that I had been*
> *but it's best to get to know you*
> *and the way your heart can sin*
> *I thought that we belonged together*
> *and our hearts fit like a glove*
> *but I was wrong, because I was watching*
> *from the window up above*

The record, which was underpinned by the subtle honky-tonk-
style accompaniment of Hal Rugg's steel guitar, Tommy Jackson's
fiddle and Floyd Cramer's "slip note"-style piano, was released in
November 1960 and quickly rose to the number two position in
Billboard. This original version of "The Window Up Above" (the
song would later be recorded by numerous artists, including Leon
Russell, Loretta Lynn, and Mickey Gilley—who revived the song in
1975 and took it to the number one spot in the country charts)
would endure as one of the most powerful and haunting vocal
performances ever turned in by the prodigal singer over the course
of his long recording career.

In April of the same year, George made another visit to Owen
Bradley's Quonset Hut studio in Nashville, where he was now doing
all of his recording. In less than two days he recorded more than two
albums' worth of the songs of Hank Williams, who'd been dead now
for nearly a decade. He recorded many of those same songs that
he'd sung so many times, so long ago, in the dingy clubs and on the
crowded street corners of Beaumont. He even recorded "Wedding

Bells," the very same song that the dark legend had sung in his presence eleven years earlier, in the small studio at station KRIC.

When George sang these familiar songs now, though, without even trying he imbued them with fresh nuances of sadness and deeper shades of mortal confusion. The languid resonances of pain and lonesomeness echoed through his voice, as if he were now gazing deeper into the same bottomless well of despair that Hank himself had fallen into—gazing far deeper into it than he even cared to.

Pappy Daily (having discovered that it was George's way to peruse the fine print of contracts with the same degree of care with which most people peruse Marvel comic books) continued to attend carefully to the wild-ass singer's business affairs for him. In 1958, he had sold his share of Starday Records to his former partner, Don Pierce, and he had solidified both his and George's relationship with the Mercury label. Pappy, in 1961, left Mercury and struck a more lucrative deal, for both George and for himself (as producer and A&R man), with the newly formed country division of United Artists Records.

Half a world away, back in Beaumont, George had found himself a new haunt, the Gulf Coast Recording Studio. It had recently been opened down on Fourth Street, and was operated by Bill Hall, an old friend and erstwhile "manager" of George's, along with Hall's partner, producer "Cowboy" Jack Clement. Clement had earlier made a name for himself with Sun Records in Memphis, where in the 1950s he'd served as studio engineer and right-hand man to Sam Phillips, while Phillips was busy recording the likes of Elvis Presley, Johnny Cash, Jerry Lee Lewis and Carl Perkins.

George liked it there at the Gulf Coast studio. He knew that Hall and Clement were always good for a laugh, and that you could get some great home-cooked Cajun food at the little joint just across the street. It felt like home.

George Washington Jones was also an occasional visitor at the new studio. Dogging his son's footsteps, he'd show up with a dirty, crumpled scrap of paper on which he'd hurriedly scrawled a few illegible lines. "Say, fellers," he'd explain in his raspy, whiskey voice to whomever he could get to pay attention, as he clumsily unfolded the paper with his gnarled fingernails. "I got me some songs h'yer I wrote. I'll sell 'em to ya real cheap!"

Hall or Clement would smile knowingly at Old George and hand him a couple of bucks.

"Thank ya!" Old George would beam happily and fondle the paper money hungrily as he hurried out the door toward the liquor store, with a shit-eating grin smeared across his face and renewed vigor in his clod-hopping gait. "Don't worry," he'd assure them as he beamed over his shoulder. "My boy George'll make good on this money!"

George's music was ever so gradually beginning to drift further afield from the ass-kicking Texas honky-tonk sound which had been in vogue at the time he launched his recording career. While still on Mercury, he had recorded a song written by Darrell that was a soulful, evocative ballad, the likes of which he'd never recorded before. It was called "Tender Years." The gentle, understated reading which he'd brought to the song's heartfelt lyrics marked another step in his gradual emergence as a smooth country balladeer. The manner in which he sang the words to "Tender Years" (which, in mid-1961, became his second number one single) was, in fact, just about enough to make the short hairs stand up on the back of one's head.

Jack Clement loved George's version of "Tender Years," and now he had another slow, soulful ballad, called "She Thinks I Still Care," written by Dickie Lee Lipscomb and Steve Duffy (two professional songwriters under contract to his publishing company), which he believed would be just right for George. Clement was so sold on the song that he started playing it for George every time he'd drop by the Gulf Coast studios. "I dunno, Jack." George would shift his weight jerkily from one foot to the other and grin that thin, inscrutable "Possum" grin of his. "I don't think I like it too much. It's got too damn many 'just becauses' in it," referring with good-natured disparagement to the song's rather insistent lyrical hook. "I don't think nobody really wants ta hear that shit, do you? . . . C'mon, let's go get somethin' to eat."

Hall and Clement both kept after him. "They had this ole, worn-out, rinky-dink tape recorder layin' around the studio that was little more than junk," recalled Raymond Nalley, Luther Nalley's brother, who was a session musician at Gulf Coast. "Every time they'd try to lay that song on George, he'd just look at that damn tape recorder and ask 'em, 'How much you sell me that thing for?'

One day, Bill Hall finally told him, 'Hell, George, if you'll record the song, I'll *give* ya the damn tape recorder!' "

Jack Clement reworked the song's melody slightly to give it a bit more of a country flavor—and after he agreed to relinquish half the publishing royalties to George and the hard-bargaining Pappy Daily —George finally relented and recorded it. When "She Thinks I Still Care" was released in April, it not only hit the number one spot in the country charts, but was received with far more enthusiasm than any song he'd previously recorded. At the end of 1962, country music disk jockeys cast their vote in *Billboard*'s annual awards poll. They not only chose "She Thinks I Still Care" as the year's Favorite Country Music Single, they also voted George in as that year's Favorite Male Country Artist. When Shirley, Jimmie Klein (one of dozens of men to be cast, over the years, in the short-lived role as George's "road manager"—a job description which, in George's case, was perhaps in itself a contradiction in terms) and Klein's wife all accompanied the prodigal singer to Nashville's annual Country Music Disk Jockey Convention that year, they gave George so many awards and trophies that it took all four of them just to carry them out to the car.

Chapter Four

KING OF THE REALM

With a spray of gravel and the harsh screech of tires against asphalt, the large, shiny, freshly purchased Lincoln limousine skidded sideways into a parking lot along the main drag that ran through Vidor, and came to rest at a precarious angle. Sitting behind the wheel, recklessly gunning the car's huge engine, was George Glenn Jones, his jack-o'-lantern grin spread widely across his face and his shotgun eyes dancing wildly, like multicolored Fourth of July pinwheels.

"C'mon, get in!" he hollered out the window at a friend who was standing at a nearby storefront.

"Where in the hell did ya get this car?" the friend asked as he stood gawking, seemingly transfixed by such a noble and magnificent construction of chrome and steel, the likes of which seldom graced the rough streets of Vidor. As he peered through the partially tinted window at George, he also noticed the bottle of moonshine whiskey, a smaller, amber bottle of pills and about $20,000 in paper money of various denominations—the proceeds of a freshly cashed royalty check. The friend saw that, as the car had skidded to rest, some of the larger of these bills had slipped out of the envelope that had contained them and were now strewn haphazardly across the seat and floorboards, mixed with some of the pills that had also been scattered from their bottle.

"I bought it yesterday," George replied absently to the friend's awestruck inquiries as to his new pleasure machine. "Bought one just like it for my band, too. . . . C'mon, get the hell in! Let's go up to Louisiana and party!"

"How much it cost ya?" The friend continued to gawk as he slid across the slippery new seat covers and marveled at the Lincoln's equally lavish and pimped-out interior.

"Hell, I don't remember." The prodigal singer shrugged. "C'mon, let's get the hell outa here!"

With one hand on the wheel and the other clutching his bottle of white lightning, George spun out of the parking lot, leaving in his wake another shower of dust and gravel. The friend held on for dear life as he roared at an alarmingly high rate of speed, up Route 105, a narrow, crooked strip of asphalt that ran northward from Vidor. Grinning gleefully, George Glenn stomped down and kicked his new Lincoln in the ass until they were doing nearly a hundred miles an hour, weaving dangerously from one side of the narrow roadway to the other, onto the rough gravel shoulder and back on the highway again.

"Hey, uh, George, I . . . uh, I can't go to Louisiana right now . . ." As his friend protested weakly and struggled to make his voice heard through the thick lump of fear that had formed in his throat, he noticed that his knuckles were turning white from clutching so tightly to the door handle. "Uh . . . you ain't in no condition to be drivin' that far either. C'mon, let's go home first, and then you can go to Louisiana."

George Glenn took a slug of the moonshine and stared blankly at his friend, as if he were struggling to decipher his words from across some great wide void of stoned incomprehension. He grinned and spoke in words of his own that tumbled out all sideways and jumbled: "O.K.! The hell with it! Fuck Louisiana! We'll go later!"

Hitting the gas and the brakes at the same time, he laughed wickedly and spun the huge car around in the center of the road, heading back down the highway toward home. A few miles farther along the road, he gently slid the Lincoln into the driveway in front of his elegant residence. He made it in the front door, up the stairs to his bedroom, and passed out.

Early the next morning, when the grass was still wet with dew and the prodigal singer was still fast asleep in his bed, the friend came around again. He peeked into the big Lincoln and saw that the $20,000 in paper money was still scattered across the seat and floor, and that the bills were now damp and soggy from the morning's wetness. Gingerly, he picked them up, one by one, put them back in the envelope, and carried them in the house and handed them to Shirley.

It was 1964 . . . or 1965 . . . or one of those years, anyway. Sometimes now, it was hard to tell, because the entire decade of the 1960s was beginning to roll quickly by, in one big confused blur.

George was now one of the hottest artists in all of country music. The trade magazines had once again named him as the year's most popular male vocalist in 1963 and had heaped their awards on him once more. He'd long ago left the rinky-dink Houston and Beaumont beer-hall circuit behind, and now was performing in coliseums and large auditoriums, all hither and yon (even Los Angeles's Hollywood Bowl and New York City's Carnegie Hall now and then), with the likes of Johnny Cash, Loretta Lynn and Buck Owens.

George was now pulling in as much as a thousand dollars a night —more cash money than his daddy ever made during the entire decade of the Great Hoover Depression, when the family had had only Mama's biscuits and egg gravy to keep them from starvation.

Even so, instead of meaning more than it did back in the old biscuit-and-gravy days, these coins of such great denomination seemed to mean even less to George. He squandered it accordingly —squandered it flagrantly and openly, as if flaunting the lack of regard that he had for it and all that it could buy. He left piles of it lying haphazardly around motel rooms, amidst the discarded cigarette wrappers and beer cans. He blew it on women, jewelry, parties, pills and gallons and gallons of vodka, Jack Daniel's, and Old Charter. He pissed it away on dozens of fancy, factory-fresh cars, most of which he merely drove for a few days or a few weeks before trading them, reselling them, giving them away or simply leaving them abandoned for the repossession agents to claim. About the only time that all that money ever really seemed to mean anything at all to him was when he was spending it on someone else.

There were some things that didn't and wouldn't change, though.

George still managed to go out and play a long string of those "thousand-a-nighters" and come back home with his pockets emptier than when he left. Even that didn't matter; he always knew there was more where that came from. He always knew that if he wanted to take his two young sons, Jeffery and Bryan, on a trip to Florida, or if he wanted a new swimming pool, or if he got behind on his taxes, he could always get Pappy Daily to advance him another $20,000 or $30,000 or more. What the hell, they were both in the chips now.

With his fancy house there in Southeast Texas, and his fancy cars and his good-looking wife, George was now King of the Realm. It seemed like there were just no limits anymore—little or nothing to stop him from doing whatever in the hell he pleased: he could get drunk and drive a lawn mower down the side of the highway to the liquor store; get mad and run a brand-new John Deere tractor through a fence; pull a concealed gun on a sheriff's deputy; go in a local bar and, with a snap of his fingers, ride off with the best-looking barmaid in the joint; or even shoot at a friend in one of his towering fits of jealous rage. He could do just about whatever in the hell he pleased, and it no longer seemed to make a fucking bit of difference. It even seemed like those were the kinds of things that people *expected* George Jones to do.

Hell, no. There no longer seemed to be any damn limits at all. Not only had his music made him rich, by Vidor's modest standards; it had even made him downright *respectable*—far more respectable than he ever hoped or cared to be. May 13, 1965, was officially declared "George Jones Day" by the mayor of Beaumont. On March 3, 1963, the Texas state legislature, in a joint resolution of the House and Senate, had even proclaimed him an honorary admiral in the Texas Navy! In 1963, he and Shirley were inducted into the Vidor Chamber of Commerce, since they had by then become the proprietors of their own little restaurant, the Chuckwagon, on North Main Street (an enterprise that, though short-lived, was still haunting George in 1968, when he was sued for $3,052.35 in unpaid back rent and damages by one M. S. Wozencraft, the owner of the land on which the Chuckwagon had stood). As the decade wore on, he had continually refurbished and enlarged his spacious ranch-style house at 165 Hulett Street until it assumed palatial dimensions. Then he bought another house nearby, and another one, until he damn near owned the whole block.

In the midst of all this affluence, a deep and abiding sense of weariness would often consume him, like some strange rheumatism of the soul. The years since his initial burst of success with "Why, Baby, Why" now weighed down upon him heavily, like the sinking weight of a huge grindstone. He had survived an entire decade since then: more than ten long years of pouring his heart out to strangers. It had been a wild, disjointed decade, full of long, lonely nights and strange faces: the faces of fans and backslappers and loose women who so often, after shows, descended upon him like a horde of hungry insects, pawing him, kissing him, cornering him and poisoning his mind with their cigarette smoke, whiskey breath and false idolatry. It seemed as if each of these insects tried to carry off a little piece of him, and dealing with them, night after night, left him feeling devoured, nervous, dizzy and depleted of some essential inner strength, which he could never get back. In the midst of these backstage hordes, he tried his damnedest not to get drunk, but it was impossible. It was just like an alcoholic singer friend of George's had once put it: "I drink to make *other people* interesting."

No matter how badly George fucked up in Nashville, he still could do no wrong. He was no longer writing songs with Darrell Edwards, the Muse from the Thicket, but now Nashville's top songwriters were personally bringing him their best songs to record. Though the increasingly influential Country Music Association did not yet— and would not for years to come—choose to acknowledge his existence by presenting him with one of their annual awards, crowds of admiring musicians, most of them with drinks in hand, often flocked to his recording sessions to hear that hauntingly powerful countrified voice of his in action. ("Even back then, George was the *singer's* singer," recalled Kelso Herston, a session guitarist who played on many of George's sessions of that era. "He's the only person I know who, every time he cut a record, people would show up in droves.") The awestruck admirers that gathered in the studio to listen would shake their heads, whisper among themselves and wonder out loud how it was possible—outside of making a pact with the devil—for a mortal man to sing that damn good.

George would always oblige these admirers of his with a spectacular performance, even if he was sometimes too drunk to even sit up straight and keep his balance. With his songwriter friends, like Earl "Peanut" Montgomery or Dallas Frazier, standing behind him, propping him up on the stool, he would pour his frazzled emotions into songs like "A Girl I Used to Know," "Open Pit Mine" and "If

My Heart Had Windows." During this time all of George's songs, almost without fail, sped right up into the country top ten, one after another.

"Back then, if you caught George at the right point, when he'd only had a few drinks, but before he'd gone too far overboard, he could just moan his ass off and just put a whole lot more feeling into those ballads," recalled piano player Pig Robbins, a regular on the prodigal singer's sessions.

With each successive hit record and with the additional exposure that came from the numerous appearances he was beginning to make on network and nationally syndicated television shows, like "The Jimmy Dean Show," George's concert price had slowly edged upward. By the mid-1960s, he got to the point where he could employ his own road band, and it was one of the best in the business, the Jones Boys. Quite a few of those among the ever-changing cast of characters in the Jones Boys' lineup ended up working with George for years, through thick and thin. In spite of the wildness and chaos that constantly flowed around the prodigal singer, many of those band members would, in later years, remember George best for his fairness and generosity; they would recall how he treated them more like brothers than mere employees.

One of the first road musicians that George ever hired was Georgie Riddle, who was then a young singer, fresh out of the Army. Riddle had met his future employer quite by accident in 1960, at the Country Music Disk Jockey Convention, a week-long drunken blowout which is held every autumn in Nashville under the auspices of WSM-Radio and the Country Music Association.

"I was walkin' down the hall of the old Hermitage Hotel when I heard all this ruckus comin' from this one room," recalled Riddle. "Out of curiosity, I stuck my head in the door, and there was George, layin' on the bed with a guitar in his hand, with a few people standin' around. I just walked in and joined the party."

When George announced to the small bedside audience over which he was holding court that he was looking for a harmony singer to go on the road with him, Riddle quickly volunteered. After auditioning on the spot, he was immediately offered the job. "George had been drinkin' some that day, and at first I didn't think he was serious," said Riddle. "But he was. We hit the road together about a day later."

Riddle soon became George's right-hand man and constant companion. Despite the fact that he was routinely hired and fired about once every two weeks, Riddle discovered, as many other road musicians after him would, that George was both a good employer and a good friend. He paid Riddle top dollar, recorded some of the songs that he'd written and even talked Pappy Daily into giving Riddle a recording contract of his own.

Though the money out on the concert circuit kept getting better and better, the wild-ass times—as Riddle nostalgically recalled—remained a constant. George would occasionally get on a tear, and Riddle would find himself driving down the interstate highway, holding the steering wheel steady with one arm and holding a very drunk and emotionally overwrought George in a headlock with the other, trying to keep him from making good on his threats to throw himself out of the fast-moving car. He also had to scrape his boss up off many a sawdust floor of some beer joint or nightclub after he'd succeeded in picking a fight with the biggest cowboy in the house. What impressed Riddle most about George was his resilience, his ability to drink and raise hell for days on end and go without sleep, night after night, and still be the first one up in the morning. "He could just go on and on and never get sick and never get hoarse," Riddle explained with amazement and a trace of envy. "It never mattered how many nights in a row we stayed up and roared, or how far we drove between shows, he could always sing his ass off when it came time."

George had by now nurtured, like the late, great Hank Williams before him, an abusive whiskey-drinking reputation all his own. It stalked him like a shadow, and there was always somebody, in every two-bit club and in every half-assed town he played, who would sooner or later challenge him to live up to it. "Sometimes he'd go two or three weeks and not drink nothin' at all. But then, sooner or later, some ole boy who claimed he knew George would show up with a jug of liquor and shove it in front of his face.

"One time, we were doing a week's worth of shows in this nightclub in Baltimore," Riddle explained. "All week long, the owner kept after George: 'Now, George, before you leave, I wan'cha to sit down and have a few drinks with me!' Well, I could see that the guy was gettin' on George's nerves, and I kept tellin' him, 'Listen, don't push him. You'll be sorry if you do,' but he kept on. On the last night, George finally did get to hittin' the bottle with him. When he started, he didn't stop: he threw chairs, knocked over tables, you name it! He just tore the hell out of the place."

In early 1963, Pappy Daily came across a song that he thought might be just right for George. It was called "The Race Is On," and it was written by a man named Don Rollins, who composed it one day after visiting the Turf Paradise Race Track in Phoenix, Arizona. The song, with its splashy, tongue-twisting lyrics, used the fast-paced images and emotions of a horse race to weave a whimsical and slightly tongue-in-cheek lament of lost love.

One warm cloudy night in June, George finally got around to recording the song at the Quonset Hut studio in Nashville. "Usually, George would have to have him a little drink or two in the studio," recalled a fly on the wall who was present that night. "Sometimes he'd have him a bottle hid from Pappy in the bathroom, and nobody'd know about it until it was too late.

"Well, the night we did 'The Race Is On,' George had been hittin' it real hard," the fly added. "If you listen real closely to that record [the original version, on United Artists], you can hear where he screwed some of the words up: like, 'lay right down and die' [in the final verse] came out 'ray right down and die.' I remember he got his vocal track down, an' then it wasn't but about thirty minutes later, he got to where he couldn't walk and we had to carry him back to his hotel room."

Despite of—or, more likely, on account of—his whiskey numbness in the moments before his final swan dive of the evening, George imbued "The Race Is On" with a masterfully frenetic, on-the-edge vocal reading, full of whining emotional ambivalence and mock sadness. By gleefully bending and stretching the notes and singing, at times, slightly ahead of or behind the song's fast-clipped meter, he embellished it with a subtle sense of tension and release that perfectly complemented the rapid-fire cascading effect of the song's lyrics. Session man Kelso Herston, playing behind him, added to the frenzy, laying down relentless, cavity-rattling rhythm and lead patterns on a heavily reverberated electric six-string ("Tic Tac") bass guitar.

After "The Race Is On" was released more than a year later, in September 1964, it galloped up to the number three position in the country charts and made a showing in the national pop charts, staying there for several weeks.

Around Nashville, George's reputation continued to spread, not only for his continuing success as a country vocalist but for his sometimes prodigious excesses as well. Always, the furiously wagging tongues of Music City—a town that is as renowned for its virulent gossip, innuendo and political infighting as it is for its music —saw to it that all of the riotous tales of debauchery which had George's name attached to them were quickly broadcast far and wide.

Once he and his close friend Peanut Montgomery, an Alabama-born songwriter who had, by now, come to be his confidant and right-hand man, got high on beer and black beauties (or "California turnarounds," as Peanut called them) in George's Nashville hotel room. It was Peanut who got pissed off at George and poured ketchup all down in his suitcase and then heaved a TV set out of his hotel-room window. But, naturally, the whole town soon got wind of the episode and quickly got it all turned around to where George was the one who actually did the damage.

But some of the increasingly bizarre "George Jones stories," when traced back to their sometimes apocryphal sources, had a distended ring of twisted truth to them that was even stranger than fiction—such as the time George was on tour in Texas with Jimmie Klein.

"I think we was in Lubbock," Klein remembered. "We had just gotten paid for several dates, and we had four or five thousand dollars stacked up there in the motel room, and George was just throwin' money all over the place. He'd been tryin' to get hold of some pills, and somebody finally brought him over a whole quart jar full of those little heart-shaped Dexedrines. Well, I saw them pills and I took 'em away from him and threw 'em in the toilet and started to flush 'em down. Naturally, that made him madder than hell. So he just picked up about three thousand dollars in bills and said, 'You might as well throw that away, too!' He tossed it in the toilet and down it went."

One typically carefree weekend in Nashville, when George was feeling no pain, Sonny Burns, a face out of his now foggy and smoke-filled past, temporarily came back to haunt him. Old Pappy Daily had tracked Sonny down, pulled him out of the long, slow slide that he was still on, sobered him up after about half a decade of drunken oblivion and brought him out of mothballs to make some more records—this time for United Artists. "I think the old man—

bless his heart!—just brought me back to kinda spook George," Sonny said, smiling. "I believe it was gettin' to where Pappy couldn't hardly handle him anymore, and he thought that maybe bringin' me back into the picture might scare him back in line, on account of I'd been outselling him back in Houston. Course, it didn't work." Sonny laughed. "It didn't faze George one bit."

One afternoon, Sonny and George, along with Country Johnny Mathis, recorded a song called "Blue House Painted White." In the studio they put George up on a box, so he could stand up on tiptoes and share the same microphone with the much taller Sonny. And for a while there, it was just like old times.

After the session, George, Sonny, Pappy and Georgie Riddle, along with a handful of other wild-ass, drink-sodden musicians and other assorted flunkies, were all together in a smoke-filled room at the Downtowner Motel. George poured himself a big water glass full of straight whiskey and gulped half of it down. Then turning to Sonny, who'd been on the wagon for nearly a year, he raised his glass and saluted him with a voice so full of rhetorical scorn that the memory of it would make Sonny shudder for years to come. The room was dead quiet as all eyes were riveted on George. "Right there's the son of a bitch that got me started on this shit." George grinned coldly, then coughed just before he tipped back his glass and emptied it in a single slug. "And now he don't even drink no more!"

By the mid-1960s, thanks in part to the omnipervasive influence of television and radio, country music had reached a new and unprecedented level of national popularity. In addition to "The Jimmy Dean Show," which was pulling down solid ratings on the ABC television network, there were now also more than a half dozen nationally syndicated country music TV variety shows originating from Nashville. The number of full-time country radio stations across the nation had also begun to increase dramatically (from 81 in 1961 to 525 in 1971).

In the forefront of this massive new wave of popularity—reaping its significant financial rewards while helping to push it along on its inevitable course—was a new generation of country music concert promoters, like the slick-tongued, hyperbolic North Carolina-born Carlton Haney. These men—Haney and his contemporaries—had come to realize that they could now book artists like George and

Johnny Cash and Porter Wagoner into large venues like civic centers and sports arenas, and with the right kind of Barnum & Bailey-like advertising and promotion blitz, they damn near always filled the joints.

With the prospects of huge profits from such shows, there also came the inevitability of much greater and potentially more disastrous financial risks. Such promoters came to realize that booking George into such places was, indeed, a calculated risk—something that one did with an uneasy feeling, like a farmer who frantically harvests his wheat while looking over his shoulder at storm clouds moving toward him through ever-darkening skies.

That was the exact situation one night in the mid-1960s, when Haney had George headlining a show that also featured a handful of other, lesser-known artists. He'd booked this country circus into a huge skating rink in Alexandria, Virginia.

"Somebody come to me just before the show and told me that Gawhge was drinkin'," the silver-tongued Haney recollected with a shudder of dread. "And I just said, 'Oh mah *Gawd!*'

"Well, as soon as I heard that, I got somebody over there to the motel to get Gawhge, and he could not *walk,*" added Haney (who, for many years after his long, slow slide from the top of the concert promotion business, still kept enshrined under glass, in the little corner grocery store he operated in rural North Carolina, a battle-worn pair of $800 ostrich-skin cowboy boots that George had once given him). "It turned out he had drank two bottles of whiskey, one right after the other. I just said, 'By Gawd, he's goin' on, and that's all there is to it!' So when they introduced him, we just dragged him out there, in front of seven thousand people, and he just fell right off the stage, on top of his *gih*-tar, and just mashed the plumb hell out of it! We got him back up off the floor, and half the people was laughin', and the other half was madder than hell. I pulled Gawhge backstage and told him, 'Now, Gawhge, you *gotta* go out there and sing or them people's gonna tear this place down!' Finally, he come around a little bit and said, 'Hell, I'm gonna do it!' And he staggered out there and somebody handed him another *gih*-tar, and he ended up playin' one of the best damn shows he's ever done in his life! He got three standin' ovations!"

There were other nights when George made it to the stage and through his whiskey numbness felt only the deep burning of his vast and abiding emptiness and confusion. He would gaze out into the swirling crowd as if he were gazing into a dark crystal ball. In the adoring, expectant faces of the strangers, he would see nothing but more of the same confusion and emptiness that dwelled within him. He fled from these visions as if fleeing from some horrible apocalyptic revelation. Quite often, he executed these escapes with disingenuous Houdini-like stealth, slipping out a backstage window and roaring off into the night in the first car that he was able to buy, beg or borrow. Other times, he would merely plant himself inertly backstage and seek refuge from his horrible visions by sinking still deeper into the shadowy amber veil of strong drink.

"One night, we was playin' a show in Winston-Salem, North Carolina," recalled Peanut Montgomery, who often accompanied George on the road, to play guitar for him, drink his whiskey, take his pills and chase the loose women that he drew like flies. "He was back in the dressin' room, gettin' drunk, and we couldn't get him to go onstage. Then the whole crowd, about three thousand of 'em, was out there clappin' and yellin', 'WE WANT GEORGE JONES! . . . WE WANT GEORGE JONES!' We finally got him out there and he started playin' 'White Lightning.' He stopped everybody and said his guitar was outa tune, and gave everybody in his band a good cussin' for not havin' it tuned up right. He started messin' around with it, tryin' to tune the bottom strings, like: 'TAAAAA-AAAA-DAAAAAAAAWWWWWHHAAAAANNNNNNGGGGGGGG . . .' till he had it tuned way up too high. Course, that made him even madder. Finally, he just took his guitar off and busted it on the floor, just like it was an ax and he was choppin' wood. Then he walked off, and we never did get him back out there again that night."

When George left his home in Vidor and was on his way to catch a plane or to meet his band in some distant city, his weariness and darkness would sometimes suddenly overtake him. When he failed to arrive in the distant city as scheduled, frantic long-distance calls would be made to his family back in Texas. Search parties would be sent out. Someone would finally manage to track him down to some well-concealed refuge in an anonymous hotel or a dimly lit lounge. He would be sitting alone in the darkness, drinking and staring blankly at the television, a look of abject misery and defeat etched deeply into his haggard, unshaven face.

It was in 1966, in Nashville, that a reporter from *The Music City News*, after several unsuccessful attempts, managed to locate

George in a room at the Biltmore Hotel. Amidst "a haze of pickers and grinners," he was holding court in his usual fashion—sprawled out on a bed, surrounded by an addle-brained gaggle of hangers-on: songwriters, fellow musicians, fans, music industry weasels and other admirers. In the crowd were Pappy Daily, Faron Young and Melba Montgomery, Peanut Montgomery's statuesque and talented sister, with whom George had begun recording love duets. Amidst the lewd laughter and boisterousness of the whiskey-swilling idolaters, lackeys and wastrels, George's weariness was now obvious. The reporter asked George if, in looking back on his career, he had any advice for a newcomer; George's reply was surprisingly to the point:

"I wouldn't advise them to. . . . Oh, I love country music, but . . . there's always somebody wanting something . . . wanting you to do something . . . you're constantly in demand . . . there's no seclusion, or rather there is, but not when you really want it. When you're out with friends or in a party, or out in the public, that's the main time you really find yourself wanting some privacy, but there's no way in the world to get it. Then, when you're not working, after about three or four days, you start getting restless, and that's all due to nervous tension. You want to be out again, moving around and seeing people, playing and singing. . . . If I could have made a living doing some other things, I know I would have been a lot happier. . . . I would have had more peace of mind. [But] you don't get that in this business."

Back in Vidor, the wild ways of old George Washington Jones had slowly but surely begun to get the better of him. He was semi-retired now, drawing ninety-five dollars a month in social security and old-age pension benefits. No longer burdened with work, the chronic and habitual curse of the drinking class, he had dived still deeper into the wine bottle, and he'd continued to make numerous repeat appearances down at the drunk tank of the county jail.

On November 22, 1963—the very same dark, doom-struck day that John F. Kennedy took his last limousine ride in Dallas, 250 miles to the northwest—the old man was committed by his family to the alcoholics' ward of the Rusk State Mental Hospital in Cherokee County, north of Nacogdoches.

Old George's stay at Rusk merely stemmed the tide without stopping the flow. After his release, he eventually raised the bottle to his lips and got his head all tore up again. He suffered a mild stroke a couple of years later, and after the doctors operated on him to repair some of the arteries in his throat that he'd burned out after his long years of hard living, they told him that if he did not set the bottle aside once and for all, he'd surely die. Old George had merely grinned his crusty, pie-eyed grin when he heard this warning. To everyone's amazement, this time the wily old man did not rush back out to the liquor store and get his head all messed up, as he usually did after one of his long dry spells. Instead, he actually did succeed in setting strong drink aside.

With his demons finally quelled, Old George seemed to find new contentment in his twilight years. Once again, he and Clara were able to live peaceably under the same roof. He began augmenting his meager retirement income with occasional salesman-type jobs, peddling Amway products and ground coffee, door to door, all back through Hardin County and the Big Thicket, where half the people in the countryside still knew him. (For a while, he even had a pretty good little old scam going, selling sewing machines. The sewing machines required a five-dollar down payment from a customer, and they netted Old George a twenty-five-dollar commission. It didn't take him long to figure out that he could pay the five-dollar down payment for a hesitant customer out of his own pocket, and then take his commission on the sale and still come out twenty dollars to the good.)

With his mind no longer clouded by alcohol, Old George did quite well for himself. After all, with his easygoing, comic ways, he was a natural-born salesman. ("If he couldn't sell ya somethin', then, hell, he'd *give* it to ya!" one family member warmly recalled.) Occasionally, he'd take a customer aside and scratch his head and grin that big, lopsided grin of his and tell him: "I wan'cha ta hear this here song I wrote for my boy, George Glenn!" Then he'd launch into one of his wheezy, half-baked renditions of "She Thinks I Still Care."

It was the little brick house that his son George Glenn had bought for him and Clara that Old George was most proud of. In fact, he was about as proud of that house as a man could be.

On August 15, 1965, George Washington Jones and Clara celebrated their fiftieth wedding anniversary, and George Glenn decided that he would honor his mama and daddy in style. He threw open his own spacious home on Hulett Street and invited all their other children, twenty-eight grandchildren and six great-grandchildren. Old George and Clara had now contributed a fine number to the lineage of old Frank Jones, a lineage which was now as vast and as widely scattered across Texas as the down from a thistle.

George Washington Jones did not speak, even at such hallowed family gatherings, to these new generations of the courage of his long-dead grandfather who'd shown such valor in the struggle for the Old Confederacy, so many years ago, back at the Hogpen Incident. Nor did he speak of old Frank's medals, which, over the years, had been handed down through the family. For just as George Washington Jones's father, Rollie, had feared, so many years earlier, when he'd attempted to pass these family tales on to his oldest son, they had merely gone in one of his big ears and out the other.

George Glenn's guests of honor that day at his mama and daddy's anniversary celebration were his family's cherished friends from Kountze, Brother Burl and Sister Annie Stephens, the evangelist couple with whom, as a boy, he'd passed so many hours singing the old Holiness songs that he loved so much. As the multitude of Texas Joneses gathered in his backyard around the swiming pool that day, many of them filled their glasses and drank deeply of strong drink. George Glenn, however, did not let alcohol touch his lips there, in the presence of Brother Burl, Sister Annie and his beloved mama. As the party loosened up, the raucous multitude of Joneses began to holler for George to get out his guitar and play "White Lightning" and "The Window Up Above." He demurred and explained to them that he would not defile the presence of his honored guests by singing anything but the old gospel songs that were so dear to his heart and theirs. The family knew how George Glenn could be about such things; they knew that he would not countenance such untoward behavior as dancing, drinking or lewd laughter when he sang these old Holiness songs. They knew that if they did any of these things, he would merely put down his guitar and walk away.

As those who were gathered all raised their voices and sang those old gospel songs together, it made George Glenn and his old mama particularly glad in their hearts. They could almost imagine that they were once again back on the porch of their humble little frame house in "Depot Town," and Uncle Litt and the Patterson sisters had all gathered once again to fill the blue skies above the tall pines with the lovely sound of their heavenly praise, just as they had once done, so very long ago.

Shirley had been a good wife to George. She had married him nearly a dozen years earlier, back when the prospect of eventual fame and affluence had been something even more remote than a dream. Over the years, almost single-handedly, she'd done a good job of raising their two young sons.

But now she and George had grown worlds apart. Shirley was as constant and predictable in her frugality and temperance as her husband was in his gleeful abandonment and wild profligacy. She herself hardly drank at all. She had, nonetheless, shown remarkable tolerance for George's drinking sprees and his unpredictable outbursts of violence. She still did not understand his wildness. For that matter, she understood little about the business that he was in or the demands that it made upon him—little more than she'd understood about it that day, more than a decade earlier, when he'd first showed up at the Princess drive-in back in Houston, waving around a shiny new copy of "No Money in This Deal." Over the years, she'd never even developed much of a fondness for country music either. She'd long ago stopped going to George's shows, and it just seemed that one too many times he'd gone off and left her stranded in some strange city, or once too often she'd found herself an unwilling spectator to the madness that swirled around him.

"One night we were doing a show up in Houston, and George was sober as a judge," Jimmie Klein recalled of one such instance when Shirley would have been better off staying at home. "She came over from Beaumont to meet us, and she was walkin' up to the room we were in. One of the band members saw her comin' and happened to slam the door in her face. Webb Pierce and some disk jockeys was in there with a whole bunch of women. Shirley thought George was up to somethin' in there, too, even though he wasn't. She ran back out to her car and was gonna drive back to Vidor. George got wind of the situation, got mad and ran out after her. He sort of grabbed her in a choke hold. He was pretty upset, and I really think that if I hadn't been able to get out there and get between them, something serious would have happened."

Shirley eventually came to realize that there were certain aspects of George's life, when he was out on the road or in Nashville, that she was merely better off not knowing about.

"George was kind of like Elvis Presley, on a smaller scale," Georgie Riddle explained with a voice full of fond nostalgia. "There was always lots of women around whenever he did a show, and he could more or less just walk off the stage and point and say, 'I'll take you and you and you and you.' He once told me, 'Riddle, I don't know what they see in me, but I'm sure glad they see it!'

"He mostly drew the partyin' type of women." Riddle grinned. "There was always a lot around, and I had a blast myself. Sometimes, back at the motel, George would get to drinkin' and tap out. And then I'd have my pick."

Up in Nashville, for a star like George, the girl singers were no more difficult to come by than was a pack of cigarettes or a cold six-pack of beer. Who the hell could blame him if he went through more than his share of them? After all, they were always eager enough to try and hitch a ride on the coattails of an artist of his magnitude—even though he seldom got around to telling them that the ride would be a short one and that most of them would merely end up discarded along the way. Few of them ever bothered to ask, either.

A different sort of girl singer came along in whom George had come to have something more than just a passing interest: Melba Montgomery, Peanut's sister. Melba was a Dobro-strumming Alabama-born beauty with a gentle disposition and a family background just as hard-core countrified as George's own. She sang in a strong, mellifluous voice that was so delightfully rural that people in Nashville's music industry eventually took to referring to her as "a female George Jones."

"Now, truthfully, Melba fit my style of singin' more than Tammy [Wynette] did," George once noted, making passing reference to his third and most famous wife. "I hate to use the word 'hard-core,' but that's what Melba is—a down-to-earth, hard-core country singer. She don't mind sayin' 'a-fore I get back,' instead of 'before.' And that's the way I am. I admire her for that, because I don't like singers who try and put on."

Pappy Daily had begun producing Melba on United Artists Records in 1962. He later decided it might be a good idea to hear how George's and Melba's voices fit together in the studio. "Our very first recording date together was at ten in the morning," Melba recalled. "I was nervous as a cat! Not only was it my first major session, but it was with *George Jones!* George had been out roarin' the night before, and nobody even knew where he was up until an hour before the session. When he finally showed up, he was in a really good mood, and the whole thing really came off well."

In May 1963, George and Melba's first duet single, "We Must

Have Been Out of Our Minds" (one of the seven chart singles that they would score together in the next four years), was released and went all the way to the number three spot. (Melba's greatest moment as a solo artist would not roll around until 1974, when she hit the number one position with a sentimental song called "No Charge.")

With the success of their first record, Melba and George soon began touring together and became close friends. Melba soon discovered that George had an almost childlike sense of humor and impulsiveness about him that tickled her. He could spend hours getting emotionally involved in "The Three Stooges," or cartoons, or whatever else happened to be on TV when he decided to watch it. When he grew tired of eating in restaurants, he'd gather the entire band and crew together and descend en masse on a grocery store, where he'd pay for all the groceries that they could gather up and carry out. Then they'd take all of it back to a motel and make an awful mess there in one of the rooms, as they tried to cook it all up home style.

Once, when George and Melba were working in the Chicago area, they found themselves with a couple of days off between shows. George decided they should go fishing on Lake Michigan. He bought hundreds of dollars' worth of fishing equipment and camping and cooking gear. Off they went and had a big time. "We just forgot all about the music business for a day or two and thoroughly enjoyed ourselves," Melba remembered. "Then, when we got ready to move on, George just said he didn't want any of that stuff anymore. He just took all the campin' and fishin' gear and dumped it in my car.

"I was close to George, off and on, for a couple of years," Melba added, "and he was never mean to me. I never saw his bad side. When he wasn't drinking, he was real shy. Usually, if he didn't know you, he wouldn't say anything at all. He'd just stand there with that little grin of his, or maybe kind of kid you a little bit about somethin' or other. Even when he was drunk, he always treated me with respect."

Melba was particularly touched by the kindness and generosity that George showed in 1963, when a niece of hers was badly burned in a fire. When George heard of the accident, he took it upon himself to come all the way down to Alabama, where the child lived, and put on a benefit show to raise money and pay her hospital bills.

Friends like Melba, Peanut and Georgie Riddle knew that beneath all his wildness, George, in fact, had the heart of the Good Samaritan. And it was a side of his character that often revealed itself when they least expected it. Sometimes, he'd pull his car over to the side of the road just to give money to someone who looked like they needed it more than he did, or to give scraps of food to a stray dog. Once he and Georgie Riddle were riding through Vidor on a cold, rainy morning. George saw an old boy named Ray that he knew standing outside the gas station where he worked, pumping gas with no raincoat on and getting soaked to the bone. This was more than George Glenn could stand to see, so he wheeled his car around, drove to a store, bought a nice new raincoat and brought it back and gave it to Ray. "He was always doing things like that," says Riddle. "That's just the way he was."

Friends like Georgie Riddle and Peanut could also see, by this time, that George was beginning to be deeply touched by Melba. He told them that he loved her. Melba, of course, knew better. She knew that George was married, and she knew how he was about women in general. She didn't expect anything permanent to ever come of their friendship, and she told George as much. Still, when Melba broke the news to their small circle of friends that she planned to marry Jack Solomon, a member of George's band, George did not take the news lightly. In fact, he was incensed. For weeks after that, when they performed together, he would whine and beg Melba, right onstage, in front of the audience, not to go through with her wedding plans. He even talked to her brother Peanut about it, and got Peanut so worked up that he threatened to whip Jack's ass if he took Melba away from George. But eventually, after Jack and Melba were married in 1968, they all became friends once again.

George and Melba recorded together at the Quonset Hut studio in 1966 (it had been acquired by Columbia [CBS] Records in 1962 and become known as Columbia "Studio A"). There was someone else sitting quietly on the sidelines with envy in her eyes, watching and waiting.

Her name was Virginia Wynette Pugh, and she was a ravenously ambitious twenty-four-year-old, ex-ninety-dollar-a-week hairdresser from Itawamba County, Mississippi. In late 1966 and in 1967, she would begin to achieve modest success as a recording artist with hits like "Apartment No. 9," "Your Good Girl's Gonna

Go Bad" and "I Don't Wanna Play House." She recorded under the name of Tammy Wynette (a name which her producer and discoverer, Billy Sherrill, had chosen for her). In mid-1968, she scored with the immensely popular hit single "D-I-V-O-R-C-E," and had her first taste of massive stardom. (She would eventually earn two Grammy awards, sixteen number one records and three consecutive Female Vocalist of the Year awards from the ubiquitous Country Music Association.) It was just such stardom and adulation that she'd hungered for so desperately all through her troubled childhood.

Before arriving in Nashville in the mid-1960s with a hundred dollars in borrowed money and the three children from her first, broken marriage piled into a 1959 Chevrolet, Tammy had struggled through a dismally unhappy early life in rural Mississippi and Alabama. Some of the high points of her formative years had been chopping cotton; a nervous breakdown, subsequent electroshock treatments (for hysteria and depression); and listening to her mother's large collection of George Jones records. (I ESCAPED MY HATED CHILDHOOD ON A FARM TO BECOME A COUNTRY MUSIC STAR, screamed one headline from the *National Enquirer*, a publication which, in later years, would delight in chronicling her romantic and marital misadventures.)

When she hit Nashville, Tammy was already on her second marriage—this one to a millstone who, Tammy alleged in her autobiography, had taken pictures of her naked in the shower and peddled them to her fans. Tammy came to Nashville, her second husband in tow, with her sights set on possessing a number of things. One of them was George Jones.

"Tammy definitely was after George back then," said Peanut Montgomery's wife, Charlene, who was usually on hand for George's recording sessions, which Tammy also had taken to frequenting. "Later, when I got to know Tammy and toured with her, she told me that even back in Alabama, when she was working as a hairdresser, George had been her idol. She knew she was gonna have him, one way or the other. She was the one who tried to work her way into his company, though at the time he didn't hardly seem to notice her."

It wasn't until 1966 that Tammy finally got the opportunity that she'd been dreaming about for so long—the chance to be formally introduced to her singing idol. Her heart was in her throat that night when she went to his hotel room, along with her second husband, who had some songs that he'd written and wanted to play for George in hopes that he could get him to record them. When they arrived, they were greeted with the din of loud horselaughs and crude whiskey talk echoing from the prodigal singer's lair. Inside, surrounded by the usual gaggle of the purblind—fans, sycophants and nonfunctionaries—George was holding court, as he so often did. (Whether day or night, waking or sleeping, the Possum had a deep, abiding dislike of being alone, and seldom was.) He was lying on a king-sized bed, dressed in silk pajamas, with a bottle of whiskey in one arm and a shapely woman, whom Tammy had never seen before, in the other.

When husband No. 2 introduced George to Tammy, George merely nodded in her direction, then turned his attention back to those other more pressing matters which he held within his grasp. In fact, he didn't hardly seem to notice Tammy at all. The brief encounter left her depressed and disillusioned for days. That, she feared, was as close as she would ever get to George Jones. So much for that dream.

In early 1965, Pappy Daily, being the wily old music business king-pin that he was, shuffled some more of those papers of his around and put together yet another deal that—on those papers, at least—was going to mean a lot more money for everybody. Jumping ship at United Artists Records and taking George with him, he joined forces with one of his former bosses at United Artists: a Chicago-born music executive named Art Talmadge who had an almost mystical ability to look at the shape notes of a country music song and see dollar signs. Under this new arrangement, Pappy would now produce George's records under the aegis of Musicor, a former subsidiary label of United Artists, which Talmadge had purchased and given both Pappy and George stock ownership in. During the next six years, with Musicor, George recorded more than 280 songs —most of which were done in rushed, sloppily produced sessions— and helped to establish for himself a somewhat unwelcome reputation as one of country music's most overrecorded artists.

Pappy Daily, for his part, had figured out some time ago that it was best to keep George on a long leash. He also discovered that to attempt to guide his career in any other manner—either to rein him in too tightly or to let him merely run wild—could be disastrous.

Pappy seemed to understand George better than just about anyone else, though even he, at times, figured that handling the prodigal singer's affairs was about as easy as riding a Brahma bull. There were, admittedly, many times when George strained even his mentor's seemingly limitless patience. It was particularly painful for the old man to endure those increasingly frequent occasions when he would fly all the way to Nashville, hire a bunch of top studio musicians and be sitting there, watching the studio time clock tick away, burning up his money like a taxicab meter, only to discover that George wasn't even in Nashville, as he'd promised he would be, but was instead off drunk somewhere in Florida.

Now, to make matters worse, there was something new afoot in country music—something that neither George nor Pappy had much use for yet knew they could not get around. In fact, it appeared to be the same kind of unavoidable evil that they had perceived rock 'n' roll to be, back in that long-gone era when they'd recorded those "Thumper Jones" tracks.

The name that had been given to this new musical threat was "the Nashville sound," and it was a trend that was being felt in country music and was beginning to affect the career of practically every artist and producer who recorded in the Nashville studio system.

The Nashville sound—as insidious as some considered it to be— had been first pioneered in the late 1950s and early 1960s by Chet Atkins, Owen Bradley and a handful of other innovative country producers who, like Art Talmadge, could look into the tea-leaf patterns of country music shape notes and conjure up visions of dollar signs. These men figured—correctly, it turned out—that they could make those dollar signs even bigger if they could produce country records that captured the imagination of the much larger urban-dwelling, pop-music-oriented record-buying public. In a conscious effort to raise sales figures and reach this new audience, they began working all manner of subtle pop-influenced permutations into the rather predictable musical embroidery of the old standard hard-core country honky-tonk sound, to which George and Pappy were so devoted.

By the mid-1960s, more and more Nashville-produced country records were beginning to feature sensuous, pop-inspired background vocal harmonies and lush violins, in place of the raunchy twin-fiddle and steel-guitar arrangements that had been the mainstay on so many of George's earlier records.

The country artists themselves, in some cases, were now being coached by these forward-thinking producers to ease up on their down-home countrified accents and to opt instead for more bland and orotund vocal readings which were free from hokey regionalisms and more like those urban inflections favored by big-city TV newscasters and weather men.

George, like many dyed-in-the-wool country boys of his era, heartily resented this intrusion of the flaccid pop music dialectic on the domain of his beloved hard-core country sound. "I've got too much respect for country music to abuse it," he once noted with a trace of bitterness. "I don't want a thousand violins and twenty trumpets on my records." But when Pappy, at Art Talmadge's suggestion, began loading down the production of his own records with these constipated-sounding string and vocal arrangements, George did not complain.

Ironically, in the midst of all this, George's own singing style was undergoing a maturation of its own. He was now in his mid-thirties, and fewer and fewer of his performances in the studio were charged with the youthful, high-whining honky-tonk fervor and raw rockabilly fire that had echoed so clearly through earlier hits. He had come to be more comfortable in the lower and mid-range registers of his voice. Ever so gradually, he was becoming less ill at ease with the mellower, "uptown"-style songs that Pappy was starting to bring around for him to record.

With his vocal style maturing like it was, George's acceptance of these musical changes, the backwaters of which were now beginning to sweep him up like a slow-rising tide, was still only begrudging, at best. This became clear to Pappy when he started coming around the studio with another song which he'd managed to corner all the publishing rights to, and hoped to talk George into recording. The song, "Walk Through This World with Me," had been written in 1965 by two songwriters from Tucson, Arizona, named Sandra Seamons and Kay Savage. It was a musically middle-of-the-road love ballad that was almost inspirational in its unabashedly optimistic and romantic sentiments—a far cry from "The Window Up Above." It was a song that fit, tongue and groove, into the new Nashville sound, which was now garnering dominant play on the country airwaves.

When Pappy first played "Walk Through This World with Me" for George, he had balked worse than a mule kicking in his stall. But

Pappy kept coming around and insisting he give the song a try anyway.

One day in September 1966 George had him a few drinks, and then a few more, until the sound of his own voice when he sang was like the faraway sound of soft music heard by a heavily anesthetized man in a dentist's chair—until he was, as Pappy recalled, "too drunk to hit the floor with his hat."

"The only reason I'm recordin' this damn song," he jeered over his shoulder at the snickering studio musicians as he struggled to keep himself vertical with the microphone, "is because every time Pappy comes around here, he brings it with him!"

But this time, as George listened to himself through his anesthetized haze, he was amazed to hear how masterfully he sang "Walk Through This World with Me." In fact, he gave it a near-perfect reading, in a rich, almost theatrically expansive baritone, with inflections so smooth, urbane and concise that he could have been reading the evening news. When "Walk Through This World with Me" was released in January 1967, George was even more surprised when it became a number one single—the first one of those he'd had in nearly five years.

Amidst all the gaudy trappings of countrified affluence in Vidor, George's home life was slowly beginning to sour, like vintage wine turning to table vinegar. Even so, he did have one dream left that he was itching to fulfill. For some time, he'd wanted a country music entertainment park—a place all his own, with his name on it in big flashy letters, where he could hold concerts, rodeos and similar festive events.

He bought himself several large parcels of land out on Lakeview Road, in the hilly countryside, only a mile or two from his big ranch house on Hulett Street. There, on Lakeview, he spent nearly $100,000 having an even bigger house built for himself—this one, a large, two-story brick manse. He had palm trees planted around it, and he even had a big guitar-shaped swimming pool dug in the back. Soon after, he spent another $15,000 having it all encircled with elaborate wooden fencing. When the fence was erected he built a guest house, a horse ring and livestock barns to keep his fifty head of Black Angus cattle and Appaloosa horses in.

He named his new spread the George Jones Rhythm Ranch, and for a time, there in East Texas, he delighted in playing the role of the

gentleman rancher—even though he did bring a few unusual variations of his own to the role. Late at night, when he came home all
worn out from one of those long tours, it did his heart good to get in
one of those big, fancy Lincolns or Cadillacs that he was forever
buying and selling, and go roaring out across his pastures and drive
all those Black Anguses and Appaloosa ponies out into the road.
Then his hired hand, Gordon Artis, had to get out of bed and go out
and round them all up again. (In October 1966, George was sued by
one Elwood Boulet, who claimed that he'd sustained $687.55 in
damages to his car after colliding with one of these stray cows of
George's. But after George had heartily protested to the court that
the cow in question was not one of his own, the case was dismissed.)

Once he'd gotten settled in on his new "ranch," George pressed
on with his plans for a country music park. He spent thousands of
dollars more building a stage and elaborate pipe-welded grand-
stands. When everything was all completed to his satisfaction, he
chose a date, July 4, 1966, for his grand opening and hired Merle
Haggard, who'd just hit with his first top-five record, "Swingin'
Doors," and some other top country artists to come down and
perform with him. The appointed day rolled around, and about half
the population from Vidor and surrounding Hardin and Orange
counties came streaming through the gates. George ended up letting just about all of them in for free. A good time was had by all that
afternoon, but when the dust had settled and the receipts were
totaled, George realized that he had lost a great deal of money—too
much, perhaps, to risk a repeat performance. With a sinking heart,
he admitted to himself that there would be no more country music
shows at the George Jones Rhythm Ranch.

For several days after that debacle, George was nowhere to be
found. He had been last seen leaving the ranch with Merle Haggard
and a bevy of female admirers, on his way to a Beaumont motel.
When this last live-sighting report reached Shirley, she was furious.
As was standard procedure, search parties consisting of band members and members of his family fanned out across the countryside,
searching every bar and hotel lounge for the errant singer and his
newfound friend Merle Haggard.

Several days later the bedraggled music star finally returned,
weaving his way slowly, erratically and without purpose down the
highway, in a new Lincoln, as he headed like a condemned man
toward the incendiary wrath of Shirley which he knew awaited him.

Though he was still wearing the expensive, immaculately tailored stage outfit he'd worn the day of the show four days earlier, it was now rumpled, torn and dirty. Beneath his several-day shadow of a beard, his skin was sickly pale, and his eyes were badly bloodshot. No longer did they dance in their sockets, but merely gazed blankly into the distance: dull, passive, without hope.

"George!" cried a friend who came running out to his car to greet him as he pulled in the driveway of his Hulett Street house. "Where the *hell* you been!?"

George did not raise his eyes to meet those of his friend. Instead, he merely shuddered and spat and continued to look away, staring disconsolately toward the sullen horizon. "I been *drunk,*" he muttered disgustedly.

By 1967, the George Jones Rhythm Ranch was no more. The big brick house he'd built for himself had been sold, and the land had been divided back into parcels and unloaded to the highest bidders. His plans for a country music park were merely added to the increasingly long list of stillborn dreams and bad memories that he was leaving in his wake there in East Texas.

Shortly after the Rhythm Ranch fiasco, life there in Vidor really started going to hell in a hand basket. It was obvious by now—even to him—that the strains in his marriage to Shirley were irreparable. (Even a brief, voluntary stay by George in a neurological hospital did not ease his drinking, quell his temperament or turn the tide.) She had received an anonymous letter that had deepened her own lingering suspicions about Melba Montgomery. And more and more, her own name was being whispered around town in the same breath with that of J. C. Arnold, a Vidor businessman who had, for a long time, been a good friend of both George's and Shirley's.

There were other rumors, too, that flew as fast and furious as the Gulf winds back and forth across Southeast Texas and Vidor: rumors of gambling, of large sums of money changing hands; and of the sound of men's voices, loud, drunken, belligerent voices hurling angry threats and accusations back and forth through the night, followed by the flash and thunder of shotgun blasts exploding in the darkness. It was all over East Texas that George, in one of his towering fits of jealous rage, had shot his friend J. C. Arnold in the ass with a shotgun and that a local physician—since deceased—had almost lost his license when he treated Arnold without reporting his injury.

In the years to come, both George and J. C. Arnold (who later married Shirley) would both deny such accusations. And a long time afterward, after they'd all become friends again, Arnold would sometimes joke about the alleged incident. "Sometimes J.C. would laugh and say, 'You want me to pull down my pants and show you my scar!?' " one of George and Arnold's mutual friends recalled, years later. "But he never did. To tell you the truth, I don't honestly know if anyone ever really got shot or not."

Sensing by now that the beginning of the end was about to roll around, George began spending less and less time in Vidor. Nobody had any idea at all where he was on that day in early September 1967 when a grim-faced, hollow-eyed man came knocking on the door of the little brick house that George Glenn had bought for his aging mama and daddy, and said that he was from a mortgage company. With a coldness in his voice that did not hold out the hope of compromise, the man informed Old George and Clara that his company, in fact, held a mortgage on their little house (which they had assumed their younger son had paid for in cash), and that the monthly note on this mortgage had not been paid in many months. With a tone of cold finality he informed the elder Joneses that their little house was being repossessed and that they had three days to vacate the premises.

It took a while for the full devastation of this unexpected news to sink in with George Washington Jones. He stopped off at the nearby home of his daughter Ruth, and was nearly out of his mind with anguish and confusion. His anguish did not subside until the pre-dawn hours of the following morning, when Clara awoke to find him butting his head furiously against the wooden headboard of their bed. She called his name and was alarmed to see that he did not respond. Looking more closely into her husband's eyes, she saw that they were unseeing—that they were flat and glazed, like the dull color of ice on a snow-swept winter pond. Old George had lapsed into a coma, and was rushed by ambulance to the Baptist Hospital at College and Eleventh streets in Beaumont. The doctors examined him, and informed the family that he had suffered a second and considerably more severe stroke.

It took the family some time to track down George Glenn, who was off singing in some strange city—although nobody, not even Shirley, seemed to know exactly which one. When he had been located and summoned hurriedly back home, his brother and sisters had already gathered at the Beaumont hospital where their father lay dying.

The air there in the hospital room was heavy with the lingering smell of impending death and harsh antiseptic. Hooked to various life-support systems, George Washington Jones lay silently on the bed, his glassy eyes staring unseeing toward the ceiling. Rattling harshly through his partially blocked windpipe, his labored breathing made a horrible gargling sound, like coffee percolating in a broken coffeepot.

The family members took turns keeping a hushed vigil by the old man's bed. George Glenn—even though he had plied himself with enough whiskey to anesthetize an ordinary man—could feel a wave of anxiety and remorse welling up within him and stabbing at his insides like sharp daggers. He realized that one by one his siblings had wandered off to get coffee or to wait in the lobby, where they could breathe easier, and that he was alone at his father's bedside. No one else realized that George Glenn had been left alone in there —not until they heard the sound of shouting and cursing and confused scuffling coming from the room.

The others rushed back to their father's deathbed, and it took them quite a while to calm their younger brother back down again.

A day or so later, on September 7, George Washington Jones drew his last troubled breath. Sadly, bitterly and still drinking heavily, George Glenn paid all the expenses and helped make the arrangements for his father's funeral at the Memorial Funeral Home in Vidor on September 9. He watched through his whiskey numbness as Old George was laid to rest in "The Garden of Prayer," out near the big stone Bible in the Restlawn cemetery, just north of Vidor on busy Route 105. Once this task had been completed, the prodigal son quickly departed. He flew off to meet his band in some strange city in Michigan, where he was already scheduled to play another road date.

For days, George Glenn's friends in the band couldn't help but notice how unusually terrible his grief seemed to be, and how lost he seemed in a veil of guilt and mortal confusion. They noticed how he would cry from time to time, and was not himself.

As time passed, George Glenn learned to hold his grieving silently within him, but even so, it did not subside altogether. There were still those occasional moments of helplessness—moments when certain sights and smells and sounds came swarming into his mind, like angry, pestilent insects: the horrible smell of medicine and death, the harsh rasping sound of Old George's breathing and memories of his glassy eyes, wide, staring, yet unseeing. Worst of all, though, were those memories of the sound of his own loud, drunken voice, full of tearful outrage and anger, echoing loudly through the sepulchral silence of the hospital corridors. Time after time, these memories cut through him like a surgeon's scalpel, and when they did, he broke down and began crying all over again.

In the weeks and months after George Washington Jones's untimely death, many accusatory fingers were pointed as attempts were made to unravel the mystery of the unpaid house note. George realized that his marriage to Shirley was over, but with the death of Old George amidst such untoward circumstances, it was firmly laid to rest.

When the terms of Shirley's divorce (in which she claimed "harsh and cruel treatment") were enumerated in her petition of April 11, 1968, they took him by surprise nonetheless. Though Dorothy and old man Bonvillion had really socked him in the ass in his first divorce, so many years ago, he could see now that it had been a mere trial heat for this latest round of strife, litigation and acrimony.

When the conditions were finally delineated and the terms were finally settled, Shirley was the proud owner of:

Three houses that they had jointly owned on Hulett Street.
Two additional lots of land that they owned nearby.
One half of all the songwriter's royalties to all songs that George had written up to that point in his career.
$10,000 in cash and $5,000 in U.S. savings bonds.
A registered quarter horse named Calhoun Star.
A 1968 Oldsmobile sedan.

George (who, according to Shirley's petition, had formally ceased to live under the same roof with her as of mid-March 1968) was also ordered to pay $1,000 a month in child support.

George, for his part, was left to pick up the scraps—which included:

One half of his songwriting royalties.
His stock in the Musicor Record label (which eventually proved to be worthless).

Equity in a house that he and Shirley owned in Lakeland, Florida, as well as additional property that they owned in Bon Wier, Texas.

His 1968 Flex touring bus and his musical equipment.

A 1968 Cadillac sedan and a 1968 Buick Skylark sedan.

The death of George Washington Jones, coming as it did in such a disquieting and sudden manner, had struck a demoralizing blow against all seven of his living children. None seemed to take it any harder than George's older sister Ruth. "When you lose one of your parents, you lose part of your strength, part of yourself," she explained. "I think when Daddy died is when my troubles started, and I think that's when my brother George's real problems started, too."

Ruth, who was three years older than George, had always been close to her younger brother. Ever since the days back in Beaumont, when she'd married a good ole boy named Buster Maddox (they would divorce two separate times, the second time in 1982, when their marriage became a casualty of the storm's eye of family jealousies and intrigues that would eventually engulf her brother) and moved out of Multimax and off on her own, she and George had never been far apart. "Ruth, the Truth," George would sometimes call her, and when Ruth had something on her mind, or had some scheme cooking, George always seemed to listen to her, no matter how ill-conceived or outlandish these notions of hers sometimes seemed to be.

After their father had died, Ruth, for her part, could not help, in her own mind, putting some of the blame for the unpaid house note on Shirley's shoulders. She knew it was in her brother's nature to be heedless of such details, but she also knew it was as much a part of Shirley's to be mindful of them.

When George's divorce came through, it had rankled Ruth even more to see Shirley end up with all the big houses, fancy cars, savings bonds and cash money that her brother had worked so hard for, year after year, as he squandered his emotional equilibrium singing his heart out for strangers night after night. In her own heart, Ruth now felt the intense sorrow and scorn known only to the dispossessed. This hurt and sorrow built up within her until she no longer seemed to care whether she lived or died. In the throes of her grief, she walked out along the highway where Shirley lived, resolved to throw herself in front of her car the next time she came driving by. She figured if Shirley really wanted to put her under, then she'd just let her, and have done with it all. When Shirley's car finally came around the bend in the road, that's exactly what Ruth did. Shirley was able to slam on her brakes and skid to a stop without actually hitting her ex-sister-in-law. Still, Ruth took a certain gleeful and perverse pleasure from the entire episode. She knew that she'd really put a fright into Shirley!

Seized as she was by this overweening scorn of the dispossessed, Ruth's bitterness festered and her suspicions grew. Only now, the source of her unrest had to do with a long-overlooked but strangely disquieting episode from the troubled history of the Jones family. It was an episode that, in her mind at least, was still shrouded in mystery, though it had transpired more than a decade and a half earlier. She figured if she could unravel this troubling conundrum, it might be the answer to the entire family's troubles.

Ruth's suspicions grew out of the time, long ago, when George Washington Jones had been called to Houston to receive the small cash settlement in exchange for which he signed away his claims to the estate of his father, Rollie Jones (who—at least by appearances—seemed to have died intestate). After all these years, Ruth could not overcome her feeling that there was something unusual about the haste and secrecy that had surrounded that transaction. It had a bad smell to it, and it rankled in her imagination until she became convinced of foul play. "My daddy was done dirty," she finally concluded. "I know that a lot of them other Joneses own oil wells over there in Houston, and somehow my daddy was jewed outa somethin', though I don't exactly know what it was."

Though she barely knew any of them, Ruth had always been suspicious of those distant "highfalutin' Joneses": those far-flung branches of old Frank Jones's vast lineage who, she knew, now resided in well-heeled affluence in Houston. The more she thought about all this, and the more she added it all up in her mind, the more her suspicions were multiplied. She'd even taken it upon herself to research some of the musty old deeds and land grants back in the courthouses at Nacogdoches and Angelina counties. She'd not been surprised to find out that Frank Jones and some of those other Joneses from the olden times of the Hogpen Incident had been pretty substantial landowners. There were even a couple of them back there in those faded old court records named John Paul Jones, and for all she could tell, Frank Jones and old Rollie Jones may have even been direct descendants of the legendary old sea captain himself.

Ruth also knew that Rollie Jones had been "a real-estater" during his later years in Houston, in an era when that city was beginning to grow by leaps and bounds, and huge fortunes were routinely being made. She knew that "he was a church figure, too . . . so he was bound to have a lot of money."

Ruth had also tried to do a little investigating over there in Houston, where Rollie had spent his final years. She'd attempted to unearth copies of those documents that George Washington Jones had signed so many years before. But she found it even more curious that the harder she looked for those old probate records, the less luck she seemed to have in finding them. Again and again, she seemed to hit a dead end with her research. It was almost as if there was somebody over there who knew what she was looking for, *and maybe had a lot to lose if the truth ever came out.*

The real pot of gold at the end of the rainbow, as Ruth envisioned it, might lie somewhere out there beyond the vast horizon, in the great coastal expanses and flat marshlands of Southeast Texas, shimmering like an emerald of hope against the wide skies. Out there somewhere, she believed, were great oil wells that were pumping day and night, pouring untold riches into the pockets of some undeserving whelp of third or fourth cousins that she'd never met—riches that should have belonged to old George Washington Jones.

Ruth figured that if she could somehow get to the bottom of all this and reestablish her familial claims on these oil wells, then maybe she could make things right for everybody—her brother George Glenn included.

Ruth had explained this situation about Rollie Jones's estate and the oil wells to George Glenn. But whether he had paid any attention, or whether it had merely gone in one ear and out the other (in much the same way that old Rollie's tales had once gone in and out of their daddy's big ears), she could not tell. She could see that her brother had little time, just then, to speculate about misplaced fortunes or mysterious oil wells. He had in fact little time or little inclination to look back at all. Almost everything that he'd once owned there in Texas—the houses, the horses, the cattle, the cars, the Rhythm Ranch—was all gone now—either in the possession of his ex-wife or sold, lost or otherwise scattered to the winds.

Still, George Glenn—heedless as he was about material possessions—knew in his heart there was more where all that had come from. He borrowed a thousand dollars in traveling money from his brother-in-law "W. T." Scroggins, packed his bags to move to Nashville and assured friends that he would never marry again. Oddly enough, he felt a sense of freedom such as he had not felt in years.

For he was untethered now, at last, cut loose from his Southeast Texas roots: drifting, floating inexorably toward something, though he was not sure what.

Chapter Five

TAMMY

*I remember when I first met Tammy on a show date, and then
I went over to her house and accidentally tore up a table. I guess
it was love at first sight.*

George Jones, 1980

The rasping drone of cicadas filled the hot, turgid air. The humid,
sweltering gauze of late summer 1968 hung over the wheat fields
and cow pastures of Middle Tennessee and the nearby subdivisions
along the wide, placid waters of Old Hickory Lake.

Amidst this torpor, George Glenn Jones, one of the newest arriv-
als in this well-heeled suburban area just to the north of Nashville,
sat in the living room of a large brick house that he'd just purchased
for $35,000 on Brandywine Drive. "I'll bet George just loves the
name of this street!" quipped a reporter from *The Music City News*

who'd driven out that day to interview the Possum—as he was becoming increasingly known to his many fans.

"Everything seems to be shaping up now," George noted with breezy optimism as he leaned back in his chair, surveying the dozens of awards and trophies which already adorned the walls of his new residence (the reporter counted twenty-seven of them) and listening to the steady pounding of the carpenters who were busy remodeling his basement.

"I'm making all my dates now," he added self-assuredly—hoping perhaps to bury forever his burgeoning reputation as a concert no-show, which promoters and booking agents were beginning to find increasingly troublesome. "I've goofed off in the past," he added. "But that's over. My intention now is to be number one again."

As the afternoon wore on, George outlined, with similar breeziness, a number of other irons that he now had heated in the fire—such as the production company through which he intended to begin producing a number of new artists. One of these was a recently acquired protégé of his, an attractive seventeen-year-old singer from Houston named Brenda Carter. Late one night the previous June, the two of them had recorded a rousing duet together called "Milwaukee, Here I Come." It was released on Musicor and went all the way to the number twelve spot in the singles charts just a couple of months later.

George also talked profusely about another entrepreneurial venture in which he'd become enmeshed—one that would surely, he felt, work out for the best, a Nashville nightclub called Possum Holler, located on Lower Broadway. The club's back door opened directly across the alley from the Ryman Auditorium, then still the home of the Grand Ole Opry. George explained that he planned not only to make frequent personal appearances there himself but also to market his own line of souvenirs, which would include an assortment of women's lingerie, called Possum Panties. These undergarments, he went on to brag, would be emblazoned, in a strategic spot, with the grinning likeness of the prodigal singer himself.

The Music City News scribe finally got around to popping the question that a lot of people had been asking one of country music's most eligible bachelors: Did he have any marriage plans?

"You can just say the ole Possum ain't gettin' married again till he's sixty-nine," said the prodigal singer with a grin. George, who was about to celebrate his thirty-seventh birthday, had recently abandoned his flattop and had started letting his hair grow out long enough to actually comb it—nurturing a new and surprisingly urbane image. "That'll be about when I'm ready to settle down!"

The passing years had, in fact, done little, if anything, to quell George's giddy and seemingly unquenchable appetite for whiskey, vodka and women—particularly those women who knew how to sing a country song. "Ya know, I don't *really* fall in love with all them girl singers," George once confided to Georgie Riddle. "I fall in love with their *singin'*."

On that sweltering late-summer day when he had waved away the reporter's casual suggestions that he might be contemplating yet another return trip to the altar, the Possum had a romantic trump card that he was not showing. The name and face on that trump card, of course, was Tammy, Tammy Wynette.

Not surprisingly, it was Tammy Wynette's voice that had first captivated George—long before he even knew her well enough to match her equally alluring face and body up with that voice. He'd first heard "Apartment No. 9," her debut single on Epic Records, on his own car radio shortly after it was released in December 1966. The rural soulfulness that seemed to resonate so clearly through that shrill, tear-stained vocal style of hers had moved George, indeed.

George—who had by now learned "you can't live with 'em and you can't live without 'em either"—was on the lookout as always for new female companionship. His path now began crossing Tammy's more and more often. They shared a booking agent (Hubert Long), they toured together now and then and along the way they had developed what Tammy—who was now actively looking for a convenient way to shed the increasingly heavy millstone that her second marriage had become—later remembered as "little more than a nodding acquaintance."

"I was on the first tour that George and Tammy made together," a local spider on the wall said, "and George didn't hardly notice her, even though it was obvious at the time that Tammy was anxious to be a part of everything that George was. They [Tammy and husband number two] would sometimes ride on the [tour] bus with George. But when they did, they invited themselves on. Tammy's [second] husband's daughter, who was a real pretty girl of about sixteen or seventeen, was along, too. And to be honest, George seemed way more interested at the time in her than he was in Tammy."

Matters had begun to change on several counts by mid-1968, however. "D-I-V-O-R-C-E," Tammy's consciously hokey lament of broken marriage, was rapidly becoming one of the most commercially successful records of 1968. That October, she released the resoundingly popular single "Stand By Your Man." It eventually became a substantial pop "crossover" hit, sold a million copies, became the theme song of the award-winning 1970 feature film *Five Easy Pieces* and afforded Tammy just the sort of country superstar status for which she'd ached for so long.

This new brush with stardom left Tammy's voracious appetite for fame, if nothing else, at least temporarily appeased. She was even more famous than George was now and no longer did she have to try and ride on anybody's coattails.

George was no longer merely "nodding" at Tammy, but had actually started talking to her. There was no question; she'd finally succeeded in catching his eye as well as his ear. After they'd done a show together one evening and were relaxing backstage as the crowds emptied out, George casually asked her where she was performing the next night.

"I'm doin' a benefit down in Red Bay, Alabama, where I grew up," she replied. "Gonna raise some money and put air conditionin' in the new schoolhouse."

"Red Bay . . . Red Bay, Alabama . . ." George seemed to ponder the name as he scratched his head and shuffled away. "Don't b'lieve I've ever heard of Red Bay."

The next night (after Tammy had slyly inquired of George's "road manager" about the likelihood of persuading George to come down to Red Bay and play at her benefit), she and her husband were sitting in their car outside the Red Bay Auditorium. They sat in silence, waiting for the right time to enter the stage door, when suddenly an elegantly glistening new burgundy-colored Cadillac Eldorado—a gleaming pleasure machine, the likes of which was seldom seen on the landlocked streets of Red Bay—slithered up beside them. At the wheel, naturally, was the prodigal singer, his close-set Possum eyes dancing gleefully and that Halloween grin spread widely across his face.

"Why, George!" Tammy gasped with breathy, wide-eyed innocence, feigning forgetfulness of the fact that he was there by her invitation. "What in the world are *you* doin' down here!?"

"I come down to do a benefit." He grinned even wider. His

Possum eyes gleamed with the gloating self-assurance of a fisherman who knows he's about to reel in one big catfish. "Y'all said ya needed some air conditionin' or somethin', didn't ya?"

George gave quite a performance that night, impressing Tammy with both his musical expansiveness and his pure generosity. After the show was over, she went aboard his tour bus, which had transported his band, the Jones Boys, down from Nashville. After thanking him profusely, she stayed to chat for a while. As she started to climb off the bus, she smiled back over her shoulder and told him, in an offhanded, rhetorical sort of way: "Love ya, George!"

To the amazement of George's manager, who had also tagged along that night, George suddenly grabbed Tammy, and the two of them embraced heartily, in a manner that was not rhetorical at all. Later, as George and his boys made the 150-mile drive northward, back to Nashville, his manager couldn't help but notice that his boss was nearly beside himself with excitement—like a hot-to-trot teenager. "Ya think she likes me!?" he kept asking. "Ya *really* think she likes me!?"

Back in Nashville, Tammy and George spoke over the telephone for a long time the very next day. Then George sent his manager out to pick her up at a suburban shopping center where she was waiting, on the sly. The manager dropped Tammy off at George's Brandywine Drive house, where the two of them spent a long afternoon, alone. Later that evening, when the manager saw George again, his wide eyes were shining with self-satisfaction, and the jack-o'-lantern grin was spread across his face wider than ever. This time, he *really* looked like the cat who'd swallowed the canary.

Several days later Tammy and George met again, in a scene that was too poignant, even, for a country and western Harlequin novel. Tammy invited George and the manager over to her house to have dinner with her and her husband. The Millstone wasn't stupid and was aware of the fact that George had more than just his professional antennas out for his wife. Joining them for dinner were Tammy's three daughters. The young girls were all sick from a recent bout of food poisoning, and were crying and yowling hideously as their stepfather continuously yelled at them to shut themselves up. Accompanying these cries of pain and suffering, on the stereo, in the background, playing over and over again was a lachrymose, dirgelike ballad called "When the Grass Grows over Me." The Millstone had written the song; George had recorded it. The four adults in this besotted gathering tried their best to maintain the rapidly crumbling veneer of strained politeness. Even so, the rancor of repressed anger and violence now hung in the hot, stale air like the smell of rotten food.

The evening wore uneasily on, George began having a few drinks, and so did the husband. For most of the day Tammy and the hubby had been involved in a marathon quarrel, much of which had hinged on his deepening suspicions of his wife's designs on George. As the liquor settled in, the couple's daggers of reproach and recrimination began flying through the air with renewed fury.

"Well, you bitch," the Millstone finally barked at his wife, for the benefit of their guests, "you ain't fit to sleep with anyway."

George had settled into one of his deceptively slothlike positions. (They didn't call him the Possum for nothing.) Restlessly crossing and recrossing his legs, he muttered softly into his drink: "Uh, you shouldn't . . . uh . . . talk to . . . uh . . . Tammy that way."

"What's it to you, anyhow?" the jealous husband fired back at his slouching dinner guest. "She's my wife. I think you better mind your own business."

With little cause and no warning, the slumbering Possum, fired by a lethal combination of alcohol and indignation (a high-octane combination which seemingly transformed him as abruptly and mysteriously as Popeye was transformed by a can of spinach), suddenly leaped from his chair. All five feet seven inches and 145 pounds of him was riveted with anger. He started cursing, screaming, yelling and knocking over furniture like a crazy man. He picked up the small dining-room table; food, drinks, cigarettes, money and glassware went flying in every direction. And as he heaved the table through a large plate-glass window, the sound of shattering glass echoed through the still night air.

"She may be your wife, goddamnit!" he screamed at Tammy's husband, "but I love her! And," the Possum added, as he turned to Tammy with only a trifle less menace in his voice, "you love me, too, don'cha!"

Tammy's lipstick-smeared mouth fell open in well-rehearsed amazement, even though inwardly she was pleased, flattered and vindicated by George's frothy display of wild emotion. Never one to hesitate to play two men off each other, she had expected—even hoped—that it would eventually come to this. But even she had not imagined that it would unfold with such an unbridled storybook intensity. "Y-y-y-y-yes," Tammy stammered in reply, as she did her best to feign a dumbfounded bleached-blonde mystification. "Yes, I do."

"O.K., then." George grabbed her by the shoulder. "Then let's you and me get the hell outa here!"

Hurriedly gathering up her three young daughters, Tammy bolted out the door with George, leaving the very stunned husband No. 2 behind, amidst the rubble of broken dreams and broken furniture . . . and on the stereo, "When the Grass Grows over Me" was still playing in the now mournfully silent room.

Outside, George was grinning victoriously as he helped Tammy and the children into his car. As the big, shiny Cadillac pulled away, it was Tammy who felt herself suddenly overcome with a nauseous wave of mixed emotions, something she had not read about in the storybooks.

Sensing her confusion, George reached over and gently patted her arm. "Don't worry, honey," he assured her. "There ain't nothin' back in that house that I can't buy you again. It ain't even worth lookin' back at it. From now on, you'll have everything you want."

As George swept her away through the night in his big burgundy Cadillac, she believed him. She surely did.

Later that evening, after George parked Tammy and the girls in a room at the Hilton Hotel near the Nashville airport, he drove back to his house on Brandywine. He arrived just in time to discover that the Millstone had already put the law on his ass for stealing his woman. His mirthful laughter could barely be concealed as the police—armed with a warrant—searched in vain through George's house, looking under beds and in closets for the two-timing Tammy. No sooner had the long arm of the law retreated from this initial skirmish than George was on the phone to his new love, making arrangements for the two of them to fly to Mexico to get her a "quickie" divorce.

A few days later, on the eve of their hasty departure for Mexico, George figured that the coast was clear enough for him to bring Tammy and her kids to the Brandywine house to stay with him. After the children had all been put to bed, George—who, after so many years of strange women in strange motels, was worldly-wise about such things—yawned and casually informed Tammy that he planned to sit up for a while in his four-poster bed and watch one of his favorite movies, *Requiem for a Heavyweight*. (A tragic 1962 film about an over-the-hill, punch-drunk prizefighter, played by Anthony Quinn, whose unscrupulous manager, played by Jackie Gleason, uses the fighter's weakness for strong drink to ruthlessly manipulate him and send him reeling down the road to personal ruin—a story that would, in later years, become hauntingly and increasingly familiar to George.)

After George had wept openly over Anthony Quinn's tragic demise, he and Tammy made love in his four-poster bed, surrounded by George's collection of broad-stroke bullfight posters and ornate hand-carved furniture. It was, indeed, just like a storybook, but Tammy was bothered that there was one thing that seemed just as out of place and intrusive that night as a pubic hair floating in a punch bowl: it was the bottle of whiskey which George brought to bed with him. All night long, it seemed to be just as much the object of his affectionate fondling and wet kisses as she had been.

In the meantime, Tammy's spouse put the law on George's ass once again. Before the ink was yet dry on Tammy's instant Mexican divorce, he'd slapped her new lover boy with a $100,000 "alienation of affection" civil suit. He'd also socked it to Tammy with a separate suit, in which he charged desertion and adultery. Through a series of complicated legal maneuvers, however, Tammy's lawyers were able to establish that, due to technicalities involved in her first marriage—to another husband, whom she'd married at age seventeen and succeeded in discarding while still back in Alabama—her marriage to husband No. 2 had never been legal in the first place. She was able to have it annulled. All of which made George Glenn rear back his head and laugh with renewed glee.

Free at last, George and Tammy—to the delight of the national gossip tabloids and fan magazines—were now able to go public with their storybook romance. Regardless of how shallow or fleeting his intentions may have been at the outset, the Possum was now madly and irretrievably in love. He began showering his new paramour with lavish gifts, including a brand-new Lincoln Continental Mark IV along with a four-carat diamond ring. The two of them told everyone—fans, friends and media representatives alike—that they were married, though they actually weren't yet. Tammy moved into George's house anyway, and there, unbeknownst to the eyes of the prying world, they lived together in sin. Though the two of them were still being pulled asunder by their separate touring schedules, George—at the cost of about $300,000 in Lear jet rental fees—was soon able to minimize the amount of time, either on or off the road, that they spent apart.

Old Pappy Daily was now in his seventies. Itching to retire from the business that had been so very good to him, he had found yet another song that he thought would be right for George. It was "I'll Share My World with You," and it had been penned by Ben Wilson, an elderly man in Miami who had made his way through life making souvenirs from seashells before turning to professional songwriting at age fifty-four. Wilson, too, had read all the fan magazines about George and Tammy. "At that time, George was just about to get married to Tammy, and was very much in love with her," he explained. "And I was also very much in love with my own wife. After talking to my wife about this, I wrote 'I'll Share My World with You.' "

Pappy, being the shrewd old codger that he was, knew how abuzz the country music world was with the latest news of George and Tammy. He figured that George singing a slow, romantic ballad like this one (which, as usual, he'd also managed to corner the publishing rights to) would sell like a son of a bitch. All he had to do now was to get George to record it.

George was still not too hot on these mushy, uptown love ballads that Pappy had begun bringing around for him here of late, and at first, he had no more use for "I'll Share My World with You" than he'd had for "Walk Through This World with Me." (The ballads were strikingly similar.) But Pappy would not let him off the hook. "I didn't get sold on too many songs," the old man explained, in justification of his relentlessness, "but those that I did get sold on, I stuck with."

On November 6, 1968, George finally knew that old Pappy had at last chased him into a corner. He laughed wearily at his mentor's almost comic persistence. After a few studio drinks, he felt his own lips begin to move and he heard his own voice as if it were coming from very far away, at the other end of a very long tunnel. He could hear sounds that once again sounded languid and expansive, like one of those big city TV newscasters. Gone now was the whining East Texas brogue that had given such raw forcefulness to those rough-around-the-edges recordings of his earlier years.

Pappy's hunch had been right, though. When "I'll Share My World with You" was released in early 1969, all the fans just assumed it was Tammy that George was singing about. Everyone bought the hell out of this new record, sending it all the way up to the number two spot in the *Billboard* charts.

Ironically, the only thing that kept "I'll Share My World with You" out of the number one position—much to Pappy's annoyance—was "Stand By Your Man," Tammy's own musical celebration of romantic lapdog allegiance. Tammy's ballad was a song that its producer and co-writer casually admitted was aimed right square at "all the women out there that have been kicked in the ass all their lives." Of course, it didn't hurt that the whole world now knew that the man Tammy was standing by—even as this new record of hers kept his record out of the top of the singles charts—was none other than the old Possum himself.

In Nashville, country music's new lovebirds relocated from George's house to Tammy's considerably larger lakeside residence. They continued to live in sin, outside the holy sacrament of marriage. This was something that bothered George Glenn at times, because he knew that if his mama, Clara, ever knew, she'd not have stood for it for one minute.

George's principal demons had been slumbering, but they had not ceased to abide within him. It wasn't until late 1968 that Tammy had the displeasure of bearing witness to them in their full fury. It sadly would prove to be the first of many times to come.

The untimely scene began to unfold one evening while they were in a Holiday Inn in the Central Florida town of Lakeland, where they hoped to find a house. The house that George already owned there —one of the scraps he'd been tossed in his last divorce settlement— was being rented at the time. They planned to move to Lakeland in order to seek respite from the fishbowl-like existence they'd been living in Nashville, where the relentless glare of the gossip machine seemed to be forever focused on them. In the process of entertaining some friends, George had been drinking whiskey that rainy night in the hotel room, until he finally seemed to pass out. When Tammy assumed he was down for the count and out of the picture for the rest of the evening, he came reeling up off the bed and charged her, like a man possessed. He heaved a bottle at her which barely missed her head before shattering against the wall. He came at her again with his fists and chased his bride-to-be, dressed only in a nightgown, down four flights of stairs and out into the rain, cursing and hollering behind her every step of the way. Across the dark parking lot they flew until the pointy toe of one of his cowboy boots got caught on a curb; he tripped, fell and broke his wrist on the slick pavement.

A few hours later Tammy summoned the courage to return to their room. She was amazed to find that the prodigal singer had once again sunk into a peaceful whiskey slumber. She woke him up and was even more startled to find that he had no recollection whatsoever of their untimely little midnight romp around the hotel grounds.

Still, as unsettling as this unexpected eruption was, it seemed but a small blemish on the exceedingly smooth complexion of their private and public life together, the pieces of which now seemed to be falling almost magically in place.

In January 1969, the two of them joined the Grand Ole Opry. (After first joining the Opry in 1956, George had left in the early 1960s, having grown weary of the strict Saturday-night attendance requirements and the other restrictions imposed by the dark-suited regime at WSM-Radio that ran the organization.) By now, each of them had also fulfilled the individual appearance obligations that stood in the way of their touring together. From now on, they would schedule all of their shows as a duet team, and from now on, they would be inseparable, both on stage and off. Surely, everything would be wonderful from here on out.

It was at one of the very first scheduled appearances that the two of them made together, at the Playroom Club in Atlanta that February, that George's principal demons, in the full splendor of their Medusa-like fury, paid a return visit. Opening night there at the Playroom had gone well for them. But the second night, as they waited outside on the $110,000 tour bus that they'd recently purchased to carry them from show date to show date (and which was emblazoned, in bright, bold letters, with the logo: MR. & MRS. COUNTRY MUSIC), George, seemingly without provocation, worked himself into a jealous rage. He began accusing Tammy of gross infidelity; more specifically, he believed she'd been getting it on with some of the boys in the band. He ended up in such a frenzied state of enraged biliousness that, at one point, he knocked his fiancée down in the aisle of the bus. As the hours passed, his physical harassment of Tammy intensified, until some of the band members had no other choice but to lock him in the bus's bedroom. They hoped that he might cool down in time for their first performance of the evening, which was less than an hour away.

When they finally hauled George onstage with Tammy, it appeared that the evening might yet unfold without further trouble. But when Tammy turned to him on stage and flashed her carefully rehearsed stage smile, she could see that his swirling eyes were still full of unvanquished rage. He sang only one song before stalking angrily off the stage, leaving Tammy to face the disappointed and hostile audience alone.

It was not until four nights later that a still very enraged and under-the-weather George surfaced again, with the sole purpose of informing his fiancée that he was still certain he could detect on her the telltale blemishes of sin and infidelity—that he no longer had any intention of marrying her. Tammy found this bit of news particularly troublesome indeed, as she was already pregnant with his child.

The following morning, the storm had cleared and George's demons had once again faded into remission. Once again, despite his obvious remorse, he was in an undauntedly cheerful and expansive mood. "C'mon," he told his wife-to-be, "get outa bed and put on somethin' nice. We're gettin' married!"

In a brief impromptu civil ceremony later that day in the small town of Ringgold, Georgia, just across the Tennessee line from Chattanooga, he and Tammy tied the marital knot. It was the third go-round for both of them.

As his new marital alliance was being consummated, one of George's most enduring friendships and professional alliances was, in a flurry of equally stormy emotions, about to come undone. After nearly a half century in the music business, Pappy Daily knew that it was time for him to hang up his gloves and cash in his chips. In his day, there had been nothing that he liked better than coming to Nashville to produce George, having a few drinks with the prodigal singer and playing the part of the crusty old music kingpin, handing out hundred-dollar bills to his favorite songwriters, like Peanut Montgomery. ("Here, kid, have a big time on Pappy!" he'd tell them as he puffed on his cigar.) But now, age was beginning to settle into his face, his hair was turning white and his joints were stiffening. He was content to sit in his Houston office and shuffle invoices, overseeing H. W. Daily, Inc., the rather extensive financial empire into which his various publishing, distributing and retail enterprises had now grown.

When George and Pappy finally parted, after a gloriously rewarding decade and a half together, there were no champagne celebrations and no gold watches exchanged. "There is no love lost between Pappy Daily and myself," George remarked with seething bitterness several years later, in an interview in which he complained at length about what he claimed to be the haphazardly uneven production quality of the records he'd made under the supervision of both Pappy and Art Talmadge. He also raised questions about all the royalty rights that he alleged he'd hastily relinquished in the mad flurry of document signing that had accompanied each of his record-label changes. "I have been kicked around worse than a damn mule," he added. "Nothing ever seemed to matter [to them] but the almighty dollar."

For his part, old Pappy—who had no fondness for George's new bride and was suspicious of the undue and perhaps unhealthy influence that she held over the wayward singer—would read such things and wonder to himself if that was really George talking, or if it was Tammy Wynette merely talking *through* George. "I like to think I did my best for [George]," Pappy responded in a separate interview. "I like to think I did my best, even in the days when he'd wreck half the hotels in Nashville, and most of 'em wouldn't even have anything to do with him."

For some time, George and Tammy, along with those who were then in power at Epic Records, a subsidiary of the Columbia record label, to which Tammy was already signed, had been kicking around the idea of having this new husband-and-wife team record some duets together. Tammy had, in fact, sung backup harmonies on *I'll Share My World with You,* George's 1969 LP on the Musicor label. (Her picture appeared on the album jacket, though she was not credited by name.) Now that the two of them were an item, both on and off stage, and now that their fans had begun clamoring for just such a musical collaboration from "Mr. and Mrs. Country Music," this seemed like a timely move indeed.

The only thing that still stood in the way of this arrangement was George's remaining contractual obligation to Art Talmadge and the Musicor label. Since there was not a great deal of time left to run on

George's Musicor contract, friends advised him to sit things out and
merely go through the motions of fulfilling his remaining inden-
turedness to that company. But that had never been the prodigal
singer's way of doing things: when he was ready to get the hell out,
he got out. He was more than anxious to be free of his association
with Musicor—which he felt had resulted in some of the shoddiest
records he'd made in the course of his long career—even if it did
mean spreading a lot of money around. He told friends later that
this freedom cost him more than $100,000, and that he had been
required by Musicor to sign away all claims to future royalties from
the dozens of albums' worth of material that he'd hastily recorded.
That was just the way the Possum was. When he decided he was
going to do something, then to hell with it. He damn well did it.

In the years before his eventual ascendance to wealth and fame as
one of Nashville's most successful record producers, Billy Sherrill
had emerged from a background that was as humble and unflinch-
ingly Calvinistic as George's own.

Sherrill's father was a Bible-thumping evangelistic preacher—a
man cut from the same stern cloth as George's long-dead maternal
grandfather, Uncle Litt. While playing piano at Alabama tent shows,
funerals and riverside baptisms by immersion where his father had
preached, he had, at an early age, learned and fallen in love with
many of the same old Sacred Harp and Southern Holiness songs
that George had first heard at the knee of his mama, Clara.

Sherrill never wavered from the strict fundamentalist faith in
which he was raised. He had, out of necessity, learned to make a
separate peace with Mammon early on. By the time he was in his late
teens, both parents had died, and as "a matter of survival," he
turned to a determinedly more secular life of sleeping under
bridges and sidestepping the flying beer bottles of the knife-wielding drunks on the Alabama-Mississippi dance-band circuit. "Back
then, I was strictly into rhythm and blues and B. B. King," recalled
Sherrill, whose speech is still peppered with the down-home patois
of a former rock-'n'-roll saxophone player. "I hated country music,
and I figured anyone who liked it was a redneck.

"But then one night, around 1960, I was driving home at about
two in the morning in my '57 Ford, coming back from a dance where
I'd just played," he added with a nostalgic grin. "And I accidentally
flipped the radio to this country station, and there was George Jones

singing 'Seasons of the Heart.' That was probably the first time I'd ever bothered to listen to a country song all the way through. And it flipped me out. That was it! I became a real country fan."

This rather sudden and miraculous transformation of Sherrill's musical tastes was made complete in 1962 when a song he'd written was recorded by an obscure Nashville artist named Bob Beckham. Like manna from the sky, a $4,000 royalty check fell into his grasping hands. Enticed by the allurement of more of this coin of such great and unprecedented dimension, he moved to Nashville that same year and managed to talk his way into a job as a hundred-dollar-a-week engineer in a small studio owned by Sam Phillips (the pioneering record producer who, in an earlier decade, had founded Sun Records in Memphis and turned the world on to such musical luminaries as Elvis Presley, Johnny Cash and Jerry Lee Lewis).

In 1963, on the strength of his work at Phillips's studio, Sherrill signed with Epic Records, a division of Columbia (CBS) Records, as a "shotgun producer." "Ten grand a year and I produced whoever nobody else wanted." He began working with the tiny roster of obscure country artists who were then signed to Epic. "I still knew about as much about country music as the Shah of Iran," he admits.

By drawing from such unlikely and disparate musical influences as Johann Strauss and "wall of sound" rock producer Phil Spector (one of Sherrill's big heroes), he gradually began embroidering his own subtle permutations on the rather predictable fabric of country record production. "I just decided I'd do it my way, and screw 'em if they didn't like it. Back then, the musicians had their own repertoire of stock Nashville licks and chord progressions that would work on any song. But I often wanted something different, and I'd make 'em play it."

It soon became clear that Sherrill possessed a gift for musical alchemy the likes of which Nashville had never seen before: an almost mystical power to gaze into the tea-leaf configurations of the shape notes and divine the essence of the music of the spheres that abided there, and use this essence to conjure up still more royalty checks with dollar signs of great dimension written on them. By early 1969, when George had finally gotten around to marrying Tammy (who was merely one of several dozen successful artists that Sherrill—only thirty-three years old—was producing by then), he was already well on his way to earning the first of his many millions and expanding Epic Records' tiny collection of second-tier country acts into a powerhouse roster of first-class talent. Along the way, working with these various artists, he eventually amassed a track record as a producer that included more than fifty number one singles and dozens of platinum (million-selling) and gold (half-million-selling) albums—a track record that, in country music, remains virtually unparalleled even today.

If it had not been for Billy Sherrill, in fact, it is quite likely that Tammy Wynette would have still been stuck wielding a hot comb and curlers in some backwater beauty salon in Shell Shock, Mississippi, or Test Site, Alabama. It was he who, almost single-handedly, guided her career from obscurity to fame. The relationship began one day in 1966 when she accidentally stumbled into his Music Row office, broke, bedraggled and—after having already been turned down by five other record labels—hungry for a deal of any kind. With typical iron-handedness, Sherrill soon invented her drugstore-sounding stage name. "You look like a Tammy to me," he assured her. He then set about personally handpicking or—in many cases—helping to write songs for her to record—all of which nurtured her carefully cultivated public persona as "the woman with a tear in her voice."

Naturally, it was to her mentor, Sherrill, that Tammy first brought her new husband, George. Sherrill, being a longtime fan of the prodigal singer, wasted little time in signing him to a ten-year contract with Epic Records on October 1, 1971, a few days after he'd extricated himself from his contractual obligations to the Musicor label.

A more unlikely artist-producer alliance there never was. For in many ways Sherrill had come to stand for all that George hated. It was Sherrill, after all, who—with his eagle eye trained on the much greater sales figures offered by the crossover pop market (which were often ten times that of the average hard country hit)—had most eagerly picked up the bouncing ball that had been kicked in motion by pioneering Nashville-sound producers Chet Atkins and Owen Bradley, and it was he who had run with it the fastest and the furthest.

By the early 1970s, Sherrill had taken the Nashville sound to its ultimate, pop-influenced refinement (or—depending upon one's musical perspective—its ultimate *vulgarization*). By then, all manner of urbane, uptown permutations had begun to creep onto the country records that he produced: orchestral violins playing full-octave glissandos, sensuous Mantovani-style background vocals and melo-dramatic crescendos of drums, cymbals and wailing, shrilly ampli-fied steel guitars. The end result was often his own countrified musical "wall of sound" production style, a sound about as subtle and understated as heavy artillery and armored tanks rolling onto the bricked streets of Berlin.

Because of his overbearing tendency to bury the fiery heart and soul of traditional hard-core country and honky-tonk sound beneath an urbane gruel of gushing vocal harmonies and double-track string orchestras, Sherrill came to be regarded in more conservative-minded musical circles as nothing less than a pariah. Needless to say, he won very few new friends among the ranks of those more tradition-conscious country artists whose records were now being routinely knocked out of the top ten by these newfangled produc-tion numbers of his. To these people, his overwrought, pop-in-spired production innovations were about as welcome in Nashville as a cholera epidemic.

In the studio, there were often clashes of a more personal nature between the wily, quick-to-anger Jones, with his unbridled hard-core country instincts, and Sherrill, the flippant pop- and classical-inspired perfectionist. Sherrill's barbed-tongued sarcasm and con-descending humor would sometimes make the shotgun eyes dance with fiery indignation. ("I'm the one person you *can't* fire!" Sherrill would occasionally taunt him.)

"George's main problem has always been that he's lazy," Sherrill laughed one day, long after the two of them had managed to resolve their initial aesthetic and personal differences, and gone on to cele-brate their tenth anniversary as a producer-artist team. "All he ever wanted to do was to just sing the damn song and get the hell out of the studio and do something else. He was just always happy with what we would get the first time through, and if he happened to mispronounce a word here and there, well, hell, that didn't bother him. But I guess I was a little bit harder to please than what he'd been used to."

George's first single for Epic, "We Can Make It," was released in February 1972. It eventually reached the number six spot in the charts. Months before George's first Epic release had even hit the record racks, Sherrill had already begun to work on a more pressing matter. He had already looked into the mysterious patterns of shape notes and divined, in tea-leaf fashion, where the real money was to be made. He knew that Tammy and George were now in the process of turning their celebrated romance into a country-music passion play. He knew they wanted to take their romantic road show out to strange cities like Sioux City and Peoria, where they would perform for all the people who'd been reading in the tabloids and fan mags about their storybook love affair. He felt that if he could come up with some good duets for them to record and sing onstage—songs which sounded like authentic slices of melodrama from the over-wrought soap opera which Tammy and George's private life to-gether was about to become—then they would probably sell like a son of a bitch.

In October 1971, with George's spanking-new Epic contract just signed, Sherrill took Tammy and the prodigal singer into a studio together and produced the first of dozens of love duets (most of which sounded like two-and-a-half-minute-long musical *Cliff's Notes* to Harlequin novels) that they recorded together over the course of the next decade. "We Believe in Each Other," "Lovin' You Is Worth It," "There's Power in Our Love," "A Perfect Match" and "You and Me Together" were just some of the more syrupy song titles from their 1972 *Me and the First Lady* LP—one of the earliest of the six duet albums that they would record on Epic. Their first hit single together, a song called "The Ceremony," was released in early July 1972 and made it to the number six spot in *Billboard*.

"The Ceremony" eventually became the perfect stage vehicle for Tammy and George in their ever more conscious and contrived efforts to go public with their fairy-tale love affair. When they sang "The Ceremony" onstage in places like Sioux City and Peoria, they enacted for the benefit of their fans an elaborate wedding ritual which, in reality, was quite unlike the quickie civil ceremony with which they'd actually sealed their nuptial bond.

When longtime fans and friends saw Tammy and George's road show, and watched them sing and perform "The Ceremony," they were startled to see a new George Jones, quite unlike the one they'd known before. Having fallen under Tammy's sway, he was now decked out in immaculately tailored suits and other fancy stage duds. He'd also begun wearing his hair in a long, urbane style that particularly shocked his old-line fans, who had grown so accus-tomed to his flat-topped "burr-head" look that they went so far as accusing him of wearing a toupee.

It was easy enough for these fans and friends to conclude that

Tammy had actually succeeded in taming the rough beast that abided within George. When they watched the two of them prancing formally around the stage, silhouetted in the bright lights, reeling off their well-rehearsed stage lines—George in his fancy suits and Tammy in a full-length gown and her hair in a resplendent bubble-gum bouffant—they couldn't help but notice, from a distance, just how much they looked like those cute little candy bride-and-groom statuettes that adorn the tops of huge wedding cakes. What they didn't know was that, before long, before the icing on that imaginary cake was barely dry, the bride-and-groom statuettes would begin to melt and crumble to the degree that they would become nothing more than pathetically disfigured parodies of their former selves, merely going trancelike through their well-rehearsed but hollow public rituals.

Due to the combined momentum of their hit records, their association with the Grand Ole Opry and the lavish homage that the fan and gossip tabloids were now beginning to pay to even the most trite minutiae from their personal lives, Tammy and George's nightly concert fee rose to $20,000 and occasionally even $30,000. Traveling in their large, elegantly appointed tour bus, they began making appearances at such prestigious venues as New York's Madison Square Garden, where they performed at a benefit for their friend, then presidential candidate, George Wallace of Alabama, and Philharmonic Hall, where they even garnered a "fave" write-up from the decidedly urban-elitist *New Yorker* magazine.

Now the money was pouring in faster almost than even George could spend it—though he still tried his damnedest. He bought Tammy a $43,000 Nautalina houseboat, which, after putting it afloat on Old Hickory Lake near Nashville, he christened *The First Lady,* in honor of Tammy, who had now become far more of a household word with the American public than George had ever been, because of the crossover success of "Stand By Your Man." He showered her continually with other lavish gifts: expensive automobiles, jewelry, clothes . . . (Once, on an impulse, he wrote out a check for $36,000 at a Los Angeles auction and bought her two diamond rings, simply because he could not be bothered to make a decision as to which of the two he liked better.)

In March 1969, Tammy and George finally managed to make their long-awaited escape from the fish-eye lenses of Nashville's ever more curious gossip machine. They moved to Lakeland, Florida, the small inland city about thirty miles east of Tampa where they'd been planning to relocate for some time.

For a while, they lived in the large, comfortable ranch-style house which George already owned there. Then during the hot summer of 1970, the two of them found the potential dream house for which they'd been searching—a pleasure palace which bespoke a countrified elegance and grandeur more in keeping with their ever-rising status as "Mr. and Mrs. Country Music." What they found was a huge moss- and oak-shrouded neoclassic house originally built in 1903. Though such luminaries as William Jennings Bryan and Thomas Edison had once slept under its roof, the noble manse had since fallen into a state of semi-disrepair, and George was able to acquire it and the surrounding forty-three and a half acres for the bargain-basement price of $150,000.

George set about restoring the old plantation-style mansion with a zeal the likes of which his friends had not seen him display since he'd undertaken the ill-fated Rhythm Ranch project. He spent $100,000 lavishly restoring and redecorating its spacious interior with ornate antiques and crystal chandeliers. He had a large kidney-shaped swimming pool installed out back, spent another $150,000 or so improving the landscaping and shrubbery and even had royal palm trees imported from South America planted in the yard. The prodigal singer knew that he had to get the grounds so they looked just right for those lazy afternoons when he could venture out to survey his new realm, with mixed drink in hand, riding astride his favorite riding lawn mower. Otherwise, he knew, true contentment would elude him.

(George was never without a riding lawn mower; it was a vehicle which he favored, not only as a good means of substitute transportation for an emergency run to the liquor store when he could not find his car keys, but also because he believed that its shaking effect, when you took it over rough terrain, was all the physical exercise that a person really needed.)

Tammy and George were still getting settled in their new residence in late 1970 when another heartwarming development occurred in their lives—something that Tammy believed would, once and for all, assuage those Medusa-like demons that occasionally burst forth from the troubled depths of her husband's soul.

George and Tammy were now overjoyed to learn that Tammy was once again pregnant. Her earlier pregnancy by George had ended in a miscarriage, and this news made them even more beside themselves with giddy excitement and anticipation.

Their firstborn—a girl child—arrived on October 5, 1970, and they named her Tamala Georgette, in honor of her famous mama and daddy. In those first weeks at the Lakeland mansion, after Tammy returned from the hospital with their newborn daughter, George seemed nearly beside himself with pride and happiness. He fawned and doted over his wife and the new child she'd borne him. He spent hours making a homecoming present for the two of them —a huge velvet-framed plaque which had their pictures engraved on it and was inscribed with love poems that he'd written to them.

To the imaginary suitor who would one day sweep away his new girl child, he wrote:

> *When young love is in bloom and happy*
> *I hope you love her as I loved her mom.*

To his third wife, he wrote:

> *This house holds a lot of memories.*
> *There are good ones and bad ones, I fear,*
> *but nothing can harm us in this house,*
> *we know, because my darling Tammy sleeps here.*

Overwhelmed with emotion, Tammy eventually reciprocated this bounteous expression of love and devotion with a prosaic tribute of her own, which she called the Husband of the Year award:

> *To the sweetest, kindest, most wonderful husband of the year. I hope*
> *you enjoy one hundred years of complete happiness. I love you.*

Those early times there in Florida were halcyon days for the prodigal singer. They were destined to be a few, fleeting months of profound optimism and contentment that would later shimmer like a backward-beckoning mirage across the troubled years of strife and unrest that were to follow.

Once George had finished refurbishing his new mansion and its grounds to his own satisfaction, he then turned his energies elsewhere. He began expanding the impressive collection of antique cars which he'd already acquired. He had already accumulated an extensive record collection that included all but one of the original 78-rpm singles which the dark archangel Hank Williams had recorded for the Sterling and M-G-M labels in the late 1940s and early 1950s. His new hobby quickly won out and he became the proud owner of a couple of dozen perfectly restored vintage pleasure machines, including a 1925 Model T Ford, a 1929 Model A Ford, a 1936 Chevrolet, a 1938 Austrian-made Steyr (which bore bullet holes from the days in World War II when it had been commandeered by German soldiers), a twelve-cylinder 1940 Lincoln Zephyr, a 1947 MG, a 1923 Cadillac and, just for fun, an ancient Rolls-Royce that had once belonged to Cary Grant.

The most prized trophy in George's car collection, though, was a custom-designed Pontiac Bonneville that he had bought from Nudie, the famous Hollywood clothes designer who made many of his extravagant stage outfits for him. (He had also made suits for Hank Williams, including the one that he was buried in.) The car—a white convertible—had 4,000 silver dollars embedded throughout the interior and in the dashboard, a huge set of Texas steer horns ornamentally mounted on the hood and a horn that, when you mashed on it, sounded just like the bellow of an enraged Brahma bull. Just to aggravate his older brother, Herman, who often came to visit, he would sometimes send him down to the car wash with his "silver-dollar car." Poor Herman, a nervous man to begin with, could just about hear his knees knocking as his trembling hands steered the garishly designed convertible through the busy streets of downtown Lakeland. Frightened half out of his wits that somebody was going to hit him over the head and pry all those silver dollars loose with a crowbar and make off with them, Herman many times never reached the car wash but stopped short and quickly drove back home.

It was obvious, though, that George's newfound inner peace flowed from emotions far deeper than the fleeting satisfaction he got from the mere accumulation of worldly goods. Deep down, he was as disdainful as ever of money and of the value of all those things that it could buy. He was clearly a man who was very much in love with life. Now in his late thirties, he seemed to find contentment in the role of husband and father such as he'd not been able to find in his two previous marriages. He'd even grown to love Tammy's daughters from her first marriage as if they were his own, to the degree that he legally adopted all three of them.

Amidst the seclusion and serenity of their Florida retreat, there were still problems, however. From time to time, Tammy had to get after George about his drinking, even though he tried his best, time and time again, to wean himself, and sometimes was able to actually set the bottle aside for months at a time. Of course, he usually kept a bottle of vodka stashed out in the nearby orange groves, just like his old daddy used to keep bottles of wine stashed in the tall hedges back at the Rhythm Ranch. That way, when he did feel the demons starting to sing too loudly in his blood, he could just get himself a glass of orange juice and hop on his lawn mower and ride out amongst the orange trees and mix himself a little drink on the sly.

Sooner or later, no matter how valiantly he struggled and railed against it, though, George would always end up succumbing to the amber-hued genie in the whiskey bottle, and his submissions would often result in acts of comic desperation. After staying straight and sober for quite a long time, he'd finally roll off the wagon for several days. He always came crawling back home again when his thirst had subsided, and was so messed up and bedraggled that all he could do was to stagger upstairs to his bed and pass out. In a futile attempt to curb further disruption one particular night, Tammy first made sure that there was no booze in the house. Then she hid all twenty-seven sets of car keys, as well as the keys to George's lawn mower; then, feeling sure that the evening escapades were over, she went to bed.

Around 1 A.M., George awakened from his slumber and found that he was once again suffering from a prodigious thirst. After crashing and stumbling around the house for a long time, searching in vain for either booze or car keys, he finally hopped aboard his trusted riding lawn mower, after hot-wiring it, and commandeered it the half-dozen or so miles to the nearest open bar.

For a while there in Florida, such misadventures were surprisingly few and far between. George seemed intent upon forging the kind of close familial bonds and friendships that had eluded him for a very long time.

One friend in whose company he took particular delight was a man that he'd first met in Lakeland, named Cliff Hyder. Hyder was badly disabled by Lou Gehrig's disease, and when George first got to know him, he was still in a state of utter despondency over the weakened and largely immobile condition in which his affliction had left him. Hyder had, in fact, become a virtual recluse, far too ashamed and embarrassed over his diminished coordination to even venture out in public. George could feel his friend Cliff's deep despair. He became determined to shake Hyder free from his depression and pessimism—afflictions which, he knew, could be even more potentially crippling to a man than his actual physical impairment. He began by inviting Hyder to go out into the world with him and Tammy—to restaurants, on boat rides—and refusing to take no for an answer. Gradually, on account of George's patience and compassion, Hyder was able to overcome his depression and once again learn to enjoy many of the things he'd assumed he could no longer do for himself. "George is the finest human being I've ever met in my life," Hyder explained. "He made me realize that I *was* still a human being, and could put my own pants on, like other people. There's no other way to say it, except that he just turned my life around."

George's mama, Clara, who was now old and gray and well into her eighth decade, came to visit her youngest son at his new lavish retreat. Clara could see that George Glenn was now living in a far different world than the strict, antediluvian realm in which Uncle Litt had raised her, back in the Thicket, nearly a lifetime ago. She knew that her youngest child was now earning more money in one night than any of her six other children (all of whom had drifted into marriage and ordinary working-class lives) made in an entire year.

Even when she came to this wondrous subtropical Babylon in which her son now dwelled, Clara was still not once tempted to falter from the strict edicts of Uncle Litt's faith, which abided in her always. She still refused to let strong drink touch her lips, and she would still not let rouge defile her face. She would occasionally venture out to the dog races with George Glenn and her new daughter-in-law, and sometimes she'd even pick a dog and let her boy put some money on him for her. If her dog won, she would never keep that money; for she knew that it was tarnished and ill gained, that it had not been earned by the honest sweat of her brow.

George took Tammy and his mama out to dinner one evening at one of his favorite fancy Hawaiian restaurants in the area. When they finished eating, the prodigal singer paid the hundred-and-fifty-dollar tab and then left forty dollars lying on the table. He was almost out the door when he turned and saw his old gray-headed mama running excitedly toward him, through the crowded room, waving the two twenty-dollar bills in the air. "George Glenn, George Glenn!" she scolded him loudly. "Honey, you done went off in such a hurry you left your money lyin' on the table!"

"Mama," George whispered, as he glanced around the crowded room full of bemused strangers and felt the flush of redness rush to his face. "Mama, that there's the *tip!*"

"The tip!?" old Clara gasped. "Well, I never!" Why, sure, Clara knew what a tip was, she always gave the boy who carried her grocery bags an extra quarter when she had one to spare. . . . But twenty dollars! . . . Why, back in the old days, she could have kept the family in biscuits and egg gravy for six whole months on that kind of money!

To the world at large, it now seemed that Tammy and George were twice blessed, that peace and prosperity were now raining gently down upon them in equal measure. They crisscrossed the country on their megadollar tours, they continued to garner rave reviews and draw sellout crowds and in their private lives they continued to luxuriate in the domestic splendor of their lavish Florida pleasure dome.

Still, all was not well. The demons and the snakes refused to sleep, and their horrible writhing movements in the depths sometimes made frightening patterns on the surface of the still waters—patterns that did not bode well for those days yet to come.

As all was not well with George, all was not well with the First Lady either. Her health, which had never been good, now seemed to be caving in under the combined pressures of trying to maintain the carefully constructed façade of domestic bliss while trying to cope with her husband's ever more erratic moods, all under the relentless scrutiny of the hungry press and public. She was suffering from a wide array of real or imagined physical ailments, which she attempted to alleviate by taking an even wider array of prescription drugs. In mid-October 1971, she passed out at the wheel of her car and knocked down two palm trees on a downtown Lakeland street. She was taken to the nearby Watson Clinic on Lakeland Hills Boulevard and was diagnosed as having "a high sugar count."

Even when George was in his most relaxed and most expansive of moods, she would even then find herself watching him and waiting uneasily. "Sometimes George would get violent, and sometimes he'd just go quietly to bed and sleep it off," she later remembered. "[But] the fear of violence was always there."

Friends also noticed that when she was under stress, Tammy's own disposition could be nearly as volatile and erratic as her husband's. More and more often, she was subject to screaming tantrums, and she vented her uncontrollable wrath against the Possum by hurling items of kitchenware at him and kicking him roughly on the shins with the toes of her high-heeled cowboy boots. "I never have met a woman with such a temper!" George later recalled in a voice still full of awestruck amazement. "It's hard to live with a woman like that!"

There were other, sometimes inexplicable harbingers of doom that were beginning to reveal themselves in mysterious ways, much like the sound of slamming doors in a dark, deserted house or tendrils of slowly creeping vines that grow only by night.

"One night, me and my wife, Charlene, was down there in Florida visiting George and Tammy," recalled George's right-hand man, Peanut Montgomery. "Me and George had been outside and we came back in through the door and didn't see anything wrong. Later, after we'd all gone to bed, Charlene saw Tammy get up and go downstairs. She was down there a while, and all the sudden, she started hollerin' and carryin' on like there was someone after her, though there didn't seem to be no one else around. We all ran downstairs, and Tammy showed us where someone had written 'PIG' in lipstick on the door."

It was shortly after Tamala Georgette was born that George's principal demons finally came forth again, and the false lull of domestic serenity was shattered, once and for all. George had fallen off the wagon again—this time with a resounding thud—and for nearly a week he'd been out running wild, mixing whiskey with the amphetamine-based diet pills that he often relied upon to combat the double-edged threat of hangovers and a creeping waistline. When the wayward singer finally came crawling home, he was in such bad shape that he fell flat on his face as he struggled to get out of his car.

Working on the dangerously unfounded premise that he was way too far gone to do any more damage that night, Tammy and a friend were able to drag him inside and up the stairs to bed. When Tammy started to take off his pants and reached down to unzip his fly, George, with possumlike stealth, suddenly arose from his feigned whiskey coma and swung wildly at his wife with his fists. Tammy hurried down the stairs to escape his wrath. She made the mistake of then stopping and looking back over her shoulder, and what she saw almost froze her into a pillar of salt. George was at the top of the stairs, his hair dangling dangerously in his face and his beady shot-gun eyes dancing wildly. Cradled in his arms was a loaded .30-30 deer rifle. "You may run out on *me*, baby," he screamed as he raised the high-powered rifle and drew a bead on her through its sights, "but you sure as hell ain't gonna run out on *this!*"

Tammy fled out into the backyard as George raced to the porch. Once again she turned, just in time to see him raise the gun again and point it at her. She screamed and ran still farther out across the yard, the deafening roar of gunfire echoing in her ears.

Instead of continuing in his heated pursuit of his terrified wife, George turned and went back into the house. Hollering, screaming and cursing like a crazy man, he turned his fury on the lavish interior of his elegant home, which he'd spent so many hours and so many, many thousands of dollars redecorating. He picked up expensive antique chairs and, one after another, hurled them at televisions and into antique cabinets containing dozens of pieces of expensive china and crystal. Picking up still more chairs and bits of expensive furni-ture, he continued to hurl, smash and chop his way through the interior of the house, bending to his task with a furious, yet strangely methodical vengeance—much the same way his old daddy, George Washington Jones, used to hack his way through those majestic virgin pines as he grinned his lopsided grin back in the Thicket. Working with termitelike thoroughness, he pressed onward from room to room with his grand tour of destruction, hacking away like a trapped animal struggling to free itself from the gilded cage in which it is imprisoned. He pulled down curtains and drapes; he demolished three television sets; he broke dozens of windows; and he reduced thousands of dollars' worth of crystalware and antique bric-a-brac to tiny glass fragments. He didn't stop until he was finally subdued by a team of medical attendants who re-strained him in a straitjacket. The raging bull was hauled off in an ambulance to a padded cell in the Watson Clinic, where he was left to dry out for ten days.

When George was released from the clinic, he took a taxicab back out to his stately manse. Arriving there, he walked gingerly inside and fell into a grim, sober silence as he quietly surveyed the destruction he'd left in his path—and which Tammy had made certain would still be there for him to see when he returned. Then he sat down on the porch steps, took his head in his hands and cried until his eyes were swollen.

On some evenings, when George was still in the throes of such extreme remorse and contrition, he would hear the demons start to sing in his blood once again. He would inveigh against their dark powers, even as he could feel them gaining strength within him. While Tammy's aging mother played the piano and sang the old Holiness songs he loved so much, he would mix tears of remorse with prayers for deliverance. But then, more often than not, the demons would ultimately win out, and he would go out and get himself all messed up again.

When Clara Jones visited, she could plainly see the towering dissipation that had now overtaken her son. It troubled her deeply. She prayed for George and took him aside, gently but sternly admonishing him not to put his third wife through the same kind of earthly hell that Old George had dragged her through with his violence and hard drinking. It even crossed George's mind, as he watched his third marriage slowly coming unraveled, that despite all his wealth and fame, he was now no different in his excesses from his old daddy. "It just don't make sense," he'd shake his head and murmur in a faraway voice as he sat quietly with his old gray-headed mama. "I hated Daddy for his drinkin' and the miserable way he treated you. Yet, now I'm makin' a bigger mess of things than he ever did."

The eleven-year age gap between George and Tammy at first had seemed to make little difference. That, too, was now beginning to exact a price on their increasingly troubled marriage. As George celebrated his fortieth birthday on September 12, 1971, he could see that his young wife's career was gaining momentum with each passing day, while his own was waning. Almost every one of her Sherrill-produced singles broke the top five. In fact, in the past four years, nine of them had hit the number one spot. His, on the other hand, in many cases merely crept phlegmatically into the bottom of the top ten and quickly fell back out again. In 1972, Tammy's *Greatest Hits* LP was certified gold when it sold more than half a million copies—far more than any one of George's albums had ever sold. Everyone could now see that George was running the risk of becoming a mere musical appendage to his younger and ever more famous wife. They could see that he was in danger of merely becoming Mr. Tammy Wynette No. 3.

The abiding weariness in George, from so many years of constant recording and touring, was never so outwardly apparent as it was now. He was overweight, languid in his speech and movements, jaded by the allurements of fame and sated with all the creature comforts that his affluence had afforded him.

Performing had now even come to be something that he endured rather than enjoyed. Throughout his career—despite his popular acceptance—he had often been subject to severe and persistent bouts of stage fright—an affliction for which alcohol, more often than not, served as the natural antidote. "Them really big shows like to scare me to death," he explained. "My mouth gets so dry I can't hardly swallow!" This phobia of his had now assumed pathological dimensions and preyed mercilessly on his deeper personal insecurities.

George could also see that when he and Tammy played places like the casinos of Las Vegas or the Palomino Club in Hollywood, the two of them were beginning to draw a whole new kind of audience that was much different from what he was used to. These weren't the gruff-voiced, woods-eyed, weather-scarred farmers, day laborers and cowboys, with their rough hands and loud, honest laughter— the kind of people that he'd sung for in those beer halls back in Texas for so many years. No, these new people were a whole breed apart. He could see that. These crowds were people whose pale skin and bland faces were unscarred by the sun, and whose soft, uncallused hands had never wielded a woodsman's ax—people who, just a few years earlier, wouldn't have been caught dead singing "The Great Speckled Bird" in the shower. These people, with their designer-brand clothes, their smooth, snake-oil salesman voices and their icy, sinister politeness, swarmed around him after a show, trying to shake his hand; and in their coldly smiling, subdued and treacherous manner, would whisper secrets to him such as "Normally, I don't like country music, but you're *fantastic!*" When George heard such backhanded praise, he would thank them and smile back with an icily polite smile. But in his heart, he did not smile.

"They use'ta call us *hillbillies!*" he spat bitterly as he once offered a fleeting glimpse at the seething snakes of resentment and insecurity that writhed within him. "They didn't wanta be associated with country music. It took us years to live down that word.

"I really get mad about it when somebody calls me a hillbilly, even now," he fumed distastefully, as if trying to cleanse his mouth of the rancid taste of bile. "It ain't the word itself. It's just the things that take shape in their minds when they use the word. . . . A lot of your so-called educated people tend to look down on other kinds of people, almost like they was peasants. Sure, we're from the country, but we went to school. I went to the seventh grade.

"Course," he added with a cold, calculating smile, as if he'd learned to savor the scorn of the dispossessed, knowing that the day of reckoning and vindication would surely roll around, "when they're talkin' like that, we're laughin' all the way to the bank!"

When confronted with the prospect of singing for one of these new uptown audiences, it made George feel like an organ grinder's monkey, like a puppet on an invisible string. As he prepared to go before such a crowd, he could feel, building within him, the same suppressed outrage and anger that he'd felt in those long-ago times back in Kountze when George Washington Jones used to yank him out of bed in the middle of the night and command him to sing on the porch, under threat of an ass-whipping.

George knew that there was nobody who was about to whip his ass now. When this outrage of the dispossessed—an overweening, impulsive outrage, like that of the poor-white sharecropper who delights in wiping his shit-stained boots on the rich landowner's living-room carpet—would overtake him, he would merely drink deeply and savor the courage that the amber-hued elixir gave him. He would then make his swift, abrupt escape. With his by now notorious magician-like stealth, he would smile and excuse himself, then wriggle out of a small backstage bathroom window. After all, they did not call him Possum for nothing.

In the wake of his sudden, unannounced departures, he would always leave behind him disappointed audiences and angered promoters who had been left holding the bag, along with his equally disappointed wife, who was left to the sorry task of making excuses for him.

In the midst of his growing apathy and disillusionment, George suddenly revived an old, unfulfilled dream which miraculously sparked him with enthusiasm. Despite the Rhythm Ranch fiasco back in Vidor, George had still not abandoned his hopes of someday having a country music park of his own. (He and Tammy, in fact, already had an interest in the Loma Linda Country Music Park just south of Dallas.) One day in Florida, as he journeyed forth on his lawn mower, surveying his forty-three-and-a-half-acre realm, he decided he would once again attempt to build himself such a park.

With childlike enthusiasm and a blank checkbook, he immediately set to work. There in his fields near Central Barn Road, at a cost of $40,000, he built bleachers to seat 8,000. Thousands of dollars more were spent on a huge amphitheater-like stage and pavilion with an expensive top-of-the-line sound system. Hundreds of picnic tables dotted the area. Another $20,000 was shelled out for a thirty-foot-tall neon sign and colossal billboards that advertised in bright, gaudy letters the official headquarters of Mr. and Mrs. Country Music. He spent still more on elaborate landscaping and shrubbery, until his total investment in his new park and his nearby pleasure dome approached the $300,000 mark.

Opening day of George's Old Plantation Country Music Park, April 4, 1971, was a gala affair. More than 12,000 fans braved the rain and mud to hear five hours of live music, played not only by George and Tammy, but by illustrious guests such as Conway Twitty and Charley Pride. Dozens of other distinguished visitors—including Billy Sherrill, country music radio personality Ralph Emery and even a reporter from the rock magazine *Rolling Stone*—were flown in to witness the event.

The opening day proved to be a smashing success, and in the following months, George had many similar shows, booking in top-name acts like Merle Haggard, Johnny Cash, Barbara Mandrell, Dolly Parton, Porter Wagoner and the Statler Brothers. For a short time, his music park—where no alcoholic beverages were allowed, as George strove for a family atmosphere—even turned a small profit. Ultimately, though, this new dream fared no better than the Rhythm Ranch project had. Boredom and unrest once again overtook the Lord and Lady of the Realm. In late 1972, the two of them made the decision to leave their subtropical Xanadu for cooler climes. They sold their Old Plantation mansion, along with George's music park and his huge car collection. Then they rushed back into the waiting jaws of Nashville's recording and gossip industry snake pit and temporarily set up housekeeping in Tammy's large house on Old Hickory Lake.

Though neither of them had the courage to put it into words just then, they could feel their dreams beginning to slide through their hands like quicksilver. Try as he might, George could not seem to stanch this slippage, could not bring himself to grasp hold hard enough or long enough to keep from losing whatever he thought was left.

Tammy and George were still riding the crest of an overwhelming wave of popularity by mid-1973 in Nashville. The American public's fascination with the fool's-gold glitter of their mansions, Lear jets, jewelry, pleasure-mobiles and fairy-tale lives had not waned; the sold-out concerts and best-selling records continued.

Billy Sherrill continued to hold up his end of the bargain, too, always coming up with ever more poignant and provocative new hits for them to record—two-and-a-half-minute musical soap operas that titillated the public's imagination and offered fleeting glimpses into their increasingly confused and twisted personal lives.

By June 4, 1973, Tammy and George had left the lakeside retreat on Old Hickory Lake and purchased a $190,000 home at 1813 Tyne Boulevard in the well-heeled South Nashville suburbs. Earlier that year, they also bought, for $300,000, a 340-acre farm in nearby Maury County, with a 140-year-old, fifteen-room, elegantly pillared and magnolia-shaded mansion that had served as field headquarters for Confederate General John B. Hood during the Civil War. On their new farm, some twenty-eight miles south of Nashville, George pulled out his checkbook once again. Before he had put it away, he'd bought himself a herd of 160 Black Angus cattle for approximately $50,000, along with a few brand-new tractors and other farm equipment.

The prodigal singer seemed to delight in playing the role of a gentleman farmer nearly as much as he'd enjoyed the role of a music park impresario—for a while. It wasn't many months before the novelty wore off of this new role, too. In little more than a year after they'd set up camp in these new environs, George and Tammy left their farm and elegant rural mansion behind.

"It seems like they played with money," recalled Peanut Montgomery, who, to Tammy's increasing displeasure, still kept almost constant wild-ass company with George. "They'd buy up everything they could get, and once they bought it, they didn't like it."

With each change of household, the two of them harbored the desperate hope that the ever more grandiose and lavish views offered from the picture windows of their ever more expensive and resplendent dwellings might somehow help to reverse the creeping terminal malignancy of disillusionment that was eating away at their marriage. George, under his doctor's orders, had begun taking Librium to smooth out his ever darker moods and ever deeper depressions. When mixed with alcohol, the drug merely seemed to unbalance his condition even more.

George was now pulling his week-long disappearing acts with increasing frequency. These often occurred after being last seen in the company of Peanut and his wife, Charlene, someone else for whom Tammy, in her infinite jealousy, had little use. Once, when George departed unannounced on one of his marathon binges, Tammy put a private detective on his ass. The detective, a short time later, informed Tammy that he had located her husband, holed up in a house with Peanut, Charlene and some other round-the-clock celebrants amidst the squalor of dirty dishes, rotten food, overturned lamps and seventeen empty whiskey bottles.

"Back then, I got drunker than George did," recollected Peanut. "We'd pile up in somebody's house and drink whiskey and beer and write songs and sing and act crazy and play the fool. There was never no orgies or dope or nothin' like that. Just drink."

It was now painfully obvious to his friends that George was falling ever deeper into the dark pit of his own dissolution, and threatened to be swallowed by it. Despite his many and varied bumpy rides on his lawn mower, he'd gained forty pounds and was smoking four packs of cigarettes a day. His doctor had repeatedly advised him that he was suffering from both emphysema and a "fatty liver," and that if he wanted to remain among the living, then he'd best stop smoking and drinking. But such advice merely went in one ear and out the other, and his health continued to deteriorate. Gossip swirled fast and furiously through the Nashville rumor mill, that George was suffering from cancer and a host of other fatal maladies, that he was, in short, knocking on death's door.

George's response to all this was to merely grin back into the smiling, beckoning face of the devil, to merely light another cigarette, tilt back his head and drink longer and deeper of the amber-hued whiskey, straight from the bottle. His benders now began to take on ever darker and more harrowing dimensions. He would return from them in rumpled, drink- and vomit-stained clothes, his eyes red and swollen and his face etched with deep lines like knife scars. His hair, which Tammy once combed so neatly for him each morning, now dangled horribly in his face, and his skin assumed the

ashen pallor of a dying man's. It was as if he had now been transformed into a bloated, slumbering, half-crazed beast that merely
masqueraded as the late, great George Jones.

Tammy, for her part, was not faring much better than her husband. She was now riddled with anxiety and had been drawn even
deeper into her prescription drugs, seeking refuge from her odd
and ever-growing assortment of chronic ailments and afflictions.
She'd undergone nearly a dozen hospitalizations in recent months
for a host of real or imagined disorders. In a nine-year span, she had
nine operations on her stomach alone. Included on her rather impressive shopping list of maladies were food poisoning, a slipped
disk, appendicitis, gallbladder irritations, bronchial infections, ul-
cers, sun poisoning and fever blisters. (This latter infirmity was one
that would often drive the Possum mad with jealousy. He was certain that these ugly sores around his wife's mouth were merely
outward manifestations of the deeper, inward blemish of infidelity.)

Friends could see that in addition to all her other aches and pains,
Tammy had contracted a new ailment: she now had a new millstone.
Not only had she grown disgusted with George's increasingly frequent concert no-shows, his towering self-abuse and his never-ending string of empty promises to rehabilitate himself; she told friends
she had also grown frustrated with the way hard liquor drained all
the interest in romantic and connubial activities out of him, for
months at a time. "Tammy didn't want it to last anymore by that
time," recalled one spider who had a particularly good spot on the
wall. "She was bored and restless. She hated George's friends, and
she knew he wasn't going to stop drinking, even though he really did
try his best . . . a few times."

On August 1, 1973, after watching one of his whiskey trips rage
out of control for nearly six weeks, Tammy, in hopes of either
scaring him off the path of doom or ridding herself of him once and
for all, filed for divorce. Her petition (which advised the process
server that George could most likely be served by night, at Tootsie's
Orchid Lounge, a famous and determinedly seedy Nashville water-
ing hole) charged that her husband "drinks to such an extent that he
becomes completely and absolutely unmanageable . . . and it is
dangerous for his wife and the minor children to be around him."
Tammy's attorneys also alleged that George "has upon his person
large sums of money which he publicly displays and squanders, and
[that he] had attempted to sell their $43,000 houseboat for $150

cash." The petition also noted that he had already sold a new pickup truck and a new Corvette at similar one-time-only cash reductions. Tammy further enjoined George from "coming about her at places of performances, recording studios, or . . . her home, while intoxicated or otherwise, for the purpose of bothering, molesting or harassing her."

When news of this new twist of contretemps reached George that same hot, muggy August day, he did not take it any too kindly. He was at the Columbia recording studios on Sixteenth Avenue South, during the midafternoon, when his friend Peanut was called to come get him.

"He was crazy drunk and runnin' his mouth and aggravatin' everybody . . . just out of his head," Peanut remembered. "I managed to get him into the back seat of my car, and I started to drive off, but then he got to pullin' at my hair, until I finally had to stop and put him out of the car. He walked the couple of blocks back up to the Columbia studios, but the guard at the door there wouldn't let him back in. So he got into it with him and ended up rammin' his fist through the glass of the guard booth and cuttin' himself up pretty bad. They ended up takin' him to the emergency room of Baptist Hospital, but they couldn't hardly do nothin' with him there either. He wouldn't even let 'em give him a shot for the pain when they sewed him back up."

After he'd been stitched and bandaged, George was arrested for public drunkenness and hauled off to the Nashville Metropolitan Jail. Around 3 A.M., when he'd finally calmed down enough for them to turn him loose, Peanut came and paid the $250 bond and hauled his wounded, hung-over friend back down to his own home in Florence, Alabama, where he hoped he would cool off after a few days.

The storm eventually subsided. Tammy and George were able to strike a fragile truce. Tammy withdrew her divorce petition, and George, with his bloodshot eyes, skin the pallor of a dying man's, and his standard-issue promises of rehabilitation, came crawling back home.

"I wasn't drinking all that much," a seemingly repentant and reformed George insisted to a *Music City News* reporter not long afterward. "But it was beginning to become a problem. I was tired of waking up sick and having people talk about me—having my wife and the children mad at me. The headaches and hangovers were pure hell. . . . I just looked at the situation and realized all the pain I was causing and all the pain I was suffering wasn't worth it. We love each other very much."

Shortly after their reconciliation, Sherrill decided to record a new duet record with the strife-torn couple. It was a song called "We're Gonna Hold On" and had been written by Peanut Montgomery from a title suggested by George. Peanut had composed the song as an act of penance one hung-over morning while on tour with George and Tammy in Pennsylvania. He'd gotten drunk the night before in the lounge of a Holiday Inn where they were staying and had charged all his drinks to Tammy's room.

When it was released in the early fall of 1973, "We're Gonna Hold On" went to the number one spot in the charts. The record's success nevertheless did little to quell the rancor of tension, betrayal, sickness (Tammy was hospitalized again in January 1974 for a gallbladder operation—her fifth hospitalization in eight months) and broken dreams that now hung listlessly in the air around Tammy and George like vile poisons.

Outside of a close circle of friends and business associates, few people realized the abject emotional squalor into which their marriage had sunk. The world at large was still deeply infatuated with their fame, their mansions and their expensive clothes and cars, and to the fans, their marriage was still a precious thing indeed. On Thanksgiving Day of 1973, the two of them rode in the annual Macy's parade in New York City. They hugged and kissed each other while smiling and waving from atop a float of a giant turtle that played "We're Gonna Hold On" over and over again.

The fan magazine scribes continued to hold up their end of the bargain as well—continued to spin out exuberant cotton-candy depictions of their fairy-tale lives and of their country and western marriage made in heaven. The April 1973 cover story in *Country Music* magazine on Tammy was entitled "Songs of Heartbreak but a Happy Home." In the article, the First Lady, with her worry lines and battle scars carefully concealed, cooed, "George and I are very happy!" But the sad truth of the matter was that their private life together had now lost whatever resemblance it may have once had to a fairy tale. It had now become a sordid nightmare—more along the lines of *The Amityville Horror*.

Ironically, amidst this maelstrom of frayed emotions, Tammy's and George's records were selling better than ever. After several years of trial and error, Sherrill was also learning how to coax rich, low-register textures out of George's powerful voice and meld them, ever more effectively, with his own heavy-handed "Sherrill-ized" production style. In the latter half of 1974, George, with Sherrill producing, scored two back-to-back number one singles, "The Door" and "The Grand Tour" (the latter of which, ironically, was co-written by George Richey, a man who, a few years later, would take George's place and become Mr. Tammy Wynette No. 5).

The gap between George and Tammy continued to widen, until it reached a point where even their fans were getting wind of the cold, hard truth. When Tammy and George sang "The Ceremony" on stage, and attempted to feign their cute little pageant of domestic bliss, more and more of those in the audience could see the sad, cold truth leaking through, like embalming fluid from an ornately mani-cured corpse. They sensed it in the icy tension that lurked beneath the surface of their carefully rehearsed stage banter. They saw it in George's bloated, beastlike dissipation, which now bulged embar-rassingly through the seams of his once flashy stage outfits. They saw it beneath Tammy's well-rehearsed smile, in the deep lines of worry and depression that were now etched across her face. From a distance, dressed in their lavish, glittery outfits, the two of them still resembled tiny little frosting-candy bride-and-groom statuettes atop a wedding cake. Only now, instead of serene and confident, these little statuettes, when silhouetted in the stage lights, looked merely pathetic and tragic: forlorn and melting, as if waiting to have their heads bitten off by some hungry and uncaring celebrant.

While they were performing in England, reenacting their sad masquerade onstage, tragedy struck—one that sliced even deeper into the heart of their marriage and tore away like a wooden stake at the ever more fragile strands of George's sanity. Word reached George there that his beloved mother, Clara, who was nearly eighty, and who had been suffering from diabetes and heart trouble for some time, had finally passed away on April 13, 1974.

With Tammy in tow, he quickly flew back home to Texas. For several days, he stayed on to attend her funeral at the Memorial Funeral Home in Vidor. Fighting back his tears, he helped see to the grim task of having her laid to rest. Clara was buried on the dark, gloomy afternoon of April 15, there by the big stone Bible in the

Restlawn cemetery, where George Washington Jones had been buried six and a half years earlier.

"George never loved another woman like he loved his mama," recalled Josie Marcontell, one of the fourteen ancient, gray Patterson siblings who survived her sister Clara. "She was his strength. When she was alive, she talked to him and straightened him out when nobody else could. But after she was gone, he just went to pieces. He didn't have nobody to love him, and he didn't seem to care whether he went straight or not."

After the funeral and back in Nashville, Tammy and George, burdened still more by this new loss, decided to once again change the view from their picture window, in a last-ditch effort to try and kill the worms of discontentment and discord that were eating away at their marriage. They moved from their resplendent French Regency-style house on Tyne Boulevard, where they'd taken up full-time residence after selling their Maury County farm. The house that they purchased this time at Tammy's bleating insistence, and with the help of a huge loan, in the form of an advance, from their record company, was a $415,000 status symbol built to last at 4121 Franklin Road in South Nashville. This new, 17,600-square-foot, Spanish-style pleasure palace—with its excessive dimensions and garish accoutrements—was Babylonian, even by Nashville's often questionable architectural standards. It came complete with twelve bedrooms, fifteen baths, an Olympic-sized swimming pool, a playground the size of a public schoolyard, nine and a half acres of terraced lawns and a decorative wrought-iron frontispiece that displayed the music notation from "Stand By Your Man."

In the huge, lavishly appointed rooms of their newest pleasure palace, they still continued to destroy each other—continued to slice and tear at each other and rip each other apart. Their marriage continued to roll on, like a slow-moving train, toward the inevitable terminus that had been in sight for many months. Tammy had played the part of the victim for George for five years now, and she'd played it well, played it to the hilt. Even she realized that now *she* had had enough. On the chilly, overcast morning of December 13, she went to the dentist and returned home to find that George had departed on what would prove to be the last of his several-week-long vanishing acts. Many days later, when he finally called, beseeching her with the same empty promises, whimpering and begging her to let him come home, she refused. Though their long-running soap opera was far from over, they would not see each other again for seven months. They both sadly realized, deep down, that they did not have the strength for yet another painful encore in the tired, tedious passion play into which their marriage had degenerated.

On December 13, 1974, the same day that George fled their new gilded pleasure dome for the final time, Tammy filed for a legal separation. She stayed on, alone, at the Franklin Road rhinestone pleasure dome. George was last seen outside a downtown nightclub that Christmas Eve—a rainy and unseasonably warm night in Nashville—drunk, in a newly purchased $29,000 "stretch" Cadillac limousine, preparing to leave for Florida.

On January 8, 1975, Tammy filed for her "D-I-V-O-R-C-E" on the grounds of "cruel and inhuman treatment." As in the old "one for me, one for you" child's game, the lavish spoils of their five-year love affair with the imagination of the American record-buying public, were divided between them:

One for Tammy: the heavily mortgaged Franklin Road love palace.

One for George: the $190,000 French Regency house on Tyne Boulevard.

One for Tammy: their $110,000 tour bus (on which she quickly painted over the MR. & MRS. COUNTRY MUSIC logo) and their road band, the Jones Boys (which she eventually renamed the Country Gentlemen).

One for George: the $43,000 houseboat.

One for Tammy: the joint property that they owned in Alabama.

One for George: $135,000 in indebtedness to Columbia Records.

One for Tammy: custody of their daughter, Tamala Georgette, and her other children.

One for George: $1,000 a month in child-support payments.

Then Tammy went back home to the Franklin Road love palace. She was all alone now in the huge rooms resplendent with gold-plated lamps, gold-gilt end tables, gold crushed velvet chairs and an ersatz gold grand piano. ("Rooms not so much lived in as decorated to meet expectations," one visitor noted.) Wandering forlornly from room to room, she took down the beautiful plaque with the adoring love poem on it which George had given her upon the birth of their baby daughter. Holding back her tears, she covered it with a sheet, as if it were a corpse. She put it away in a closet where she would not have to look at it again.

In interviews with the Nashville newspapers and the fan magazines, Tammy attempted, as best she could, to sum up her mixed emotions about her five-year whirlwind marriage to George Jones.

"I honestly didn't realize until recently that George is one of those people who can't tolerate happiness," she said. "If everything is right, there is something in him that makes him destroy it . . . and destroy me with it.

"I'll have to say that I nagged him a lot about the drinking," she added later, "because he had a bad liver. It got to the point where every doctor was telling him, 'Listen, man, unless you quit, you're gonna die.' . . . [And] that was the hardest thing I've ever gone through in my life . . . to sit and watch him have fun and laugh and have a good time, yet knowing that every drink that goes down—he was slowly digging his own grave."

George, too, was alone now. Night after night, he sought refuge in either Tootsie's Orchid Lounge, the Hall of Fame Motor Inn Lounge, the swanky after-hours clubs along downtown Printer's Alley or other familiar stops along Nashville's seedy, neon-soaked Desolation Row. With no home to go crawling back to, and the snakes in his head seething out of control, he was somewhat more forthcoming in his bitterness—as he made clear in one magazine interview.

"[Tammy] never did like the friends I had," insisted the wayward singer, who in February 1975, brought suit against Tammy and the booking agent that they'd formerly shared, charging them with "conspiracy to damage his career." "She tried to change me," he added. "She *did* change me. But you just can't change a person in all the ways you want to.

"Still, I figured I done my part, I figured I done everything I could," he snarled with barely concealed anger. "I even quit drinkin' for almost eighteen months, to satisfy her. Not even a beer. Nothin'. Then one night, she kept me awake all night, cryin' and worryin' because she had not had a hit single in eighteen months. And it got me so depressed, I said, 'I've got to have a drink!' . . . and I wound up gettin' drunk that day.

"I don't call that love"—he glared—"when a man tries to do all the things a woman wants, even gives up drinkin', and then goes out and pulls one on for just one night. Then they wanta spend the rest of their lives without you.

"*Mental cruelty!*" He spat out the words viciously, almost as if he'd discovered a fly floating in the Jack Daniel's and 7-Up he was drinking. "I think that term should be taken out of the law! What gives a woman the right to say, 'Well, he beat me up all the time . . .' Well, I'll be honest with you, a lot of 'em needs to be whupped a few times. . . . But no offense to just one sex," he added with a smile as ingratiating as the skull and crossbones on an iodine bottle. "Sometimes we menfolks do too!"

The tabloids and the ragpicker press, which had chronicled their marriage with such inexhaustible zeal, now had a field day with Tammy's divorce: "I Thought I Found My Prince Charming, but Oh How Very Wrong I Was" *(TV Mirror);* "I Love a Man Who Almost Destroyed Me" *(Movie Life);* "Country Music Killed My Marriage" (San Antonio *Light*). Nashville's morning paper covered the divorce with similar unrestrained glee. Because of its proximity to the action, the city room there was inundated each day with dozens of phone calls from people all around the country inquiring about the latest blow-by-blow details. "A voyeur's delight," is how one *Tennessean* editor described it.

After the divorce, the demand for concert bookings with either Tammy *or* George, *separately,* fell off drastically. This meant little to George. He'd already decided that he'd had enough of the road for a while . . . maybe forever. Tammy was terribly distraught when her longtime booking agent, Shorty Lavender, informed her that about 90 percent of the concert promoters had decided that if they couldn't have both Tammy *and* George, then they didn't want either one of them by themselves. On those occasions when she did perform alone, Tammy found herself strangely ill at ease in front of the disappointed and often angry audience members, a few of whom never failed to holler and scream, even in the middle of one of her songs: "Where's George!?"

Now with ex-Millstone No. 3 out of the picture, there was none of the buoyant weightlessness of freedom that she might have expected to feel. She experienced instead a horrible sinking feeling, and began suffering from chronic fatigue and persistent insomnia. One night, in hopes of easing her fears over facing the future alone, she took two sleeping pills and lay down. Her fear still clung to her, so she took more sleeping pills. Her pain and fright persisted. So she took some Valiums, too, and then some more barbiturate-based sleeping pills, until her pain and dread were no longer a crushing weight, but merely an intense blue light, high above her, receding and growing ever dimmer in the vast darkness that beckoned. Vaguely, as if in a dream within a dream, she heard the distant sound of sirens. Then she felt the unpleasant sensation of someone forcing something down her throat.

When she woke up, she was in the hospital, having her stomach pumped.

Those who watched George, cut loose now and floundering in his own monumental self-abuse, felt that this could be the end of the line for him. For the next few months, when he even got up the enthusiasm or strength to go to the recording studio, the records that he cut merely entered the charts like sluggishly bouncing balls, made brief showings in the top twenty before sinking like stones into bottomless waters with barely a ripple. Only three of his single releases would even make the country top ten in the course of the next five years.

There were those—even George himself—who figured that if he didn't drink himself to death in the coming months, then he'd probably fade back into the same vast obscurity that had swallowed up so many other gifted but troubled Texas troubadours, such as Wynn Stewart and old Sonny Burns himself—to name but two.

"I was feeling sorry for myself," he later admitted. "I was at the point where I didn't care if I didn't record again or not. It had a lot to do with the way [country] music was going, this middle-of-the-road kind of thing. The radio stations had gone to where they weren't even playing a lot of real country acts. . . . Some big businessmen out of New York and the West Coast had taken over Nashville, and it's nothing but a syndicated rat race now."

But obscurity was not destined to be George's lot. In small record company offices, over lunch in four-star restaurants and across transcontinental phone lines that connected cities many miles apart, the voices of record company executives and music critics were now beginning to buzz like stirred-up insects, all of them speaking his name: speaking it not as if it were a mere two-syllable symbol of backwoods commonality—the name of a dispossessed woodcutter's son—but speaking it in tones of hushed reverence, as if it were the name of the royal lineage of some arcane realm.

As George fled from the bad debts, bad blood and bad memories that he was now leaving in a trail behind him, somewhere, far away, still waters were beginning to churn and quietly take the shape of a wave. Slowly, but inexorably, that wave was beginning to rise and gather speed and move in his direction.

Though George Glenn Jones had no way of knowing it, his fate was already out of his own hands. Even in his most profound moments of terror and despair, he had no way of knowing that the best —and, by far, the worst—yet awaited him.

Chapter Six

ALL THE KING'S HORSES
AND ALL THE KING'S
MEN . . .

It was to northern Alabama, the land from whence old Frank Jones had come so long ago, that George now fled, as he searched desperately for a place to hold his ground amidst the confusion that now swirled around him like a rising tide.

The countryside around Lauderdale and Colbert counties felt comfortable to the prodigal singer. He fell in love with the irregular lay of the land, the ruggedness of the deep pine forests and cotton fields and the bedrock simplicity of its hard-shell Protestant churches and quiet hamlets. (The region boasts the world's largest

coon-dog cemetery.) He told friends the area reminded him of
Texas.

It is a land where, on a Sunday morning, sinners can appease their
guilt and supplicate their harsh Protestant God by switching on
their radios, flipping across the AM airways and listening to a hundred and one different perfervid, self-ordained "Gawd-ah-mighty-
ing" backwoods preachers offering up a hundred and one different
variations on the pathway out of eternal damnation. It is a land
where, during the other six and a half days of the week, these same
sinners can defile their harsh God with an array of readily available
late-twentieth-century peckerwood transgressions, such as gambling, cockfighting, drug running, poaching off the thousands of
acres of national forest in the region, political skulduggery and (at
least until recently, when Colbert County went "wet") bootlegging.
It is only fifty miles to the northwest, as the crow flies, where the
legendary Sheriff Buford Pusser—immortalized in the *Walking Tall*
movies—waged his violent crusades against the Dixieland Mafia of
McNairy County, Tennessee—a county no more or less rife with
down-home-style organized crime than its counterparts just across
the Alabama state line.

The city of Florence (pop. 34,000) and its rustic environs—
though only a two-and-a-half-hour drive from Nashville—afforded a
peaceful refuge from the fool's-gold glitter and the vicious, relentless star-making gossip machinery of Music City.

The people at George's record label—who could see the waters
churning in faraway places and were now starting to crank up their
own wave-making machines—would often try in vain to track down
the errant singer for a recording session or an appearance on "The
Merv Griffin Show." George was usually far out of their reach, off
with friends like Peanut Montgomery (who was born and raised near
Florence and whose presence there had prompted George to relocate to the area) and songwriter "Wild Bill" Emerson. Together,
they whiled away their days catfishing on the muddy banks of the
wide Tennessee River, riding jeeps on the fire trails that ran through
Freedom Hills (an isolated region that, in earlier decades, was particularly noted for its many illegal moonshine stills) or driving aimlessly in one of the singer's shiny new Cadillac or Lincoln pleasure
machines, exploring the back roads of the Natchez Trace. (These
nearby federal parklands encompass segments of the original
Natchez Trace, the early-nineteenth-century trade and travel route

which was the pathway that Frank Jones, in another century, had most likely followed southwestward to the promised land of the East Texas pine forests.)

It actually seemed that George would, for a while, learn to flow with the quotidian tranquillity and languid pace of life there in northern Alabama, as he tried desperately to escape the abiding veil of the sadness with no name. On October 4, 1975, he assumed the mortgage on a stately residence in the Sherwood Forest subdivision near Florence. He also paid $13,000 for a lot on the secluded, pine-shrouded banks of Wilson Lake, about a dozen miles east of town off Highway 72. He swung a short-term $50,000 loan from a Nashville bank and made plans to erect an A-frame there.

For a time, the Possum even became immersed in more high-minded civic affairs. He donated his time and talents so extensively to the local cerebral palsy telethon on WAAY-TV in Florence that they even considered naming it after him.

Friends like Peanut Montgomery knew, however, that such com-passion and generosity of spirit was not out of character for George. Around this time, he'd had his ass hauled into court when he'd refused to play a show which reportedly had the financial backing of Dewitt Dawson, a local gambling and bootlegging kingpin who, at least once, had crossed swords with Sheriff Buford Pusser himself. George had bolted in his car at the last minute, when his agreed-upon cash fee was not delivered beforehand as had been promised. As the prodigal singer sat waiting in the courtroom with Peanut and Charlene, he seemed nonchalant and disinterested as to the out-come of his own case. Before his own session with the judge, he'd watched with dismay as a black teenager went before the magistrate and was fined $500 for deer hunting out of season. When the youth said he did not have the $500, the judge remanded him to jail for thirty days. It was far more than George could take. "He may have been huntin' them deer because it was his only way of gettin' food for his family," he whispered to Peanut. George jumped up, paid the boy's $500 fine out of his own pocket, and the errant hunter walked out of the courtroom a free man.

The wheels continued to turn in Nashville. It looked for a time as if George might hold his own there, too. On March 13, 1975, just a few days before a new version of George's "The Window Up Above" was released by Jerry Lee Lewis's piano-thumping first cousin, Mickey Gilley, he announced the reopening of the Possum

Holler nightclub. He'd disassociated himself from the nightclub business shortly after his marriage to Tammy, and had been itching to get back into it for a while. "It'll be a place for those who love the kind of music I love—pure country," he announced. He explained to reporters that the menu at the 450-seat club would feature ham and biscuits, white beans and corn bread. Offered for sale in the club's lobby were the infamous Possum Panties—the scanty women's undergarments which were strategically adorned with the prodigal singer's smiling likeness.

On August 25, with considerable fanfare, he also announced the signing of a new deal, with yet another manager: a Nashville businessman of murky repute and questionable competence named Alcy Benjamin ("Shug") Baggott, Jr. The arrangement also involved the Roy Dean booking agency, in conjunction with a wealthy Indiana venture capitalist and motel owner named Bob Green. It guaranteed George $750,000 worth of personal appearance bookings over the next calendar year. George, in preparation for hitting the concert trail again, purchased a new tour bus from singer Mel Tillis for $65,000.

"I've always listened to other people, and I've been took by just about everybody I've been associated with," the prodigal singer explained in an interview with the *Tennessean.* "But I can assure you I'm associated with some very fine people right now, and there's no way I can be took. I feel like I'm in control for the first time in my life."

Music City had become, in the meantime, obsessed with persistent rumblings of a possible reconciliation between George and his ex-wife. Tammy had been hospitalized that October with a "nervous stomach" while on tour in Wyoming, and was hospitalized again, a few days later, in Nashville for unspecified illnesses. The seven-month estrangement between country music's most gossiped-about couple ended accidentally on October 13, when the two of them bumped into each other backstage at the annual Country Music Association awards show. Despite their widely publicized divorce, and their long separation, the two of them had been nominated for the Duet of the Year award. Rumors were fanned still further when George visited Tammy's bedside in Nashville, where she'd been hospitalized again in early November and undergone surgery for "adhesions." A few days after her release, Tammy surprised everyone, including George, when she surfaced unexpectedly to sing harmony with the Possum at a show in Richmond, Kentucky. She even rode back to Nashville with him on his bus. Tongues wagged even more when the two of them showed up together again the following Saturday night and sang their famous love duets at Possum Holler. "I'm having a date with Mr. Jones tonight," the First Lady cooed to reporters. She was dressed in Ultrasuede boots and an expensive cream-colored leather outfit that George had bought for her to match his own brightly festooned stage garb. "We are still good friends."

"They'll get back together again," one unidentified friend of the couple noted assuredly for the benefit of the press. "They both love each other very much. It's just a matter of time."

It seemed so to George, too. After all, he now understood just about as much as he'd ever understood about womankind: You can't live with 'em, and you sure as hell can't live without 'em either.

In Alabama, unbeknownst to much of the outside world, the prodigal singer had found new romance. His latest flame was a modest and unassuming young woman named Linda Welborn, the sister of Peanut's wife, Charlene. They had first met in late 1974, when George's marriage to Tammy was still in the process of coming unraveled. After moving to Alabama, George took to Linda right away, and since she'd just gone through a painful divorce of her own, they found they had much in common. "I guess loneliness is more or less what brought us together," she later recalled with a trace of sadness.

Linda moved in and set up housekeeping with George at his Florence house in February 1975. "I know that don't sound too good," Linda noted of their live-in arrangement. "But it was completely honest, and we respected each other." George's affection for her quickly deepened. After all, she was a refreshing change from the sleazy show girls, ambitious Printer's Alley songbirds and other female opportunists who were forever throwing themselves at him up in Nashville. He liked Linda's countrified naïveté, the way she got words messed up and said things like "George, that new suit's as sharp as a *tick!*" Or "George, the *reality* company called you about that there new house . . ." He would sometimes tease her about that, and tell friends how much he liked his "little dumb woman."

Despite his hair-trigger temper and his dark, volatile moods, George treated Linda with kindness and consideration. "George never beat me, though it seemed to come out that way in the papers later," she recalled. "Oh . . . he did bite my lip once and it bled real, real bad. And he did slap my face a few times, too. But who don't do that when they're married or living together and get themselves into an argument?"

With Linda, George found the freedom and companionship to share in the simple, everyday pleasures that there'd never been time for in his highly pressurized fishbowl marriage to Tammy. They would go catfishing at McFarland Bottoms on the Tennessee River —though the Possum had little patience and grew disgusted if his line got snagged or he had to wait too long for a bite. They bowled together nightly at the Fountain Lanes on Florence Boulevard. One night, even though George had rolled an impressive 149, Linda beat him soundly. It angered the Possum that he had been defeated so easily at the hands of a woman, and he thought this was not how it should be. He tried explaining this to Linda, but to no avail. He put his expensive bowling ball and bowling shoes back in his black leather monogrammed bowling bag and dropped the whole works off in a garbage can outside the door as they left. They never bowled again.

To pass the time, they would often drive over to Colbert Park on the Natchez Trace or out into the nearby national forests. They'd grill pork chops and green tomatoes, or merely go walking, arm in arm, out into the deep piney woods, take their shoes off and wade in the clear-running creeks. They'd lie on blankets listening to the soothing trill of the songbirds and the gentle buzz of the bees. George's daughter Tamala Georgette—now a lovely child of six— would occasionally come visit them, and the three of them would be just like a little family. It was on one of these blissful outings that George asked Linda to marry him, and they became engaged.

Linda grew to love George's easygoing sense of humor and his amazing generosity. First he bought her a Lincoln Mark IV, then a Cadillac, then a Chevrolet Monte Carlo, then a Ford Thunderbird, then a Corvette and then a Lincoln Town Car. She recalls that he bought and sold at least twenty-seven cars during one year-long period that they were together. He showered her with other lavish gifts as well—just as he'd once done with Tammy.

But his characteristic generosity was not reserved for Linda alone. More than once, George stopped his car in the middle of the poorest section of Florence and, on a whim, walked up to an old black man on a dilapidated porch, handed him a wad of folding

Looking unusually dapper in a dark suit and tie, "the Possum" warms up
backstage at the Grand Ole Opry, in the Ryman Auditorium in Nashville,
on November 1, 1968. (Photo by Les Leverett)

LEFT (Circa 1969) George and his third wife, singer Tammy Wynette, in go-go boots and bouffant hairdo, make an early appearance on the Grand Ole Opry. (Photo by Owen Cartright, Nashville *Banner*)

ABOVE George and "the First Lady" at a TV taping in the early 1970s. Outwardly, their stage show was all kisses and smiles and "oohs" and "ahs," but the tension and worry lines, particularly on Tammy's face, were beginning to show through their sad masquerade as "Mr. and Mrs. Country Music." (Photo courtesy of *The Music City News*)

RIGHT Tammy combs George's hair backstage before a show in mid-June 1974 as the two of them share an uncharacteristically quiet and peaceful moment during the final stormy and tumultuous months of their six-year marriage. (Photo by Jill Krementz)

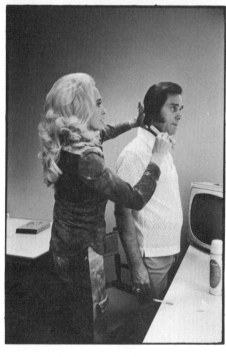

LEFT George and Tammy performing at Lincoln Center in New York City in the early 1970s. Their show was part of a concert series called "Country in New York." People had come to see Tammy, whose popularity had assumed immense proportions as a result of her million-selling hit "Stand By Your Man," but they ended up calling George back for two encores. (Photo by Jim Fitzgerald)

ABOVE George, solo once again, performing at the Willie Nelson Picnic, a huge open-air music festival held in Gonzales, Texas, on July 4, 1976. As he stepped onstage before 80,000 youthful, rebel-rousing fans and a large gathering of national media representatives, he was nearly paralyzed with fear. By the time he walked offstage after being called back by a thundering demand for an encore, he had the audience in the palm of his hand, and was suddenly on his way to superstardom. (Photo by Charlyn Zlotnik)

ABOVE The lonesome bank where the Cypress Creek empties into the wide Tennessee River outside Florence, Alabama. As George's personal problems deepened, he would often come here to sit in his car and meditate with his .38 caliber pistol and a bottle of Jack Daniel's by his side. He watched the swirling, swift-flowing waters and listened to the cars pass overhead on the Savannah highway bridge.

RIGHT The demons were finally unleashed in September 1978. Brother Peanut Montgomery sits in his car and shows the track of the errant bullet which George fired at him with his pistol late one night as they sat in their cars on the bank of Cypress Creek. "See if your God can save you now!" the enraged singer shouted as he pulled the trigger. The bullet missed Montgomery, who was seated in his car just as he is in this photo, by inches. (Photo by Bill Jarnigan)

ABOVE Jimmie Hills at his barbershop in Florence, Alabama, where George often hid out from his real and imaginary pursuers. A kind, gentle man, Hills began as George's barber and occasional traveling companion. Eventually he became a trusted friend and confidant whose compassion and understanding helped guide the singer through his darkest hours.

LEFT George with his daughter (by Tammy Wynette), Tamala Georgette Jones. While still a small child, Georgette often accompanied her famous mother and father to their shows and joined them onstage. Later, she occasionally appeared with George on television and on records as well. (Photo by Charlyn Zlotnik)

RIGHT George in concert at the Wembley Music Festival in London in 1981. Jones has enjoyed enduring popularity in Britain, where, in a 1983 poll, he was named as that country's favorite male country artist. (Photo by Kathy Gangwisch)

ABOVE In the lobby of a London hotel in 1981 with British rocker Elvis Costello. A dedicated Jones fan, Costello recorded *Almost Blue,* an album of country songs which was produced in Nashville by Jones's longtime producer, Billy Sherrill, and which included two of Jones's early standards, "Color of the Blues" and "A Good Year for the Roses." Costello also wrote a song especially for Jones called "Stranger in the House," which the two of them sang together on Jones's 1979 *My Very Special Guests* LP. (Photo by Kathy Gangwisch)

ABOVE RIGHT George at the Country Music Association's televised awards show at Nashville's Grand Ole Opry House on October 12, 1981. The singer, who was awash in a sea of legal and personal problems, stumbled nervously onstage to receive his second consecutive Male Vocalist of the Year award. Singer Gail Davies, the awards presenter, is visible in the background. (Photo by Robin Hood)

BELOW RIGHT George with pop artist Andy Warhol backstage at New York's Bottom Line in 1982. George was joined onstage by guest artists Linda Ronstadt and Johnny Paycheck.

ABOVE The raging bull in custody, May 25, 1982. Jones, who was now more popular and selling more records than ever before in his career, and who was already facing indictment in a separate arrest for possession of cocaine, is placed under arrest by Brentwood, Tennessee, police officer Tommy Campsey after being apprehended for drunken driving on Interstate 65 about five miles north of Franklin, Tennessee. A half-empty bottle of whiskey was also found in the car. This was the singer's third such arrest in less than two months. Lengthy video footage of his arrest was shot by a roving TV news crew. When the footage was aired on a Nashville station as well as cable network news, it raised a furor of protest from his fans. (Wide World Photos)

RIGHT In a Tennessee motel room while on tour in July 1982. Though the long years of travail are evident in the lines on his face, he remains like a tarnished diamond in the rough—scarred, but still shining on. (Photo by Bill Thorup/Nashville *Banner*)

LEFT Jones in performance at the Bene Supper Club in New Jersey in late 1982. (Photo by Jim Fitzgerald)

ABOVE Two American vocal geniuses: Jones with Ray Charles in Nashville in 1982. Rick Blackburn, head of CBS Records, Nashville division, is on the left. In late 1983, Jones and Charles, under the tutelage of producer Billy Sherrill, recorded a hit duet single together called "We Didn't See a Thing." (Photo by J. Clark Thomas)

RIGHT George visiting with Johnny Cash backstage at the Tennessee Performing Arts Center in July 1982. Jones and Cash were headlining a benefit for the families of firemen and policemen who had been killed in the line of duty. (Photo by Bill Thorup/Nashville *Banner*)

Holding ground against the darkness in August 1983. Jones with his
fourth wife, Nancy Sepulveda, at Jones Country, his country music park,
deep in the piney woods of his native East Texas, where he attempted to
start life anew. Peace at last? (Photo by John Yearwood/Woodsman Publishing Company)

money and then walked away without saying a word to him. That was just the kind of man that he was.

During their first months together, George set the strong drink aside for weeks at a time and tried his damnedest to dry out. Sooner or later, something would aggravate him or depress him, and he'd get himself a bottle and go off the deep end once again. "Hell," he'd complain to Linda as he related his theory as to how he mainly drank to make *other people* interesting, "I just can't *communicate* with people when I'm straight. . . . Besides, I just ain't no fun to be around when I'm sober either."

Even in the midst of their best times together, Linda could see other telltale symptoms of his deepening suspicions toward those in whose hands he'd now placed his erratic career. She noticed how sometimes—in his Nashville office, at Possum Holler or at home in Alabama—he would "play possum": he would lie on the bed or the sofa with his eyes closed, pretending to be asleep. All the while, he would really be wide awake and listening to every word that those around him might venture to say about him when they thought he couldn't hear them.

George's A-frame on the banks of Wilson Lake was finally completed in early 1976, and he and Linda moved in. If ever there was a natural sanctuary where a man might stand his ground against adversity, then surely the new A-frame was it. It was firmly nestled in the pine trees, several miles from the nearest highway, in a secluded neighborhood called Brooks Acres. There was a small pier out back where a man could sit at dawn and watch the sun slowly burn its way through the thick veil of mist that shrouded the wide, placid waters.

George quickly set about elegantly furnishing and decorating the interior of his new home. He always bought *new* furniture each time he moved to a *new* home—the Possum had no more use for used furniture or carpets than he did for used cars. After everything was in order, he settled in to weather the storm.

But his peace still did not hold, and gradually he began to lose ground to the immense restlessness and sadness that dwelt within him. Day after day, often for weeks at a time, he drove aimlessly to Nashville and back. (Sometimes he enlisted Peanut as his chauffeur, and during one two-week period they made the 250-mile round trip so frequently that they put 10,000 miles on Peanut's '73 Cadillac.) When he arrived in Music City, the prodigal singer, more often than not, would merely circle Music Row (the approximately ten-block-long and three-block-wide area, intersected by Sixteenth and Seventeenth avenues South, that contains the bulk of Nashville's music industry) once or twice. Then he would make one quick loop around the driveway of Tammy's Franklin Road pleasure dome, and after casting a fleeting, wistful glance over his shoulder, he'd merely head back down Interstate 65-South and across winding old state Highway 47 to Florence again.

Being alone was now more difficult than ever for George. Solitude was a painful thing to endure. At night, in the isolation of the A-frame—even when Linda was there—he would keep all the lights burning brightly, talk on the phone incessantly and keep the TVs running constantly as he struggled to fend off the demons that lurked in the ether of the night. The A-frame was soon overrun with guests, invited and uninvited, who were only too eager to drink his whiskey and help him pass the terrible hours between dusk and dawn when George's thoughts weighed most heavily upon him. In the late night, the quiet pine copse along the lakeshore would often echo with harsh voices, drunken laughter, the sound of loud music emanating from the ancient, scratchy records of Hank Williams and Jimmie Rodgers, and random gunfire. These round-the-clock whiskey-soaked revelries would roar on for days at a time.

Peanut—who was usually in the midst of this wildness—could see that his friend's somber, faraway moods and propensity for sudden outbursts of casual violence were deepening. George had now gotten to where he'd just as soon kick in a TV set as he would change the channel, and he'd also taken to carrying a loaded pistol with him everywhere he went. One day, Peanut was out at George's house, along with a half dozen or so other guests, when, without warning, George—as he all too often did—picked up his loaded handgun and fired several shots into the wall. Peanut couldn't help but notice later that one of those random bullets had gone clear through a wall, into the bathroom and on out through another wall. If a man had been standing in there taking a pee when George fired the shot, he would have gotten it right in the back of the head.

On many Friday and Saturday nights, George and Peanut would pay an informal visit to the home of Bobby Womble, a jovial, mandolin-playing factory hand who worked at the huge R. J. Reynolds plant near Florence. Womble, along with another guitar-picking drinking partner of theirs named Mickey Mobley, often hosted informal weekly gatherings of local country and bluegrass musicians.

At Womble's modest suburban house near Florence, they would all gather and barbecue chickens, fry fish, drink, sing and play their instruments until the wee hours of the morning.

George, too, would often kick off his boots at Womble's and play his guitar late into the night. He would reach far back into his past and play the old American folk song, "In the Pines," which was recorded and popularized by Bill Monroe in 1941, or the old Hank Williams and Jimmie Rodgers songs he'd once played on the Beaumont street corners, or the old Southern Holiness songs he'd learned at his mama's knees. "I've seen George just sit there and pick his guitar and sing them old songs for two or three days at a time," Peanut remembered. "He wouldn't do nothing but sit on the sofa and sing, day and night, and never even get up, except maybe to go to the bathroom or eat a cracker or somethin'."

Sometimes, very late in the evening, the gathering there at Womble's would fall silent and Mickey Mobley and his wife, Jane, would sing a haunting duet rendition of "A House of Gold." It is an eerie old song of redemption and salvation, written by the dark archangel, Hank Williams, in 1951, in the melodic and lyric tradition of the old Holiness songs.

> *I'd rather be in a deep, dark grave*
> *and know that my poor soul was saved*
> *than to live in this world in a house of gold*
> *and deny my God and doom my soul.*

As George listened, his eyes would become filled with the sadness with no name, and tears would roll down his cheeks. He would ask Mickey and Jane to sing the song over and over again. "It was as if he had some great pain inside him that he couldn't get out," Jane Mobley recalled.

Directly, as each of those gathered fell into his or her own silent contemplation on the eternal certitude of sin and redemption, George would pick up his guitar. Strumming an open chord, he would sing a mournful song fragment of his own, which he often sang at such times:

> *I work in a cemetery*
> *caretaker they call me*
> *In the summer I cut the weeds*

> *in the winter I rake the leaves*
> *and when people come to bury their dead*
> *I hear every bad and good word that's said . . .*
> *Oh, who's gonna cry when old George dies*
> *who's gonna cry when old George dies . . .*

One morning George and Peanut—who then was still a drinking man—decided to ride over to Hamilton, Alabama, to visit their friend "Wild Bill" Emerson. They loaded the car up with a good supply of Jack Daniel's whiskey and ice-cold Miller beer and headed southward across the countryside.

Peanut, who'd been watching George closely, could feel a song coming on just about then—a song about George, "about how when he drinks, he sometimes changes into another man, another being."

The two of them foxed around with the song's lyrics all day and finally finished writing it back at home in Florence later that night. They titled the song "A Drunk Can't Be a Man." It later appeared on George's 1976 *Alone Again* LP and was as painful and precise an autobiographical confession as he'd ever had a hand in writing. When George recorded it in Nashville on June 14, 1976, he imbued it with the stone-cold conviction and embitteredness of a man who is afraid to look over his shoulder, afraid to admit that his demons are gaining ground on him:

> *He embarrasses his child and wife*
> *Lord, he leads a miserable life*
> *But still he thinks the bottle is his right hand*
> *Yes, he can tear down more*
> *than he's ever built before*
> *A man can be a drunk sometimes*
> *but a drunk can't be a man*
>
> *He goes from Dr. Jekyll to Mr. Hyde*
> *He seems proud to have the Devil for his guide*
> *Still, he keeps reaching out*
> *Lord, he needs a helping hand*
> *Lord, a man can be a drunk sometimes*
> *But a drunk can't be a man.*

Tammy Wynette, in her aloneness, had by now embarked upon her very own version of the "Celebrity Dating Game." Her private life now included well-publicized trysts with an array of famous personages, among them actor Burt Reynolds, New England Patriots football tackle Tom Neville and twenty-three-year-old Rudy Gatlin, a singer ten years her junior whose romantic ties with the First Lady were bitterly disapproved of by his older brother, the obnoxious, whiny country music prima donna Larry Gatlin.

Alone in her pleasure palace, on many nights Tammy was now finding herself engulfed in a madness all her own. More and more often, there swirled around her a series of grotesque manifestations and mysterious events, the likes of which had first revealed themselves a few years earlier at the Florida Xanadu that she'd once shared with George. They'd once again begun to rear their ugly heads in early 1975, after her separation from the wayward singer.

Lying awake at night, she would hear the sound of unexplained footsteps on her roof. Notes bearing death threats began appearing on her wrought-iron gate, outside burglar alarms were deliberately tripped and the wires of inside alarms were repeatedly slashed. In the still silence of the night, her windows were smashed with rocks, and once her kitchen sink was plugged, the faucets were turned on full blast and the entire room was flooded. Though nothing was ever stolen from her home, she reported seventeen break-ins during one nine-month period. She would be terrified when she found epithets like "whore," "slut" and "pig" smeared in lipstick on the mirrors throughout her house—even on the mirrored ceiling of her canopied bed. Throughout all this, she called the police repeatedly—so often that they got tired of coming. No suspects or motives for these disturbances were found, although the police did find it puzzling that Tammy was nearly always at home when they allegedly took place.

On a dark night in May 1976, three separate fires broke out in different rooms of the pleasure palace and did an estimated $100,000 worth of damage. Investigators quickly concluded that the fires had been deliberately set by someone inside the house. Tammy, her children and other live-in friends and relatives were interrogated for hours on end. The investigations dragged on for months before they were finally mired in inconclusiveness. Lie detector tests were administered, and eventually the police suggested that the First Lady take one of the polygraph examinations herself. She refused.

On April 28, 1976, Tammy was once again hospitalized—this time for "bronchitis." On May 8, Mother's Day, George presented his ex-wife with a brand-new gold Thunderbird and a matching gold ring.

Shug Baggott and Jones's new booking agency were by now going through the motions of lining up a lucrative series of concert dates for the prodigal singer in the British Isles. George knew that his mama had died the last time he crossed the great waters to sing for the strangers with their tweedy coats and funny accents, and this time he had forebodings of a similar disaster.

Another face from George's past now drifted back into the picture for what proved to be the final time. Sonny Burns, who was still not drinking and who was finally at peace, safe in the arms of Jesus, returned to Nashville to make one more feeble attempt at cracking back into the record business. George gave him a job singing at Possum Holler. It was to Sonny that George confided that he did not intend to cross the briny seas, on account of his dead mama and on account of those wild goings-on in Northern Ireland, where a feller could easily get his head blowed off. Sonny was not surprised when, on the eve of his scheduled transoceanic flight, the Possum, driving a Cadillac that belonged to Shug Baggott, fled Nashville for the safer shores of northern Alabama, where he grabbed Linda Welborn. Knowing that Shug and his "Nashville Mafia" would soon be hot on his trail, he headed for the hills.

In short order, Baggott, armed with a registered .44 magnum pistol and accompanied by his associates in a small fleet of shiny Cadillac limousines, arrived on the scene. They wasted little time in enlisting several carloads of Alabama state troopers and a police helicopter to aid them in their "Possum hunt." But George, who'd now traded the borrowed Cadillac for a faster, sleeker pleasure machine, knew those Alabama back roads, fire trails and wooded cul-de-sacs far better than his pursuers did, and with great stealth and glee, he eluded them. Shug and his hastily enlisted posse spent many sweaty and anguished hours gingerly steering their oversized limousines down the rutted dirt roads and dusty pot-holed lanes that they knew to be George's favorite hiding places. All the while, they kept their Citizens' Band (CB) radios turned to Channel 22, which they knew was the Possum's (also his CB "handle") favorite channel.

"We'd drive about ten miles down the road, and then all of a sudden George would come on the radio, laughin' and carryin' on," recalled Mickey Mobley, who was induced by Shug to join in the futile manhunt. "He'd say, 'This y'here's the Possum . . . Where you all at!? . . . Y'all can't find me!' Then we'd drive back maybe twenty miles in the other direction, and he'd come over Channel 22 again, just laughin' and hollerin', 'Hey, you all are goin' the *wrong damn way!* I told ya you couldn't find me!' "

George fled to the Huntsville, Alabama, airport, then was heard over Channel 22 no more. A day or so later, he called another close friend there in Florence, Jimmie Hills—who was also his barber and occasional traveling companion. He explained to Jimmie that he was in Florida, and he asked his friend if he could pick up his new Fleetwood Brougham Cadillac, which he'd so hastily abandoned at the airport.

When Hills found the Cadillac, it was right where George had left it a day or so earlier, double-parked in a tow-away zone directly in front of the busy air passenger terminal. The back seat was littered with empty 7-Up bottles, empty Miller "pony"-sized beer bottles and wrappers from the dried beef jerky, roasted peanuts, peanut-butter crackers and canned Port Pride brand sardines that he subsisted on for weeks at a time when he was on a tear. On the windshield of his car, the singer had left a hastily scrawled message: "I am George Jones, a member of the Grand Ole Opry. Please do not tow my car away!"

Eventually George returned to his home in Alabama, where his immense restlessness merely deepened. After explaining to Linda that the A-frame was just too small, he sold his lakeside sanctuary in the spring of 1976—less than a year after he'd moved into it. He bought a $100,000 brick home in the nearby Kendale Gardens subdivision—one of more than a half dozen expensive homes that he randomly bought and sold during the seven years he was in and out of northern Alabama. On April 20, he was sued by a Nashville couple who claimed he reneged on a written agreement to buy their $179,000 home.

Adding to George's anguish was his long-running soap opera with Tammy, which was now going into disheartening new installments. Briefly, the two of them had again been reunited—both inside and outside the recording studio. On April 22, a warm, sunny spring day in Nashville, Billy Sherrill had brought the two of them together to record a spirited, gospel-flavored ballad of tragic love called "Golden Ring," which had been written by Nashville songwriters Bobby Braddock and Rafe Von Hoy. Like many of the duets that the two of them had recorded when they were still husband and wife, "Golden Ring" resonated with an authentic sense of romantic tragedy and irresolution that was hauntingly similar to the real-life timbre of their troubled, on-and-off-again love affair.

To George's dismay, however, Tammy had found herself a brand-new millstone—this one an opportunistic, thirty-one-year-old real estate dealer named Michael Tomlin. When Tammy announced her plans to wed this new millstone, no one was more disturbed than George. Night after night, in the stillness of the late hours, Tammy's phone would ring. It would be George. In a tearful, imploring voice, he begged her not to go through with these new plans of hers—much in the same fashion he had once begged Melba Montgomery not to marry Jack Solomon.

Tammy, however, did not heed her third ex-millstone's warnings. She was married at her Nashville pleasure palace on July 18, a bright, sunny day, in the midst of lavish festivities and ornate ersatz Hawaiian decor. The wedding party was later trashed by a mad stampede of drunken guests including David Blanton, son of the then reigning Tennessee governor, Ray Blanton, was was later deposed from office, convicted in federal court on various criminal charges, and ordered to prison.

On her wedding day, Tammy switched on her car radio and heard the news that "Golden Ring," her duet with George, which had been released the month before, was now the number one country single. Even she couldn't help but notice the irony of that.

Feeling more alone than ever now, George sought solace from his wounds and drove aimlessly around the northern Alabama highways and back roads with a bottle of whiskey and his .38 caliber pistol on the seat beside him.

On many quiet, starry nights, he would drive past the huge ancient Indian mound that loomed over the banks of the Tennessee River, where the prehistoric Indians who'd built it had now slumbered in the cold ground for more than a millennium, still waiting for the return of whatever harsh God it is that the Indians wait for.

George would then ramble a mile or so farther down Highway 20, where it ran along the river, just outside of Florence. He would end up at one of his favorite spots, underneath the bridge on the Savannah highway, where the swift-flowing Cypress Creek, bounded on both banks by thick stands of oak and cypress trees, emptied into the Tennessee River. The late-night silence there under the bridge, on the steep, muddy creek banks, was broken only by the sound of cars passing on the busy highway overhead. Sitting there in his car, George would gaze out across the dark waters and silently study the strange swirling configurations that the creek's swift currents made —much like his maternal grandpa, Uncle Litt, had, many years before, stood at the edge of his fields in the Thicket and studied the distant skies for signs of an impending storm.

Only now, things were much, much different for George, much, much worse really. Uncle Litt had been anchored firmly in his faith, secure, with the heavenly firmament above him, and with his own little patch of God's flat, green Texas earth safely beneath his feet. But now, as George sat there on the Alabama creek bank, near the concrete bridge abutment—adorned as it was with gaudy spray-painted testimonials of teenage love and lust, sentiments which, in most cases, probably faded before the paint had even dried—the earth and the firmament seemed wildly out of kilter, gyrating madly off on some insane, misguided course, threatening to break apart at the center. He would gaze into the silent swirling waters, thinking, perhaps, that if he stared long enough, he would find some answer there, and all things in heaven and earth would once again right themselves.

In Nashville and in other faraway cities, those silent, slow-moving waters that had been churning for some time had now gained force and gathered speed. They had formed a wave that was now rolling relentlessly in George's direction. In air-conditioned offices, the voices of promoters, bookers, journalists, press agents, disk jockeys and record company executives continued their insect-like buzzing as they spoke the prodigal singer's name across transcontinental phone lines in tones of hushed reverence usually reserved for minor royalty.

The people at CBS (the parent company of the Epic record label, to which George was signed) could see and feel this wave building. So they cranked up their own wave-making machines once again to hurry it along. Willie Nelson, the red-headed, bewhiskered king of Texas music—also a CBS artist—who just a year or so earlier had launched himself into the rarefied ozone of national superstardom with his album *Red Headed Stranger,* was planning on holding one of his huge annual Fourth of July picnics and outdoor music festivals down in Gonzales, Texas. The people at CBS knew that thousands of people would turn out for this star-studded event, including a huge battalion of national press, TV and other media people—far greater in number than the ranks of old Frank Jones's 17th Texas Cavalry, which had once stormed those dark hills. The CBS people figured that if they could wangle a spot for the prodigal hard country singer up on that stage, and if he went over well in front of the huge crowd and did not wilt under the fish-eyed scrutiny of the national media, then they could bring new heights and dimensions to the wave, such as it had never had before.

When Independence Day, 1976, rolled around, George's trepidation over the prospect of singing before a massive audience so strange and so different from the older, more countrified beer-hall crowds with whom he felt most comfortable, coupled with his unease over the thought of sharing the same stage with an assortment of latter-day country-rockers like Willie Nelson, Kris Kristofferson, Leon Russell and David Alan Coe, grew to ever greater dimensions. He found himself consumed with fear and dread.

"The closer I came, the more nervous I got," he later admitted. "I just felt like I was the oddball of the whole show. Then word got to me on my bus, where I was dressin' for the show, that they was throwin' firecrackers and beer bottles on the stage, and I almost had a heart attack! I thought maybe I oughta bow out while there was still time."

Wearing a resplendent black leisure suit with a flowery print shirt and carrying his favorite guitar—which had his name engraved in large letters on its leather shoulder strap—George gingerly picked his way around the perimeter of the sweating, beer-drinking multitude of 80,000 people—most of them young and long-haired. He stood nervously in the backstage area, grimly surveying the vast sweltering sea of crazed humanity—with its restless numbers in all manner and degree of undress, drunkenness and depravity—which threatened to engulf him. He saw before him a legion of gape-mouthed, hirsute motorcycle riders and lizard-skinned, glassy-eyed, darkly attired cosmic cowboys. With them were their women: bare-breasted troglodytes with their faces defiled with thick coats of rouge and mascara; sloe-eyed, sultry demimondaines and assorted jailbait in their mirrored sunglasses, wet T-shirts, "ass-grabber" cutoffs and slinky, skintight leather britches. Just when he thought he was about to succumb to a lethal combination of heat and hypertension, someone finally brought him the stiff drink that he'd requested. And he drank deeply from it and shuddered. Surely, he thought, this must all be some horrible mistake; his being here, some cruel joke. His shotgun eyes were now wide and round with fear, and he looked down at his feet, as if hoping they might take off running of their own accord and carry him away from this horrible latter-day Sodom and Gomorrah. He knew that it was too late; he knew that there was no Cadillac, no matter how fast or sleek, that could deliver him to freedom from where he stood in the midst of this huge throng. And for all his Houdini-like stealth, he knew it would do him little good to try and wriggle out of the window of a Port-O-San portable toilet.

Then they came and told him it was time for him to go onstage, and he found that his fear paralyzed him. He moved like a man walking underwater; his hands trembled and his mouth was dry. When he reached the parapet of the stage, he gazed again out across the vast, swirling, dancing, sunburned, beer-drenched and perspiring multitude, which seemed to stretch all the way to the distant, hazy horizon, all beneath the relentless glare of the hot Texas sun. His heart nearly stopped and abject terror seized him. Far below him, near the front of the crowd, he could see dark tufts of unkempt pubic foliage and patches of bare human flesh winking at him from beneath the folds of sweat-stained tanktops and T-shirts that bore inscriptions like "If You Don't Like Texas, You Can Sit on My Face" and "Jesus Is Coming and Boy Is He Pissed!"

He raised his right hand to strum the first chord on his guitar. For an instant, it seemed to him as if the final verdict between hellfire and redemption was being awaited and vindication and disaster hung delicately in the balance. There was an instant of hushed, painful silence that was deep as a stellar black hole and broken only by the sound of the soft wind that rustled through the sagebrush and fluttered through the Lone Star flags that hung like banners over the huge crowd. Only the soft click of dozens of camera shutters punctuated the vacuum created by this vast silence.

Far off in the distance, a firecracker exploded, and from far below him, in the front of the crowd, George heard an unkind remark about his leisure suit. He opened his parched mouth to sing, believing, surely, that the sound of his own voice would quickly fade to nothingness in the vacuum of the crowd's cold indifference. Then he heard his voice, strong and surprisingly confident, singing "Ragged but Right," a fast-paced, rambling old 1930s pop tune that he himself had recorded in a decidedly more countrified vein in the small Goldstar studio back in Houston, many years ago.

The multitude before him, despite his fears, was anything but indifferent. Beneath their long hair, beads, sweaty T-shirts, mirror sunglasses, braids and rumpled clothes, many of these people who sat under the Texas sun and listened to George that day were really, in their hearts, not all that different from the people who'd once thrown their coins to the young prodigal singer on the Beaumont street corners. They, too, could hear in his voice all those same powerful truths: the ghostiness of the Thicket, the fervent emotionalism of Uncle Litt's religion, the mournful wail of mortal despair, the primal outrage of the child thrust too early into the world of strangers, and the sadness which had no name.

George finished singing "Ragged but Right," and there was a crescendo of hoots, hollers, rebel yells and applause so huge and thunderous that it seemed to shake the skies. Smiling widely now, his shotgun eyes dancing with both relief and gratified delight, George sang more. He sang "The Race Is On," "White Lightning," "The Grand Tour," "Picture Of Me Without You," a great and diverse number of other songs that he'd made famous over the years. The applause and shouts of approval grew louder and more intense with each one that he sang. He finally wrapped up his part of the show with two spirited verses of the old Little Richard rock 'n' roll classic, "Long, Tall Sally." He even shook a leg and threw in a few fancy twists and dance steps, just like he used to back in the days when he'd try and aggravate Elvis and steal his thunder, back on the Louisiana Hayride.

When he left the stage, he was sweating heavily and was nearly numb with relief. He had just collapsed in the back seat of the chauffeured limousine his record company had waiting for him when he was summoned back to the stage once again. The delighted multitude had been screaming, yelling and stomping for him to do an encore.

The brigade of media people on hand (people who, with their

cassette recorders and video cameras in hand and harried glazed looks in their eyes, seem to be always running around frantically searching for "The Real Thing"—whether it be a farmer's wife's recipe for burdock salad, a dog that rides atop a car, or an armless man who plays mandolin with his teeth) took note of all that transpired there that torpid afternoon. As these members of the Fourth Estate watched George sing his heart out to this seething mass of strangers, they could see that it was almost like watching a grown man cry. They cautiously read the crowd's spontaneous reaction—much like an amateur-hour show host reading an applause meter. There was no doubt now, they assured each other, this *was* the Real Thing. Their cameras continued to click and whir as George sang, and they raised their pens to their note pads, hastily scribbling down phrases of superlative admiration, some of which surfaced in the national press in the months to come.

> *"He was the undisputed star of this year's Willie Nelson Picnic . . . one of the greatest."*
>
> (Houston *Post*)

> *"He is the spirit of country music, plain and simple, its true Holy Ghost."*
>
> (*Penthouse* magazine)

> *"As a singer, he is as intelligent as they come, and should be considered for a spot in America's all-time top ten."*
>
> (*Village Voice*)

> *"What a voice . . . a triumph of style. . . . George Jones is as soulful in his way as Otis Redding was in his."*
>
> (Boston *Phoenix*)

> *"[His] uncompromisingly country voice captures both the fire and the sorrow of life, putting more feeling into single bars of music than many other stars manage to get into whole albums."*
>
> (Chicago *Tribune*)

Weeks after the picnic, George sat alone, safely back on his favorite Alabama creek bank, on a warm late summer's night. He surely must have reminded himself of God's assurances to Noah that the world would never be drowned in a huge flood again. He was truly confused and bewildered by this huge wave of praise, adulation and media attention that was now moving inexorably his way, threatening to carry him off, to he knew not where.

In the years since 1963, when they first met, Earl Omar (Peanut) Montgomery and George had grown to be closer than blood brothers. They were two footloose and fancy-free wild-ass country boys who had popped pills together, recklessly drunk and sung their way through many a long, dark night. Together, they had also written dozens of songs—songs of lost love, loneliness, despair and redemption.

In the midst of their wildest times together—the purposeless road trips, the weekend excursions to Florida and the two-week whiskey binges in Nashville—Peanut often felt something nagging at him from within, some strange movement of the human soul which he could not fathom. It was a deep and abiding heartburn of the spirit that lingered long after the Alka-Seltzer and milk of magnesia tablets had cleansed his flesh of the more worldly impurities which he so often inflicted upon it.

When this feeling hit Peanut the hardest, he would get in his car and drive, drink beer and roam his native northern Alabama countryside like a restless phantom haunting a cathedral. Sitting alone in empty churches, in some old abandoned country cemetery or on the hood of his parked car in some lonesome gravel pit along the Natchez Trace, he struggled to put this gnawing feeling inside him into words. He came close to doing just that with the songs that he wrote, like "Let's All Go Down to the River," "One of These Days" (which was recorded by George and also by singer Emmylou Harris, who turned it into a top-five country hit in 1976) and "Small Time Laborin' Man" (a haunting, mystic-tinged paean to the common man which George released as a single in 1968, and which rock visionary Bob Dylan named, in an interview with the rock magazine *Rolling Stone,* as his favorite song of that year).

Peanut came to be more and more of a witness to the madness that was slowly starting to envelop George. The strange heartburn in his own soul nagged at him with ever greater intensity, until at last he recognized that what he felt was God and the devil fighting within him. On the morning of April 17, 1976—a date that he will never forget—his struggle was finally resolved, and Peanut was saved.

He had been drinking beer the night before in Birmingham. He was still half drunk and hung over that Sunday morning when he stopped by George's house on his way back home and drank up all the beer in George's refrigerator, too. As he was riding back toward Florence in his car, throwing up on himself while still clutching an unfinished beer in his hand, the face of Jesus visited Peanut, and the gnawing restiveness within him suddenly dissolved into the warm, joyous glow of salvation. Peanut threw that last unfinished beer out the car window, and he threw his cigarettes out the window, too. And he did not raise either of them to his lips again.

When Peanut, after his deliverance, would no longer drink with him, George made light of his friend's salvation. When George realized that it was not a joke, he began taunting his friend. Peanut had taken to reading the Bible to him and talking incessantly, babbling for hours on end to him about the face of Jesus.

"He'd call me Little Jesus," Peanut recalled, in the mild voice of the forgiving. "I had me a beard back then, and he'd tell me he was gonna hold me down and pluck it out. Sometimes he'd get up in my face and be wavin' his finger at me and say, 'Aw, c'mon, son, you don't really believe in all that, do ya?' "

Peanut and Charlene decided to hang a big sign on the door of their house that said: NO DRINKING ALLOWED ON THESE PREMISES, and it angered the hell out of the Possum. One day, George went to visit Peanut and Charlene, who were not at home. He got to drinking whiskey and dropped a big 7-Up bottle through the top of their glass coffee table. Then he left a package of cigarettes and the empty Jack Daniel's bottle on their front lawn as his calling card. Despite his Christian tolerance, this aggravated Peanut. As retaliation, one day when George was not at home, Peanut went to his house and turned all his furniture upside down, which merely made the Possum laugh with glee.

George's impatience with Peanut eventually deepened into outright scorn. "He'd get to drinking and askin' me things like, if there really was a God, then how come there was crippled children," Peanut remembered. "And then he'd get mad and get to cursin', and he'd say things like 'Well, if that blankety-blank so-and-so is really up there, then why don't he show hisself? How come he don't come down here!?' "

Peanut saw the problem as clear as the biblical writing on the wall spoken of in the Book of Daniel; his friend George had given his life to the music business the way a person ought to give his life over to Jesus Christ. The music business had anointed George as a king, a false prophet, much like King Belshazzar. He, in turn, had become lost in idolatry, and had borne witness to and worshipped the false saviour of the music business. "God created singin', but the perversion of the music business is somethin' the devil has done," Peanut knew, "just like the devil has perverted love and money and can use his antichrists and evil spirits to pervert anything. And that old music business had just chewed George up and spit him out and made a wreck out of him."

Peanut had also seen on television where the Right Reverend Jimmy Lee Swaggart—Jerry Lee Lewis's Bible-thumping TV evangelist first cousin—had gone down to Tahiti and filmed those people worshipping voodoo and biting the heads off chickens and drinking the blood. Peanut knew that such things were not godly.

Peanut knew almost by heart the place in the scriptures about the man who dwelt in the tombs at Gadara, "a man with an unclean spirit," who could not be bound by "fetters and chains . . . [and] neither could any man tame him. . . . And always, night and day, he was in the mountains and in the tombs, crying and cutting himself with stones." And when Jesus asked the man his name, the man replied, "My name is Legion, for we are many." Peanut knew how Jesus had exorcised the unclean spirits sent by Satan into the man and sent these malefic demons into a great herd of swine. The swine had run violently down a steep place into the sea and all drowned.

Peanut knew that his friend George had come to be like this man Legion. He could see now that George was "demon-possessed. He is demonic. He has demons in him, and I've confronted them. I've seen them."

Despite his friend's angry defiance, Peanut merely intensified his efforts to save George's soul. Peanut loved George, and he knew that with his legion of fans and his considerable influence as an entertainer, "George would be a number one witness for the Lord right now. Maybe," Peanut thought to himself, "maybe God called me to get George started on religion."

The Tammy and George saga still raged on back in Nashville. After five weeks of marriage, Tammy divorced Millstone No. 4. When her birthday rolled around, George sent her eleven red roses—as he always did—and threw a surprise party for her at her favorite four-star Italian restaurant in Nashville. In early September, she was hospitalized for "complications" following gallbladder surgery; she was hospitalized again just a week or so later, at the Mayo Clinic, for "severe abdominal pain."

On November 8, while touring England, the First Lady was again hospitalized—her sixth hospitalization in six months—purportedly for acute bronchitis. To the utter delight of their fans and the gossip tabloids, George quickly caught a plane and rushed to her bedside, where he declared his love for her anew. "There will never be anyone else for either of us," he told reporters. "No one for her. No one for me. No one either of us can get along with." As the prodigal singer sat vigilantly at her bedside, "Near You," a duet version of an old 1940s big band hit by the Francis Craig Orchestra, that they had recorded earlier in the year, rushed toward the number one spot in the singles chart.

His troubles deepened, though, and the weight of old transgressions was tightening around his neck like a noose. On December 17, he was sued for $102,000 by two Nashville women who claimed they had been assaulted by George at the home of another one of his many interim managers, Billy Willheit. The two women charged the prodigal singer had "physically and forcibly embraced them," and "viciously and maliciously" struck one of them in the face with his hand, and "forced her to ingest . . . vodka from a large bottle, then commenced to pour vodka all over her clothing . . . shouting expletives and obscenities all the while . . ." They further alleged that George had picked up a briefcase and hit one of them in the back with it as she fled, "causing her severe bodily pain and injury." Denying all these charges in George's behalf, Billy Willheit explained to the *Tennessean* that "they [the women—who were later awarded $11,800 in damages when George failed to show up in court to defend himself] made the statement that they didn't particularly care for country music, and Mr. Jones kindly told them to get the hell out."

In the midst of the prodigal singer's deepening worldly travail, the rest of the great wide world beyond Nashville and beyond those remote Alabama riverbanks and back roads was continuing to pay increasing attention to him and his music. The wave grew higher. In October 1976, a new LP called *Alone Again* was released. Produced by Billy Sherrill, the new album—which included "A Drunk Can't Be a Man"—was a remarkably austere return to the musical basics of George's honky-tonk roots. Instead of the multi-tracked strings and violins with which Sherrill had weighted down many of George's earlier Epic releases, the familiar strident cadences of steel guitars and twin fiddles were once again heard. *Newsweek* called *Alone Again* "a jaunty, unassuming country masterpiece." A single released off the album, a lively novelty tune composed by songwriter Bobby Braddock, "Her Name Is . . . ," went all the way to the number three spot—higher than any of George's records had gone in nearly two years. When the fans heard this song with its veiled tongue-in-cheek references to a mystery lover, they just knew the old Possum was still singing about Tammy.

There also came lavish praise from yet another unlikely source. *Rolling Stone,* the widely read rock magazine, named George in its annual critics' poll as Country Artist of the Year.

As 1977 rolled around, George's personal problems continued to pour down on him like Morton's salt. In February, a $12,765 federal tax lien was filed against his fancy Alabama residence.

CBS Records around this same time had once again attempted to crank up the wave-making machine. Hoping to capitalize on the momentum they'd created at Willie Nelson's picnic the year before, they decided to showcase the Real Thing for the sun-pale, soft-palmed, bland-voiced ranks of the national music critics and show business cognoscenti at New York's prestigious showcase club the Bottom Line. CBS spent more than $20,000 on the show, flying in a formidable roster of leading media figures and distinguished guests, including Walter Cronkite and John Chancellor, along with CBS Records president Bruce Lundvall. George had bad portents about playing at such a far-flung place. He became filled with fear and dread at the prospect of singing for a roomful of these snake-oil-smooth and icily polite city folks whose hands had never wielded a woodsman's ax and whose coin was not earned by the sweat of their brow. At the last minute, he found himself another bathroom window to wriggle out of, and with his magician-like guile, he fled away to freedom, and failed to show for the already assembled guests.

No matter how far or how fast George fled, there was no longer sanctuary to be found—not even on his favorite Alabama creek bank. His close friends could see that his "nerve troubles" were now beginning to manifest themselves in new and disturbing dimensions which could not be accounted for by strong drink alone. Linda Welborn and Peanut both noticed how, mornings, when he was badly hung over and depressed, he would leave in his car, returning a short time later, with his shotgun eyes gleaming wildly, and he'd be nervously chain-smoking, waving his hands furiously, laughing and talking a mile a minute. He was at home with Linda one day when she couldn't help but notice how quiet he'd become. When she went back in the bedroom, she found him snorting cocaine. She desperately pleaded with him not to take on a new problem when he had so many of them eating away at him already. George calmly assured her that he was not about to get hooked, and that maybe the powdery drug might serve as a substitute to help him cut back on his whiskey drinking. It did not take her long to realize that the cocaine, when mixed with whiskey, brought a wild new edge to his paranoid rages.

"A month or so after I first saw him use it, George was at the house and he decided he was gonna show some of his friends what reality was," Linda recalled. "So he got one of his guns out and shot it off in the house a couple of times. His sons from Texas were staying with us, and it about scared them to death. I left and they called me later and said, 'Please come back over here! Daddy's tearin' the house up!' "

Friends also noticed that since he'd lost the boozy companionship of Peanut, George had acquired two new friends who were with him constantly. He named them "Deedoodle the Duck" and "the Old Man." Both were invisible to everyone but George. Though they spoke through George's mouth, these two demented alter egos of his seemed to have voices and minds all their own. "Deedoodle" sounded much like Donald Duck—and he was, in fact, as George explained, first cousin to his more famous cartoon counterpart. But "Deedoodle" was of a reckless nature, and sometimes he squawked and cursed like a malevolent banshee. "The Old Man," on the other hand, possessed a voice much like Walter Brennan's; he was often a benevolent font of home-fried paternal wisdom. When George was driving alone or even when he was partying with friends, "the Duck" and "the Old Man" would get into heated arguments, and they would sing, banter, tease and bicker with each other for hours at a time, hardly letting George get a word in edgewise.

Even "Deedoodle the Duck" and "the Old Man" could not hold back the rising waters. George was again sued in August, for $75,000, by the same Nashville couple who claimed he'd signed papers to buy their house a couple of years earlier. He was sued for another $20,000 a few weeks later for an unpaid debt to an Iowa businessman. The prodigal singer's immense restlessness once again got the better of him. He sold his large brick house in Kendale Gardens and assumed the mortgage on another stately home in the swanky Twin Brooks subdivision, a few miles away.

The wave rolled on. In June 1977, Epic Records released *All Time Greatest Hits,* an LP's worth of Sherrill-produced remakes of the biggest records from George's long career, which received extensive critical praise. In early 1978, the record label released another single, "Bartender's Blues," a soulful confessional of beer-stained pathos that sounded as if it had been taken directly from the annals of George's increasingly troubled life, and which had been written especially for him by one of his ardent admirers, rock balladeer James Taylor. The song, which featured Taylor singing elaborate, overdubbed background harmonies, climbed to the number six spot in the singles charts.

On July 6—even as the rumors concerning an impending George-and-Tammy reunion continued to swirl feverishly—an old friend of George's, a songwriter named George Richey, who had written many of his and Tammy's biggest hits, became Mr. Tammy Wynette No. 5. Mr. Richey's preference for ornate gold neck chains and open-chested, rhinestone-studded leisure suits of varied and incandescent hues had also earned him a reputation as the Liberace of Music Row.

Shortly after the marriage ceremony, Tammy's $110,000 tour bus was mysteriously gutted and destroyed by fire.

After many months of serious discussion on the matter, George and Linda Welborn decided that they, too, would tie the knot. They made hasty plans after the decision was made to drive to Ringgold, Georgia—where he'd married Tammy seven years earlier—to get an overnight marriage. Linda requested only one thing of her husband-to-be, that he stay sober for the brief ceremony.

"Well, uh, I dunno." He shrugged and grinned his shy, inscrutable Possum grin. "I've always been drunk when I got married before. But I'll sure try!"

The appointed day rolled around. George went out and had his hair done and rented a tuxedo. Linda went out to buy a new dress. Upon returning she saw that George's speech was slurred and his freshly coiffed hair was already dangling loosely in his face. She could smell bourbon whiskey on his breath, and she saw that strong drink had lit yet another soon-to-be-raging fire in him. He would never make it to Georgia that day as far as she could see, so she called the marriage off.

The Possum merely grinned: You can't live with 'em, and you can't live without 'em either.

George had had a falling out of sorts in the late spring of 1976 with his latest interim manager, Shug Baggott, and they temporarily parted ways. He then struck a separate deal with a wealthy Dallas businessman named Caruth Byrd. He sold his house in Twin Brooks, where he'd lived for less than nine months, and moved himself and his few worldly possessions to Dallas, Texas.

Now that George had once again become a force to be reckoned with in the singles charts, and had become the focus of such unrelenting media glare, Caruth could see that it was time to send the Real Thing back out on a national tour. George's barber and close friend in Alabama, Jimmie Hills, was recruited—for a fee of $125 a day plus expenses—to go along as George's guardian and traveling companion.

Jimmie Hills was a kind and gentle man—and a friend in need, if ever there was one—who first met George when Peanut sent him down to his shop near Florence for a haircut. George had called and made at least a half dozen different appointments, but had not shown up for any of them. Finally, he just wandered in off the street one day, sat down and chatted with the other customers while he waited his turn like everyone else. This had impressed Jimmie.

Jimmie and George grew to be close friends. The first night that he visited Jimmie and his wife, Anne, at their house, George pulled $8,000 from the small shaving bag where he kept his cash reserves hidden. He offered the money to Jimmie—almost as if he were testing him. "Hell, put that away, George," Jimmie told him. "You don't have to *buy* my friendship. You've got it for free."

As the two of them embarked together on the new Caruth Byrd

tour, it became painfully obvious to Jimmie that his friend was in no shape to be traveling, much less performing. The cocaine had heightened the prodigal singer's abiding fear of the ethers of the night. He found it impossible to sleep at all in the strange motel rooms without all the lights on, the TV going full blast and somebody like Jimmie sitting in the room with him. Sleep eluded him for days at a time. "The Duck" and "the Old Man" argued, quoted the scriptures and spoke of matters both frivolous and profound—the whole night through. When George did sleep, the face of Jesus with its ethereal luminosity would disturb his dreams, and he would vividly recollect it for Jimmie the next day.

Just a few hours before one of the first scheduled shows of this long tour, which was to open at Hollywood's famed Palomino Club, George turned up missing. Jimmie and the rest of the crew frantically fanned out from the Sportsman's Lodge Motel in North Hollywood, where they were staying, hoping to track him down. After hours of searching, they finally spotted him, standing alone and disoriented at a downtown bus stop, a few blocks away from the motel. Reluctantly, he agreed to return with them and perform at the show that night at the Palomino—but only after he had them promise to charter a plane afterward and fly him to where his friend Willie Nelson was performing at one of the large casinos in Las Vegas, the Nugget.

Very late that night, after George had halfheartedly faked his way through the show at the Palomino, they arrived in Vegas just in time to catch Nelson's last show of the evening. While visiting with his friend Willie, George grew bored, then wandered off to his room, only to stay awake until dawn, lost in deep debate with "the Duck" and "the Old Man" regarding the fate of man, God and the universe.

The next day, when it was time to board a plane and go to his next scheduled show, in Phoenix that evening, George had still not slept, and still did not want to leave Las Vegas. While the others were going through the boarding-gate procedure, George was able to give Jimmie and the rest of his entourage the slip, and with his typical stealth, he vanished.

The others in the entourage decided that they would fly on to Phoenix, try and get the wayward singer's scheduled show in that city postponed for a night, get his tour bus (which had already transported his band directly from Los Angeles to Phoenix) and come back for him. Though he'd lost all his money—nearly four hundred dollars—playing blackjack the night before, Jimmie Hills was elected to stay on in Vegas and find the errant singer. After searching in vain through the labyrinth of airport corridors, shops and rest rooms, Jimmie walked the mile or so back down to the main strip. Flat broke, he did not have money for a cab. A couple of blocks from the Nugget, where they'd stayed the night before, he spotted George, who had not slept now for nearly three days, and was once again standing alone and dejected on a street corner.

"George, where the hell are you goin', anyway!?" Jimmie asked his friend.

"Colbert Park," George replied, referring to his favorite riverside haunt on the Natchez Trace. "C'mon with me, Jimmie? Let's go grill us some pork chops and green t'maters."

Realizing that it was not an appropriate time to explain to George that they were in Nevada rather than northern Alabama, Jimmie half led and half carried his friend back to the lobby of the Nugget, and made reservations for both of them for one more night. After signing the register, Jimmie looked up and saw that George had again fled. He found him this time wandering in dazed, confused circles, on another street corner, three or four blocks down the gaudy Casino Row.

"I wanna see ole Willie," George told him in a sad, tearful voice. "Take me to see Willie, Jimmie."

Jimmie took George up to the room he'd gotten for them at the Nugget and promised him that if he tried to get some rest, he'd go find Willie for him. George agreed and Jimmie walked up several flights in the huge casino and knocked on the door to Willie's room. He was startled when Willie himself answered. Willie merely grinned his omniscient grin and shook his head knowingly when he saw Jimmie. "He didn't go to Phoenix, did he?" Willie laughed.

Without even having to be asked, Nelson came down to George's room, sat on the edge of his bed and talked softly with the troubled singer until he finally calmed down enough to drop off to sleep.

Sleep did not hold George for long. Nor did it hold "the Duck" and "the Old Man." The next morning, George still did not want to leave Las Vegas. Jimmie and another crew member were forced to carry him bodily onto his tour bus, which had returned from Phoenix to pick him up.

When everyone finally got together in Phoenix, things went

smoothly for the first few hours. George was hungry, so he sent Jimmie down to the hotel dining room to order him something to eat. When Jimmie returned to the room, the singer of course had again vanished. The search parties fanned out again but this time to no avail. The evening's show was canceled once again—this time for good. A few hours later, the phone rang in Jimmie's hotel room. It was George. "Hey, Jimmie!" the prodigal singer informed his friend in a voice full of unrestrained glee. "I'm back up in Vegas!"

This ill-fated tour, which ultimately deteriorated into a long string of similar no-show concert cancellations, was the last of George's association with Caruth Byrd. The wayward singer fled from Texas and back to the familiar shores of northern Alabama.

Against the advice of an increasing number of his friends, George once again entrusted his floundering career to erstwhile manager Shug Baggott.

Back in Alabama, insanity now seemed to dog George's every move and intensified still further. "The Duck" and "the Old Man" cursed and argued more feverishly than ever. Rumors swirled that his cocaine was being laced with rat poison and cyanide. His paranoia was not alleviated when a $650,000 life insurance policy was taken out on him by Shug Baggott. Poisonous snakes—copperheads and "ground rattlers"—were found in his carport and in the swimming pool behind his new house. In the middle of the day, he would often show up at Peanut's house, his hair disheveled, his swirling eyes full of wild paranoia and his trusted .38 caliber pistol in hand. "He'd get to cursin' himself in that duck voice, and he'd tell me that 'the Duck' was sittin' on the hood of his car and 'the Old Man' was in the trunk, and that the Mafia or somebody was after him, trying to kill him—though I never saw anybody," Peanut remembered. "And he'd come in and pass out on my couch or in an easy chair, still holdin' a loaded gun in his hand."

One dark and windy night, after George had been debating bitterly with "the Duck" and "the Old Man" on matters both temporal and eternal, he asked a friend of his to drive him far out into the countryside, to an abandoned old graveyard that he often visited. Sitting in his friend's car, he once again fell to cursing and crying and railing against the terror and darkness in his spirit, which he could feel pulling him down. Those remote graves, with their faded and illegible tombstones, reminded him of other graves—those graves back in the Big Thicket, where his dead sister Ethel and Uncle Litt and his mama and his daddy now lay. What kind of God, he wondered aloud, would leave the dead to slumber for so long in the cold ground: perhaps leave them there even until the stars above had ceased their cold shining and the very fulcrum of time and eternity had swung back on itself to begin anew.

Out of the stillness of the night, a bee suddenly flew in the driver's side of the car. George ceased his cursing and looked fearfully at the bee. "Ya know what?" he whimpered to his friend. "That there bee's gonna sting me!"

No sooner had he voiced his fears than the bee flew out the window, around the car and back in the window on George's side. It stung the prodigal singer, and with a wail of repentance, he knelt down on the floorboard of the car and began praying up a blue streak, praying every bit as fast and fervently as old Uncle Litt ever had.

But the dead, rotting in those ancient graves, slumbered on. Overhead, the stars and constellations of the southern skies shone on—those same stars that had shone down on old Frank Jones at the Hogpen Incident, and on George Washington Jones when he'd come staggering up the moonlit lane in Kountze a half century ago and had made his young son sing on the porch under threat of an ass-thrashing. Now, these same stars shone down on the prodigal singer in his hour of abject misery, still silent, still unblinking. Still making him wonder, surely, if all his long years of mortal confusion, outrage and travail were all less than a single heartbeat lost in the horrible void of eternity.

Sensing his friend's deepening torment, Peanut Montgomery now intensified his somewhat relentless efforts to open George's tormented soul to the beckoning luminousness of the face of Jesus. He visited him at his new residence at the Georgetown Apartments, on Chisholm Highway, where he'd moved after selling his recently acquired house. He knelt with him on the floor and prayed for him. "Sometimes George would be on his knees, just cryin' and singin' for the Lord, with the tears and mucus just streamin' all down his face," Peanut recalled. "Sometimes he'd get to singin' them old gospel songs, and cryin', even though I never could tell if that was really George cryin', or if it was the devil in him cryin' because he was losin' ground."

Peanut never had seen a man struggle so fiercely to come to terms with the Protestant God as George did. The frail vessel of his troubled soul would seem at times to waver on the very brink of salvation, but his conviction would not hold. Peanut would visit George after these near-salvations and find that he'd once more fallen to cursing and railing against the Saviour and the very ravelments of destiny which now ensnared him like a trapped animal. Twice, Peanut saw George fall into a drunken rage and rip expensive Bibles into pieces. One of those Bibles had been a gift to George from the Reverend Bob Harrington, "the Chaplain of Bourbon Street," another colorful TV preacher who was perhaps most famous for preaching the sermon at the 1975 funeral of Audrey Williams, widow of the dark archangel. (At the ceremonies he recited the lyrics to Hank's song "Hey, Good Lookin', What Ya Got Cookin' " over her casket as they lowered it into the ground.) In his rage, George angrily hurled the torn, bedraggled pieces of the Good Book out the door and onto the lawn. Sadly, Peanut would go outside and gather up the pieces, and wonder how long his friend could hide from the brightness of the eternal light, which visited him so often in his dreams.

Still, George wavered on the brink. He showed up at Peanut's house one Monday morning looking relieved and at peace with his demons. "Boy, I'll tell you what!" he explained with a bright smile, the likes of which Peanut had not seen on his face in a long time. "I seen Jimmy Swaggart on TV last night, and he really preached a message! He *changed* me!" the prodigal singer assured Peanut. "I'm gonna quit my drinkin' and just quit this whole mess."

This set the wheels in Peanut's mind to turning. If he could not save George's soul, then maybe Jimmy Swaggart could. Peanut figured that if he could get ahold of Jimmy Swaggart, then maybe the two of them could pray together over the phone for George. Peanut called Swaggart's headquarters in Baton Rouge, Louisiana, and asked to speak to the TV evangelist. Instead, they let him talk to a secretary, and then the secretary in charge of that secretary, right on up to the top secretary, whose job it was to see that Swaggart got to the TV studio in time to put on his five-hundred-dollar suit and his makeup and go on TV and praise the Lord and holler for people to send him money, so he could hire more secretaries. The top secretary would not let Peanut talk to the Right Reverend Swaggart, but merely took Peanut's number and told him that she would try to get him to return the call. Swaggart never did call Peanut back, and Peanut realized that a prime opportunity to save George's soul had been lost. Such an opportunity, Peanut figured, might never come round again.

George was convinced more than ever now that someone was out to kill him or at least run him crazy. He kept constant companionship with his .38 Smith & Wesson. He came by Jimmie Hills's house one evening and angrily explained how he'd gotten drunk and passed out the night before. A mutual acquaintance of theirs, George complained, had rolled him for $3,500. "Will ya buy me some supper, Jimmie?" George sadly asked his friend. "I don't have any money left."

With Jimmie driving, the two of them headed down Nathan Boulevard, past the huge Indian mound and across the Tennessee River toward the Bonanza Steak House in Muscle Shoals. As they neared the center of the tall O'Neil Bridge, which connected Florence with Muscle Shoals, George suddenly pulled his gun out from under the seat and put it to Jimmie's head.

"George, please," Jimmie told him in a voice that was soft and calm, and did not reveal the abject terror that he felt inside him as he looked over the bridge at the waters far beneath them. "Put the gun down."

"O.K., Jimmie," George replied as he laid the pistol back down on the seat. "I know you're my friend. But you're gonna take me to that guy who took all my money, and I'm gonna kill him."

Jimmie drove aimlessly around the Muscle Shoals area for three nerve-racking hours, pretending he'd lost his way, scrupulously avoiding the street where he knew George's alleged transgressor lived. He spoke calmly to his friend, trying to bring him to his senses. Finally, George seemed to come around a little and put his gun down on the car seat, and Jimmie figured if he could get him to eat something, he might get drowsy and give up his ill-conceived quest for vengeance. Jimmie stopped at the Omelet Shop on Woodward Avenue, and Jimmie left George alone in the car while he went in to order sandwiches to go. As luck would have it, some other acquaintances of George's pulled up beside him, got out of their car and walked inside the restaurant. Through the window, Jimmie saw George get out of his car and follow them inside. As one of the men —with whom George had earlier had a falling out—took a seat,

George walked up behind him. Pulling the .38 from his belt, he held it to the man's head and drew back the hammer.

"You was at a party at my house one night," George muttered darkly at the man. "You don't know it, but I saw you stealing some money out of Linda's purse."

Sensing disaster, Jimmie quietly came up behind George and grabbed his arm and pulled it down until the .38 dropped from his grasp and hit the floor with a loud clatter. As the manager of the Omelet Shop summoned the police, Jimmie hurriedly pulled his friend toward the car and they sped away into the night.

Slowly but surely, as George's soul twisted painfully in the wind, dangling between redemption and denial, it was upon his friend Peanut that he turned his stormful wrath.

"People don't realize the problems I got, Peanut," he'd tell his friend in a voice full of anger and desperation. "I got a Jesus, too. Why can't you see my Jesus!?"

" 'Cause he ain't my Jesus," Peanut would reply in a voice full of calm reverence and quiet certitude.

"But I can't see your Jesus!"

"I can't see him either, but I see him the way the Bible sees him. I understand him."

George renewed his taunts of "Little Jesus" and again warned Peanut that he was going to hold him down and pluck his beard out. Peanut continued to turn his cheek to this abuse, "seven times seventy times." "George is jealous of what I got, and he wants what I got," Peanut thought to himself. "He wants peace with the Lord, but he don't know how to get it."

George put the word out through their mutual friends in the area that he was laying for Peanut and that his number was about to come up. His anger was allegedly underscored by a decidedly more pragmatic and temporal misunderstanding that had arisen over some earnest money he'd given Peanut for a house he'd intended to buy from him before changing his mind. On the night of September 13, one of the last sweltering, thunderstorm-swept, 90-degree dog days of the long, troubled summer, Peanut picked up the phone and called George, who was at home alone in his unit at the Georgetown Apartments.

"I hear ya been lookin' for me," Peanut warily told his friend.

"Yeh, that's right."

"Well, then, get outa your apartment and meet me down on Cypress Creek."

It was about 1 A.M. when Peanut wheeled his silver Trans-Am off the Savannah highway and down the rough dirt road that led to the muddy bank below the concrete bridge that spanned the wide Cypress Creek. Peanut could see the tan Lincoln Town Car that George was now driving already parked near the creek bank. He pulled his car up next to it so that the two of them—each one sitting in the driver's seat of his own car—faced each other. They were about twenty feet apart. For a moment or two, they heatedly exchanged words. Suddenly, George, whose anger was now burning as hot as the biblical lake of fire prophesied in Revelations, picked up his .38 Smith & Wesson off the seat beside him. Then he drew back the hammer and propped the gun on the door of his car so that Peanut was looking down its barrel.

"All right, you son of a bitch!" George screamed. "See if your God can save you now!"

The roar of gunfire shook the late-night silence, like the slow-motion sound of glass shattering into a thousand fragments.

Even as George was pulling the trigger that night on the banks of Cypress Creek, his worldly troubles continued to multiply. On September 19, his tour bus was stolen in Nashville. It was recovered a short time later, slightly damaged, on a nearby interstate ramp. Two days later, a Nashville circuit court judge, Hamilton Gayden, issued a warrant for the prodigal singer's arrest. Earlier, George had ignored a court order to pay $36,000 in back payments on his $1,000-a-month child-support obligation to ex-wife Tammy. The $43,000 houseboat that he'd been awarded in their divorce settlement was now docked at the Anchor High Marina on Old Hickory Lane. One carefree, whiskey-soaked afternoon, he'd inflicted minor damage on it when he'd commandeered it, ramming it into the pier and then into another pleasure craft. But now, the court ordered it impounded as collateral for this unpaid debt.

Another Nashville judge ordered George to pay $13,554.35 for some furniture he'd purchased from the John F. Lawhon Furniture Company in Nashville in 1975 and 1976 but had never got around to paying for. It was also adjudged by the courts that he must immediately repay a $20,000 debt he'd incurred to an Iowa man some months earlier, along with $4,000 in interest and attorney's fees.

On October 4, two Virginia promoters were awarded $29,654 in a default court judgment. George failed again to show up before the judge to give an explanation for his failure to appear at the two scheduled singing performances in Virginia some months earlier. Failure to appear had by now become one of George's newest anthems.

Earlier that same day, in an unusually bizarre incident, ex-wife Tammy was abducted from the parking lot of the Green Hills Shopping Center in suburban Nashville by a masked assailant. At gunpoint, she was forced to drive in her own Cadillac about eighty miles south on I-65, to a secluded spot along State Highway 31A in an isolated rural section of Giles County, Tennessee, not far from the Alabama state line. There, before being thrown from her car bruised and hysterical, with a fractured jaw (which later required surgery), she was beaten around the head and nearly choked to death with her own pantyhose, which was wrapped around her neck.

The Nashville police, unable to find either a suspect or a motive in Tammy's kidnapping, found the entire episode quite puzzling. Tammy had been neither robbed nor sexually molested. They theorized that the incident might somehow be connected to the earlier disturbances at her house, including the three fires in 1976, which they'd speculated to have been set by someone with easy access to the premises. Then, a short time after the violent abduction, a note written on a page from a yellow legal pad was found on the front door of Tammy's Franklin Road pleasure palace: "We missed you the first time," the note warned. "We'll get you the second time."

As well as keeping tabs on George's misadventures, Nashville's morning paper also breezily noted that the prodigal singer had recently been back in the country top-twenty once again—this time with a single called "I'll Just Take It Out In Love."

Back on the Alabama creek bank, at the instant that George fired his pistol point-blank at him, Peanut felt himself overcome by a deep sense of peacefulness, much like the day that he was saved.

"He couldn't have killed me and he knew it. He could've run at me with his car and he wouldn't have hit me." The bullet had torn through the car door and lodged itself in a thick strip of metal inside the doorframe, a few inches beneath Peanut's chin and clasped hands.

After George fired the shot, he threw the gun down and flung his hands up in dejected resignation. "People just don't know what the hell I go through!" he sighed bitterly. Then he roared off down Highway 20 in his Lincoln and disappeared into the night.

Peanut went down to the Lauderdale County district attorney's office and the sheriff's department in Florence to relate his account of the grisly creek-bank confrontation. The Alabama police officers wanly scratched their heads, furrowed their brows, issued a collective sigh, and reminded him that shooting a gun off outside city limits—no matter how close the speeding bullet might have come to hitting its intended victim—was merely a misdemeanor. Peanut was finally able to persuade the officials to draw up a warrant on George for assault with intent to murder (a felony). He saw that they were none too anxious to be burdened with the thankless task of arresting a man who was one of the country's most popular country entertainers.

When word filtered back to Peanut that George was running around the countryside telling people he intended to finish the job he'd started, Peanut nervously pressed on with his efforts to get the arrest warrant served.

On the afternoon of Sunday, September 17, yet another torpid, 90-degree-plus dog day, as Peanut monitored developments via his police band radio, Lauderdale County Sheriff's Deputy Milton Borden showed up at unit A-15 of the Georgetown Apartments on Chisholm Highway, where the prodigal singer was still ensconced. He knocked on the door for an exceedingly long time. The Possum did not answer.

"I thought I was going to have to get more officers to help me arrest Mr. Jones," Borden recalled. George finally did respond to the loud, insistent knocking. As he opened the door he smiled his inscrutably innocent Possum-like smile and insisted, "I've been taking a shower and didn't hear y'all. . . ."

"He didn't look like he was taking a shower," Borden observed.

He was taken away to the sheriff's department in Florence, and after posting a $2,500 bond, he was quickly set free again.

The turbulent waters continued to rise. On October 10, a sunny day with temperatures in the mid-70s and autumn in its incipient splendor, George returned to Nashville. (There had been four additional court judgments ruled against him—totaling $80,000—in cases where he'd failed to show up in court to defend himself.) Filing a petition in circuit court, he begged for mercy from the judge who'd ordered him to jail for nonpayment of his child support to Tammy. In his petition he explained that he was "addicted to alcohol" and that he had "placed himself under psychiatric care."

Eleven days later, on a deceptively mild and cloudless 80-degree afternoon, George, with the poisonous serpents still writhing loose in his head, surfaced again in Nashville. In the storm's eye of the twisted web of lawsuits and arrest warrants that now threatened to strangle him, and amidst the tangle of increasingly vicious and virulent rumors that now swirled about him from one end of Music Row to the other, he agreed to give an interview to a country music magazine. In the shabby, dimly lit office/apartment of Shug Baggott, just across the alley from CBS's "Studio A," on Sixteenth Avenue South, where he'd recorded all his famous duets with ex-wife Tammy; as a football game flickered unwatched on the giant screen of an Advent color TV, George fidgeted restlessly. As the interview began, he nervously stirred a tall glass of Jack Daniel's and 7-Up with his little finger.

George's expensive and once immaculate clothes were rumpled and had been slept in. His skin was the wan color of rotting parchment. As he chain-smoked filter cigarettes and ran his fingers frantically through his disheveled hair, he had the fatigued and tortured look of a man imploding under the weight of his own depression and exhaustion.

GEORGE: I only slept about two hours last night. I laid down on this couch here, about seven-thirty, and slept two hours. (*He flicked the palm of his hand nervously across his face, as if trying to shake himself free from the thick, glassy-eyed fog of his own confusion. He stirred his drink over and over again with his finger and sipped lightly from it.*) Then this little gal come and knocked on the door, and we went upstairs and got it on. Then I needed some rest, but the son of a bitch kept me up talkin' religion till about twenty minutes till six this morning. . . . Then my manager come and give me a "sopor"—one of them sleepin' pills. But I only slept an hour or so. I got a show tonight, but I don't know if I can make it or not.

REPORTER: Why did you shoot at Peanut?

GEORGE: Well, he's supposed to be a Christian, and I believe he's a good man, and I considered him my closest friend. . . . He knew the problems I was havin', and he knew that I was drinkin' more, and the shape I was in, just worried to death about things. I was already messed up in my mind about things, and boilin' over, and he called me and said the wrong thing. I'm sorry for what I done. Peanut knows I didn't intend to hurt him. I'm just thankful that he's still alive. . . . You get all those things on your mind like that, you become a crazy person.

REPORTER: You've been described as a Jekyll-Hyde type of personality—the sort of person who stores anger up for a long time and then lets it loose.

GEORGE: One time I went to a special doctor at the Watson Clinic [in Lakeland, Florida]. He typed out three or four pages, in his words, describing this person that was me. He started off saying I was a shy person. I disliked violence but took a lot of abuse, just to keep from havin' problems. I'm the type of person who kind of lets people run over me . . . until I've had me a few drinks, or when I get mad. I get in my car, and get to thinkin' on some subject. If I'm lucky, I'll forget it. But then [other times] after I've done this thinkin', and if [somebody] says the wrong thing to me, and I've had a drink, then I'll just as soon try and whup 'em as not. The only time that I would try to do that was when I'd had a drink. Of course, all that stuff that is stored up then would come out.

But there have been times when I've been as high on whiskey as you can get, and I'll just be sittin' around, playin' the guitar and enjoyin' myself. Somebody might smart off and say the wrong thing to my wife or girlfriend. And, naturally, I get to wanting to whip the butt of this other guy. . . . But what the heck. That'd make you a little violent too, I guess.

REPORTER: In a recent newspaper report, you were described as having sought psychiatric counseling for your problems.

GEORGE: I tell you. I'll talk to people about my problems. But I still think the best counselor in the world is yourself. That's the reason I do a lot of drivin'. People think you're crazy if they walk by you on the street and you're talking to yourself. One of my doctors says that the best thing is to talk to yourself about something . . . you done something wrong, and remember it better and think about it, and try not to do it again.

REPORTER: Do you actually drink sometimes for weeks at a time?

GEORGE: My problem is—if I ate like other people I wouldn't have this problem. I go three, four, five weeks at a time without eating right and my stomach shrinks down so small . . . if I get me a hamburger I can only eat about half of it. I wake up in the mornin' knowin' I am sick. And I've just got to have something to settle my stomach, unless I want to fight it out. Well, that's the hardest thing to do. I wind up sayin', "Well, maybe just one . . ." I don't know. *He stirs his drink again with his little finger.* You just get so far down and your mind gets so screwed up, you just don't care sometimes.

REPORTER: It's hard for people to understand. You have the power to earn more money in one night than many of your fans make in an entire year. You have the capability of earning several million dollars a year. Yet now you're in debt and missing shows. Money actually seems to mean very little to you. In fact, you hardly seem to care about it at all.

GEORGE: I don't. People in the entertainment business, most of 'em, are after the glory and the almighty dollar. I love country music more than the dollar. I went through all of my first years playing my guitar and singing. I didn't make no money. I didn't want no money. Even now, as long as I have a bed to sleep in, and I've got a few bucks and some wheels to get around in, and a guitar, that's enough. If I have to sing out on a street corner, next to a hot-dog vendor, I'm not too good to do that. I feel like this because I love country music. You've heard of the man who just loved a woman so much he just worshipped her? Well, that's the way I am about country music. Country music is in your *heart*, it's in my *soul*.

REPORTER: Are you aware that some people have tried to implicate you in Tammy's kidnapping?

GEORGE: Really, it's all over town that there is that possibility. *Glares bitterly.* They're sayin' that I been disturbed and everything. Anybody who would say that just don't know George Jones the way they think they do. That's a woman who was a good mother . . . a warm person . . . gave me a lot of happiness. [Jones was later cleared of any involvement in the incident.]

REPORTER: Are you on good terms right now with Tammy and her new husband?

GEORGE: Well, it's a funny thing. For a coupla years, right up until she and George Richey got married, Tammy and I had a very good friendship. I'd call then and sometimes I'd stop by and have a cup of coffee with her. Sometimes, if she felt like it, she'd come down to the Possum Holler and sing a couple of songs with me. Mr. Richey has been a friend of mine for many years. I love him to death, and he's always helped me in any way he could. Then he told me on the phone one day, "We don't want you callin' here no more, and we don't want you around here no more." I thought to myself: What's wrong with you, Richey? I wasn't jealous because he was marryin' Tammy. I wanted her happy. I wanted them to be happy! I mean, it was over for me and Tammy. I was just callin' to check on my child. Richey said, "Yeh, and that's another thing. We want you to stay away from her, too." I said, "I'll die and go to hell first!" I hung up the phone. I ain't done nothin' to that man. But just because he got married to my ex-wife, he hates me.

I don't know. I think people need to know both sides of things before they read something about a man and condemn him and say, "Well, my God! Look at how he treated that poor little woman!" Or "He must be the sorriest thing in the world! I ain't never gonna go out and buy any more of his records!" People will condemn somebody when they don't even really know what happened. It's just like that old Hank Williams song ["Be Careful of Stones That You Throw"] where he says, *Who am I to cast the first stone?"* We just can't condemn people like that.

Even as George spoke to the reporter on that beautiful autumn afternoon, there were still more assaults that ripped and tore at the ever more fragile and frayed strands of his sanity. Earlier on that day, a gifted country singer named Mel Street whom George had publicly praised and personally befriended (he'd even recorded a song of his, "Borrowed Angel," on his 1975 *Grand Tour* LP), celebrated his forty-fifth—and what would prove to be his last—birthday. After eating breakfast with his wife and children in their suburban Nashville home, Mel excused himself, went upstairs, put a .38 revolver in his mouth and blew his brains out. A friend later attributed his death to a "severe state of depression brought on by coming down off pills."

George attended Mel Street's funeral at the Cole & Garrett Funeral Home in nearby Hendersonville, Tennessee. At the end of the service, he stood and sang the old Holiness song "Amazing Grace" for the roomful of mourners. His voice, at first, was tear-choked and faltering, but then it quickly rose, like a mournful clarion call of mortal outrage, calmed and tempered by the eternal promise of divine deliverance. It brought tears to the eyes of all those who listened, and lifted their spirits like a rising tide. After the service was over, the grief-stricken prodigal singer, his eyes still full of tears, lingered at the funeral home and was the last to leave—lingering and staying with his friend Mel right until they closed the casket lid on him for the last time.

Street's death must have given George pause. As he looked around himself, he noted the other spaces in his thinning ranks of friends: Darrell Edwards, the Muse from the Thicket, was gone now as well. He had died on June 10, 1975, also violently and by his own hand—the victim of a self-inflicted shotgun blast to the head.

The earth and the firmament swirled wildly out of kilter and did not right themselves. The waters rose.

The Third National Bank of Nashville on November 7 brought suit against the prodigal singer, seeking $56,966.70, in unpaid loans, and also claiming that he had defaulted on payments on the houseboat. The boat had already (ostensibly) been ordered seized and impounded by the circuit court as collateral for the $36,000 in support payments that he still owed Tammy. But Shug Baggott later explained to the court that the Possum had nonetheless managed to sell the boat to an unsuspecting customer (who was apparently unaware of the jumble of liens and encumbrances against it) for the one-time-only, cash-and-carry price of $5,000.

One cold morning in mid-December George woke up and discovered that his pockets were once again empty. He'd signed away what few claims to future royalties that he still had left, for similarly low, one-time-only, cash-and-carry prices. He had sold everything else that he had to sell; he had borrowed and borrowed until he could borrow no more. Seeing no way out, he got dressed, went to downtown Nashville and reluctantly filed a petition for bankruptcy in federal court. As grounds for the petition he cited his $1.5 million in debts, which included $680,811 in secured loans from friends and his record company as well as more than $300,000 in default court judgments that had now been awarded to promoters at whose shows he had failed to appear. The prodigal singer went on to admit that he'd missed fifty-four performances in the last two years, due to "exhaustion." He itemized a total of $64,500 in assets, including: a mobile home in Lakeland, Florida; unimproved property in Alabama and Texas; assorted furniture (including "two bedroom suites and an assortment of lamps and pictures"); jewelry (including a two-carat diamond cluster ring, two gold rings and a Bulova Accutron watch) worth $1,500; and two guitars worth $1,000.

"I feel like a drowning man who's just been pulled to the beach and rescued from death," he told gathered reporters after filing.

But he barely had time to breathe even a short sigh of relief. The waters were still rising and the sand was shifting under his feet. Later that month, he learned that a grand jury in Alabama was about to bring a formal criminal indictment against him for assault with a weapon. This came as a result of his creek-bank confrontation with Peanut. Peanut's original complaint had been dismissed on September 27 on payment of thirty-five dollars in court costs. His old friend Peanut had again gotten the law on his ass, with an additional arrest warrant for the misdemeanor charge of telephone harassment.

"[He] calls about every twenty minutes," the warrant alleged. ". . . [He] calls and sometimes he talks, and sometimes he laughs, and sometimes he just sits there and calls the name Earl (Peanut) Montgomery over and over again."

Heaped upon all these new troubles was still further bad news: His ex-fiancée Linda Welborn, from whom he had been estranged for several months, had also obtained an arrest warrant against him. She charged that on November 25 and 27, George had "assaulted and beat" her, "hit [her] in the face with his hand and shoved her across the table. He had made threats about things he was going to do [to her]."

He was arrested on this new charge on December 22. After posting the $300 bond, he was promptly released.

The final affront particularly wounded George's pride. Bad enough that Linda should beat him at bowling. But now *this*. He immediately took back the new Corvette that he'd bought her. Out of fear for her personal safety, Linda moved in with Peanut and Charlene. George hid the car behind Jimmie Hills's house, where it would also be safe from the bankruptcy court trustees who were now initiating efforts to seize his various pleasure machines.

Looking over his shoulder, George could now see the rising savage waters moving swiftly toward him, threatening to engulf him. It was a wave of frightful proportions, such as he had imagined only in his most terror-stricken nightmares. As it encroached upon him, it bore in its wake a ravenous descending legion of Alabama state troopers, Lauderdale County sheriff's deputies, process servers, bill collectors, irate ex-managers, distraught booking agents, hysterical kinfolk, Bible-toting proselytes, newspaper reporters, TV camera crews, gossip columnists, public relations agents, gape-mouthed Polaroid-toting fan club officials, awards presenters, divorce court judges, bankruptcy attorneys, ex-wives, ex-girlfriends, snuff queens, record company reps, auto repossessors, tax agents and pearly-teethed local politicians. With "the Duck" and "the Old Man" squawking furiously at each other like twin parrots perched one on each shoulder, he jumped into one of his shiny new Lincoln Town Cars. Stepping on the gas, he tore out in a spray of gravel, fleeing for his life, wondering to himself if there was still dry land left anywhere.

This time, the prodigal singer's circuitous ramblings did not take him to Nashville or Florida, as they so often did. Instead, after many hours of driving he found himself back in Southeast Texas, the Big Thicket region where he'd drawn his first breath in this harsh world, where many acres of the once vast sea of majestic pine trees had since fallen to the woodsman's ax. Hoping against hope, perhaps, to find among the canebrakes, palmetto and wild honeysuckle a fleeting glimpse of the childhood serenity that he'd once known but had lost somewhere along the way, he drove past the old White Oak Baptist Church, where he and the Patterson sisters had once raised their lovely voices heavenward. That joyful sound was not to be heard there anymore. In its place there was only a harsh, unyielding silence, broken only by the occasional sad, lonesome trill of a mockingbird.

Driving on, he came to the Phelps Cemetery, where the ghost winds still whispered through the pines. With grim silence, he surveyed the faded, weather-scarred graves of Uncle Litt, and of Ethel, the older sister whom he'd never known and who had slumbered in death's cold, silent repose for years before he was even born—through all those years which were now starting to turn his own hair gray.

Under ever-darkening skies, he rode on through Saratoga, with its abandoned frame houses—remnants of the long-gone boom-town days—and its deserted streets. It was little more than a dreary ghost town now. In the nearby pine forest, with the saw briers grabbing at him, he searched in vain, amidst the uprooted stumps and petroleum-tinged drainage ditches left by the lumber and oil excavators, for the spot where he was born.

Steering his car a half mile or so further down another seldom-used mud lane, he came upon the old Saratoga City Cemetery. He found that heavy rains had caused many of the crumbling markers and little stone lambs of Jesus to topple and sink beneath the viscid marsh waters; and as he walked among the ancient burial plots, he could feel the mud of the swamp sucking at his boots and pulling him down. He paused at the timeworn gravestone of his paternal grandmother, Mary Killingsworth, which lay in the shadows of the nearby pumping jacks whose clatter and cacophony filled the air with a din that disturbed everything—everything except for the cold slumber of the dead beneath him.

So much lost, yet still more: He also knew that his sister Ruth had even more bad news. Her diligent search through the confusing tangle of old land grants, faded property titles, musty court documents and probate records of the estate of old Rollie Jones had hit a dead end and trailed off to nothing. It was clear now to Ruth that her hopes of recovering the imaginary fortune haphazardly signed away by their father, so many years ago in Houston, were illusory. The prospect of those mysterious oil wells believed to be shimmering somewhere in the vastness of East Texas, which she'd hoped might someday pump untold wealth into their own empty pockets, was indeed merely a mirage—no more palpable than the glistening puddles of water that seem to beckon from the horizon on a hot, dry Texas roadbed, but then vanish into nothingness as one approaches closer to them.

The valor of old Frank Jones, once the glory of the Texas branch of the Jones family, now seemed faded and lost. His medals from the Old Confederacy, once handed down through the family like sacred talismans, had been forgotten and misplaced. There was a new generation of Joneses now, nameless to one another and scattered across East Texas like thistledown, whose ears had never heard the tales of old Frank, and whose lips no longer spoke of his courage at the Hogpen Incident.

George drove on until he found himself just north of Vidor, by the big stone Bible in the Restlawn cemetery, where his mama, Clara, and his daddy, George Washington Jones, now slept in the cold ground. He knelt and placed flowers on their headstones, and felt the darkness descend upon him, as if it were night. He looked at his own gnarled hands and thought again of the grayness in his own hair, and then wept bitterly, overwhelmed as he was by the sadness of all that he'd lost and of how little there seemed left in this harsh world to replace it with.

The prodigal singer returned again to Nashville, merely to discover that there was no rest for the weary—and that he was merely like Jonah, who flees only to find himself in the jaws of the Leviathan.

In January, 1979, Shug Baggott had also filed for bankruptcy. This was his second bankruptcy claim in seven years.

On January 26, George's former booking agent Shorty Lavender accused Shug Baggott of various deceptive practices, including "falsifying documents" and the "double booking" of George. He claimed that Baggott had willfully—and, in some cases, without George's knowledge or consent—contracted the wayward singer's services to several different concert promoters in several different cities, on the same night; and had then merely pocketed the advance cash deposits. Lavender then sued Baggott, claiming he had "falsely represented" his authority to negotiate performance contracts for the wayward singer, and that he had interfered with a three-year booking contract that Lavender had earlier signed with George. "He [George] was all right till he got with that sonofabitch," Lavender angrily told reporters.

The bankruptcy courts, in the meantime, were also taking a closer look at George's purported assets and debts. A few of the latter were: $398,561 owed to CBS Records, $100,000 to Caruth Byrd Productions in Dallas, $70,000 to the Commerce Union Bank in Nashville, and $1,200 to Ramada Inns for unpaid motel bills. . . . "The rest of the petition reads like a lawyer's two-aspirin headache," one court reporter noted.

Members of the press hovered around Nashville's federal courthouse on downtown Broad Street like circling buzzards; and at one point, the Possum avoided the elevator and fled down seven flights of stairs in order to evade waiting news photographers. The reporters raised questions as to why, if George was about to go bankrupt, he had been recently seen around town, driving, at various times, a freshly purchased 1979 Lincoln Continental and a shiny new 1978 Corvette.

"Even with his problems, would you expect to see Mr. Jones in a

Volkswagen!?" erstwhile manager Shug Baggott replied, blowing smoke with the misplaced hubris and comic self-righteousness that is often the last resort of doomed politicians and petty schemers as they stand trapped in the shadow of the gallows. "This is a man whose income is $200,000 [a year] when he isn't working, and a million when he halfway works!"

The federal bankruptcy judge ordered on February 8 that the artist and songwriter's royalties allegedly owed to George by CBS Records, United Artists Records, Pappy Daily, and the Broadcast Music Institute (royalties which, in most cases, he'd already managed to sign away) be turned over to the court and applied toward payment of the beleaguered singer's $1.5 million in debts.

On February 28, a court-appointed trustee for Jones filed two suits. One, against Peanut Montgomery, sought to set aside the transfer of a Florida lot that George had allegedly sold to him the summer before. The other, against Linda Welborn and the First Colbert Bank of Sheffield, Alabama, sought to recover some $7,000 that she had allegedly received from George "without performing any services."

George was homeless now, and living out of the trunk of his car, or staying at various Nashville hotels, like the elegant Spence Manor on Sixteenth Avenue South or the Hall of Fame Motor Inn near Music Row. (These were places where his credit was still good.) Often, late at night, he would pick up the telephone and call Linda Welborn, who—he was now certain—was secretly conspiring with Shug Baggott to drive him crazy. In an anguished voice, full of the anger of a trapped animal, and the despair of one who feels he has been betrayed by destiny itself, he would threaten her and warn her that such a conspiracy—to put someone "in the insane asylum"—carried an automatic fifteen-year prison sentence. He pleaded with Linda to assuage his dark suspicions by taking a polygraph test.

The wave rolled on. On May 15, a request was filed in bankruptcy court that George's bankruptcy appeal be overturned. His original petition, his creditors complained, was riddled with "omissions and irregularities including the failure to list various depreciable assets that had been listed on his recent income tax returns." The motion concluded that "Jones is unable to provide any explanation [documentation] about the depletion of his assets." The court ordered the prodigal singer to hand over two gold rings that he'd been wearing, for liquidation.

In a confused flurry of petitions, suits, countersuits, restraining orders, motions and countermotions, George's bankruptcy case dragged on for weeks. Depositions were filed in the nearly futile attempt to fathom the creative bookkeeping that had led to his massive indebtedness. The bankruptcy bid was finally overturned. The court noted that, in 1977 and 1978, while Shug Baggott had had full power of attorney to sign the wayward singer's name to checks, contracts and other documents, Jones had received more than $2 million, but could account for only $30,000.

In early June, George and Waylon Jennings surfaced together on the syndicated radio show of veteran country disk jockey Ralph Emery. Facing this dynamic duo across from him in the microphone stand, Emery (another bloated fixture in Nashville's Mount Rushmore of countrified egotists, whose torpid interview style brings new meaning to the radio concept of "dead air") found that he had more on his hands than he'd bargained for. When the transcription of the program was later sent out to affiliate radio stations, he even issued a disclaimer. "The show this week is rather free-wheeling, to say the least," he wrote. "All I did was try and make sense out of what was going on."

With George, Jennings, "the Duck" and "the Old Man" all laughing and talking in a disjointed and occasionally incoherent manner, Emery probed George's personal life with typical opaqueness:

EMERY: George, can you cook?

GEORGE: No, but "Deedoodle the Duck" can!

EMERY: Did you bring "the Duck" with you today?

GEORGE: Yeh. Oh, yeh! I just couldn't leave home without him. "The Old Man," too! They just stay with me all the time.

EMERY: Deedoodle?

GEORGE: Yeh. He's first cousins to Donald.

EMERY: Does he sing?

JENNINGS: Yeh, he sings. Make him sing, George.

"THE DUCK" (*in the Donald Duck squawk*): I love you so much it hurts me!

GEORGE: Aw, that's all. He's been up all night and he's tired. . . . HELP, WE'RE BEIN' HELD PRISONER!

JENNINGS (*laughs*): It's lonely at the top!

GEORGE: Yeh. It's lonely at the bottom, too! Real, real lonely, Waylon!

Later in the show, George and Waylon played a tape of a song that they'd recorded together in Waylon's studio at four o'clock one morning after they'd been up all night. It was "Pictures from Life's Other Side," which had been written and recorded by Hank Williams in 1951. As the two of them sang it, their voices blended in the thin, hauntingly ethereal harmony of two wayward souls lost in a sea of confusion.

"Ya know, ole Hank missed a lot of shows," Jennings remarked offhandedly during the broadcast.

"Well, me too, boy!" George interjected strenuously—as if to make sure that credit was given where credit was due.

As they spoke, the waters outside swirled higher.

George was indicted by a grand jury back in Alabama on charges of selling $13,484 worth (twenty-seven individual pieces) of mortgaged furniture, which was already covered by a lien filed in earlier attempts to recover it.

Four days later in Nashville, Shug Baggott (whom Jones's lawyers had accused of "misappropriation of at least a million dollars" in the earlier bankruptcy hearings) was arrested, along with two accomplices. All three of them were carrying handguns. FBI agents charged them with selling two pounds of cocaine. Later, after Baggott had been convicted and received a three-year prison term, he was still blowing smoke out his ass. He told the court that he'd only trafficked in drugs in order to "keep a certain artist off the streets."

"Shug got me started on it [cocaine] to keep me all messed up, just the way he got me drunk all the time," the prodigal singer told a writer from *Penthouse* magazine a short time later. "He's a crook. He robbed me blind."

All the while, there had also been more bizarre eruptions out at Tammy's gaudy Franklin Road manse. Incoming phone lines had reportedly been tapped. The *Tennessean* had reported that—despite the platoon of around-the-clock security personnel, bodyguards and watchdogs that now surrounded the First Lady—mysterious footsteps had again been heard on the roof, and her new Cadillac had been splattered with eggs. Mr. Tammy Wynette No. 5, however, contradicted several other well-placed flies on the wall, angrily denying these reports. "I say none of this is true," he told a reporter in a particularly wary and ominous tone of voice. "It could be," he added—in reference to the fact that none of the other well-placed flies who'd been interviewed seemed to know of Tammy's whereabouts—"that I told them to keep their mouths shut as long as they're on my payroll."

On October 4, yet another arrest warrant was issued against the wayward singer. It was discovered that he'd fled from a small apartment he'd been renting at 270 Tampa Drive in Nashville, and that he still owed two months' back rent. Before he'd so hastily vacated it, this same apartment had been illegally entered—presumably by someone who had been looking for the $35,000 in cash money which Waylon Jennings and Johnny Cash had given to George in his hour of need.

Back in Alabama, Linda Welborn dropped her assault charges against George in the fall of 1979. He gave her back the Corvette he'd taken from her, and once again, the two of them were reunited. "Even though he gave me the 'Vette, I didn't want that," she recalled, "because what I was losing was his love, and that meant more to me." Linda could see now that, as deep as George was in his mortal despair and confusion, her words could no longer reach him. She could see that he was a drowning man.

On some Sunday mornings George would rouse himself out of bed early. He would get Linda up, and they would go to church. For a while after they'd returned home again with the preacher's sermon still fresh in their minds, George seemed as if a weight had been lifted from his shoulders. "You know," he'd tell her in an agonized voice, with the tears welling up in his eyes, "I'd give anything if I could be a preacher. But if I was to become a preacher, people would laugh at me."

"But, George," Linda would tell him gently, "wouldn't it be better to make people laugh than to make 'em *cry?*"

When the ethers of the night crept through the seams of the windows and the cracks in the doors and descended like a veil upon them, George often fell victim to the principal memories from long ago—memories that had haunted him through the years. Memories that smelled of death and antiseptic: memories of the hospital room back in Vidor, more than a decade earlier, when his daddy lay dying, and he had stood looking into his glassy, unseeing eyes, listening to the rasping death rattle of his tortured breathing. He would remember, too, the sound of his own voice that night: loud, harsh, angry, echoing sickeningly through the hospital corridors. He'd recall how the anger, grief and outrage had welled up inside him and caused him to curse loudly and cry out that night about how *maybe it was best if the old man did die, seeing as how he never did anything much but give his mama an earthly hell to live in.* He'd hollered and screamed at the old man to stop fooling around and get the hell up off that bed (much as Old George had once hollered at him in the middle of the night to get the hell out of bed and sing). He had shouted desperately, angrily, for his father to get the hell up again and *not leave him*—to get the hell up and *not die.*

Brother Peanut—as Earl Montgomery, safe now in the arms of Jesus, had come to be called by many of his friends—had also, by now, dropped all his criminal charges against the prodigal singer. And the two of them became friends once again. Peanut prayed for his friend's soul with renewed intensity, and set about trying to rescue him from the swirling, deepening waters.

One drizzly autumn morning, a Sunday, when the clouds hung low in the sky, the two of them rode together to a tent revival meeting being held up on Hawk Pride Mountain, just southwest of Tuscumbia, Alabama.

Gathered beneath the tent were about fifteen people, and after the preacher finished his sermon, he gave a call for all those who wished to receive the spirit of the Holy Ghost in their bodies to come forward to the altar. Suddenly, George opened the car door. "I'm gonna get out," he told Peanut.

As Peanut watched his friend walk slowly toward the altar, he felt his heart jump for joy. "After all my prayin' for him, I could see that this man was finally fixin' to be saved," he remembered. "He went right up to the tent, and he knelt down and prayed, with the rain falling right on him, and I went over there and put my hand on his back and I prayed, too. After the altar call was over, he knelt there for a long time. He finally got up and went back out to the car and was sitting there, crying. I really believe he had an experience with the Lord that day."

But that Sunday's conviction did not hold; the poison snakes were still running loose in the prodigal singer's head. He was now going through ever more massive amounts of cocaine—snorting it, spilling it or giving it away. "Some nights, he'd heave a bunch of it out the window and say, 'I'm through with this damn stuff!' " one friend recalled. "Then, the next day, he'd be out in the yard on his hands and knees, trying to scrape it up again."

Looking gaunt and tortured, George surfaced briefly in mid-November to play a show at a club in that dreary corner of the world known as Texarkana. Though he was in no shape to be singing, he knew that it was the only way to lay his hands on the kind of quick cash money he needed to keep him in whiskey and shiny new cars. The audience was well aware of his well-publicized trials and tribulations, and those gathered now seemed to hang desperately on every twisted sinew of pain that echoed through his drug- and smoke-ravaged voice. "You're lookin' at the one in country music who's messed up more than any of 'em," he told the crowd—almost as if they were his demons and he was now smiling at them.

"We've had a lotta requests," he added as he brushed aside pleas for him to sing the famous duets he'd once sung with Tammy. "But I ain't got the right sex up here with me tonight. . . . Bless her heart. She'll come back to me someday!"

Often, it was George's habit in the middle of the day to show up at Jimmie Hills's barbershop in the big shopping center near Florence, Alabama. Jimmie could see that his friend was weakening badly. He was subsisting off a diet of crackers, roasted peanuts and canned sardines for weeks at a time. He had walking pneumonia, his gums would sometimes bleed from malnutrition, his weight had dropped from 145 pounds all the way down to 98 and now he was nothing but skin and bones—now he looked exactly like Hank, the dark archangel, in the picture taken of him peering out from behind the bars in the Alexander City jail, less than five months before his death.

With pursuers, both real and imaginary, now hot on his trail, he pulled his Lincoln Town Car back in the narrow alley behind Jimmie's shop and parked it there, next to the garbage dumpsters. There, he sat alone in his car for hours as he, "the Duck" and "the Old Man" debated furiously among themselves.

Linda Welborn, too, could see George's immense suffering; she saw that the sadness with no name was now consuming him, pulling him down, like those lost souls which are spoken of in Revelations: the ones raised from the dead only to be cast into the bottomless pit, the lake of fire, in what is referred to as "the second death."

Hoping to calm George down, Linda one evening suggested that they go out for a drive. George agreed. As they left the house, he grabbed the loaded .38 pistol, which he still carried with him everywhere he went.

For nearly two hours, as the gathering shades of early evening gradually enveloped the countryside in a deeper darkness, the two of them drove aimlessly out toward Colbert Park and the Natchez Trace. They drove out across the gravel roads and twisting highways that crisscrossed the northern Alabama wilds. By mere chance, they turned up a narrow, winding lane, and continued on until they came to an old abandoned house, with trees and grass grown up tall and mysterious, all around it. George told Linda to stop the car. He switched off the headlights and let the shadows of the chilly late autumn night encircle them. Then he took his loaded pistol and put it to his right temple. "I think I oughta blow my head off right now!" he sobbed.

Linda was terrified. She knew that the worst thing she could do was to show her fear. "George," she told him calmly, "put the gun down and stop talking that way. Let's don't do this.

"Say," she suddenly suggested, trying her best to act cheerful under the rather dire circumstances, "you know what we oughta do! We oughta drive to Florida—leave tonight. We won't tell anybody, and we'll make 'em all wonder where we're at!

"That caught George's enthusiasm," Linda recalled. "He put the gun back down. Then we drove back to my house and got some clothes and started driving south. But then we got as far as Birmingham [about 110 miles], and he changed his mind. So we headed back up I-65, and we were almost all the way back to Florence, and he changed his mind again. So we turned around and got as far as Birmingham again, and he changed his mind one more time. Finally, I told him, 'George, we're *goin'* to Florida!' So we finally did."

The warmth of the subtropical sun proved to be no help. The prodigal singer's condition continued to worsen. Upon George's return to Florence, Peanut saw he'd now become a threat, not only to others but to himself as well. As they sat together one day in a little restaurant, it saddened Peanut almost to the point of tears to watch as his friend dropped his sandwich, and then ate it off the tabletop with his mouth, like a wild animal. The end of the line had come for George, and he could run no further.

Peanut Montgomery contacted Lauderdale County probate judge Will Duncan on December 10 and requested that the documents be drawn up to have his friend committed to the nearby Eliza Coffee

Memorial Hospital. On December 15, George was transferred to Hillcrest, an exclusive $300-a-day private psychiatric hospital on Fifth Avenue in Birmingham, which specialized in the treatment of alcohol and drug abusers.

Peanut spent a thousand dollars of his own money getting George checked into Hillcrest. After George had been formally settled in, Peanut made some telephone calls, attempting to get through to Tammy Wynette, who'd earlier offered her financial assistance if matters ever came to this. But when the $10,000 arrived from Nashville, it was not delivered by Tammy, but by the brother of Mr. Tammy Wynette No. 5, Paul Richey—a man who seemed to have developed a sudden interest in George's life and career.

The doctors at Hillcrest diagnosed George as suffering from "an acute paranoid state with suicidal and homicidal potential to a high degree . . . [and] . . . delirium tremens, secondary to chronic and acute heavy intake of alcohol . . . [and] . . . suspicion of chronic use of cocaine." They also told him that if he had continued abusing himself at the rate he was going, he would have been dead in another two months. George ended up staying at Hillcrest for only twenty days, even though, in the following months, many would argue that he should have stayed much longer. But it was not to be.

The wave was still rising; the waters were higher than ever. And there were those people—those who are always drawn by the alluring scent of quick profits and coin of great dimensions—who knew that there was lots of money to be made off of George Jones. As he lay in his bed there at Hillcrest they came to visit and he could see these people smiling down at him with dollar signs in their eyes, smiling down at him hungrily, like turkey buzzards perched on a telephone line.

Chapter Seven

VERTIGO

It was a seemingly rehabilitated George Jones who emerged from Hillcrest Psychiatric Hospital in mid-January 1980. Yawning and blinking, he walked back out into the world like a child abruptly awakened from a peaceful, dreamlike slumber and thrust suddenly into the harsh light of day. The churning, rising waters were still pressing forward with relentless force, and even though he was under strict doctors' orders to limit his stress, the wheels were once again beginning to turn at an unmercifully furious pace.

In a flurry of contract signing, Paul Richey—a man who was himself a reformed alcoholic and a purported "born again" Christian—became the newest addition to the prodigal singer's long list of managers. Richey, along with the others who now had a hand in guiding George's career, knew that the world had been captivated by the sheer pathos and undercurrents of tragedy in the beleaguered singer's well-publicized decline and fall. These people also knew that there was a lot of money to be made in staging what would prove to be one of the most widely trumpeted and most short-lived "comebacks" in popular music history.

The momentum for all this had actually begun building while George still lay in his hospital bed in pajamas and cowboy boots. On December 1, 1979, Epic had released *My Very Special Guests,* an LP which, due to George's poor health and even poorer state of mind, had been two years in the making. The album consisted of duets (almost all of them overdubbed) that featured George singing with a carefully chosen collection of country and rock superstars who numbered themselves among his admirers—who had seen fit to come to his aid during his hour of need—artists like Linda Ronstadt, Willie Nelson, Waylon Jennings, James Taylor, Emmylou Harris, Johnny Paycheck, ex-wife Tammy and British rocker Elvis Costello (a dyed-in-the-wool hard country fan who even wrote a song, "Stranger in the House," especially for the occasion).

My Very Special Guests met with weak sales, contained no hit singles and was, at best, a lackluster, spliced-together musical effort featuring George at his bronchitis- and emphysema-ridden worst. The LP, due to its distinguished lineup of artists, nonetheless was the object of considerable media attention; it caused George Jones's name to be reverentially whispered on lips where it had never been whispered before.

"I won't even listen to it," George admitted in an interview with Los Angeles *Times* music columnist Robert Hillburn a few weeks after his release from Hillcrest. "It's eerie looking back on those days. I was at a point in my life where I didn't care anymore. It was real scary.

"I'd been about five years in virtually another world," he added tentatively, as if he himself was still trying to fathom the meaning of his long, shadowy journey. "It's hard to explain how it felt. Imagine yourself going to bed at night and staying in the darkness for five years."

In late January, George was once again back in the Columbia studios. There he was reunited not only with Billy Sherrill but also with Tammy Wynette, whom he'd not seen at all, and had barely spoken to, for nearly two years. They recorded a duet called "Two Story House," which Tammy had co-written especially for them to sing together.

Oddly enough, in the three years that had passed since George and Tammy had last recorded together, it was Tammy's records that had taken to sliding silently off the charts, like smooth stones sinking into still waters. When "Two Story House" went to the number two spot—higher than any record with the First Lady singing on it had gone in more than two and a half years—it made her and her cowboy-hatted court jesters very happy indeed.

"[George] is still the greatest voice in country music," cooed Tammy, still on her fifth marriage, still making frequent return appearances at the hospital and still rushing forward in her headlong pursuit of happiness—much like a bedraggled moth beating its head against a light bulb. "Even though we couldn't live together, he'll always be my favorite singer."

The ever-resourceful Billy Sherrill had never relented in his deep, purposeful gazing into the mystical tea-leaf patterns of the musical notes. During George's darkest hours, he'd never ceased to spend hours listening to the hundreds of demonstration tapes of unrecorded songs that had come across his desk at CBS. He was always looking, always listening, always hoping for still one more potential smash hit that might be right for George.

One day in early 1979, Sherrill yawned, lit a cigarette, fixed himself a cupful of J&B scotch and water and picked up a tape box that had the names of Bobby Braddock and Curly Putnam on it, two eminently successful Nashville songwriters. The song on the tape was "He Stopped Loving Her Today." It was a mournful, slightly morbid tale of a man so devastated by the breakup of a romance that his only escape from his lingering heartbreak turns out to be death itself.

When "He Stopped Loving Her Today" first came across Sherrill's desk in early 1979, the song was already more than two years old. It had already undergone numerous permutations, including several rewrites—it was one of those songs that *almost* never happened at all.

"To tell you the truth, I never really did think it was all that great of a song," admitted Bobby Braddock, the co-writer of "He Stopped Loving Her Today." "It started as just a little bit of black humor. Curly and I started fooling around with all the old clichés about dead people, like 'Don't he look natural! . . . Well, you shoulda seen him a week ago!' And from there, we just kinda schmaltzed it out."

When Sherrill first heard it, two different versions of "He Stopped Loving Her Today" had already been recorded by singer

Johnny Russell on two different record labels. Both versions, shortly after they were released, were—in record industry jargon—"DOA."

As Sherrill sat puffing on his cigarette, sipping his scotch, listening to the song and letting its sad, soap-operatic sentiments wash over him for the first time, he too had his own misgivings about it. "It just didn't flow right," he recalled. "They had the guy dying too quick."

Even as he took note of the song's serious flaws, he did not toss it into the large metal trash can that normally served as his reject file. Instead, he felt himself becoming infatuated with the song's *idea.* Despite the murky lyrics, the garbled story line and the overwrought sentiments, he was sure that he could hear dollar signs echoing around in there somewhere.

"Billy called us and asked us to rewrite it," Braddock remembered. "We showed him another version that we'd already rewritten for Johnny Russell, but he didn't like that version either. So we rewrote it again, and he still wasn't satisfied. This went on for about a half dozen rewrites, until finally he called us back and told us, 'That's it! You got it!' "

Sherrill first played "He Stopped Loving Her Today" for George in mid-1979, and the prodigal singer's reaction, too, was considerably less than enthusiastic. "He thought it was too long, too sad, too depressing and that nobody would ever play it. He was going through hard times then, and I was having a hell of a time even getting him into the studio at all. He hated the song, hated the melody and wouldn't learn it. Every time I'd try to get him to sing it, he'd end up singing the Kris Kristofferson classic, 'Help Me Make It Through the Night.' This went on for a long time. He just couldn't seem to get it in his head."

As a light snow fell outside the Columbia studios on February 6, 1980, Sherrill finally coaxed the ambivalent singer into laying down a serviceable vocal track on "He Stopped Loving Her Today." George still referred to it disdainfully as a "sad, slobbery tearjerker." "I was afraid people would think I was feeling sorry for myself," he sheepishly admitted.

When George finally got ready to leave the studio, late that cold, dreary afternoon, he was visibly aggrieved at having been forced to waste the better part of a day at what he considered, by and large, to have been a profitless endeavor. "I remember his last words to me about the song that day were 'It's too damned depressing!

Nobody'll ever play that thing!' " Sherrill recalled with a gleeful grin. "I bet him a hundred bucks it would go to number one, and he took me up on it."

"It was a nightmare," George told a reporter who asked him about his long, harrowing journey through the darkness. The reporter was one of a couple dozen journalists who'd braved the icy, snow-swept highways to attend a January 30 press conference at ex-wife Tammy's Franklin Road pleasure dome. George himself had been two hours late because of the icy conditions. Those who manned the wave-making machines at his record company and at the offices of his new management team were urging him to do many interviews again, hoping to herald far and wide the full drama and miraculousness of his "comeback."

"I've lived a bad life," he admitted woefully. "But I read the Bible a lot while undergoing treatment. Now I can see all the way down the highway.

"I've got my thinking cap on straight now," he added cheerfully. His weight had now ballooned back up from a skeletal 98 pounds to a robust 145. "I know what drinking will do to you," he assured his audience. "If I thought for one minute I'd have to go through that again, I'd jump off a cliff."

One of the first people to see George on the day that he returned from the hospital to his home in northern Alabama was Linda Craig. She was an attractive, intelligent ex-barmaid from the Hall of Fame Motor Inn Lounge in Nashville. Linda had first befriended him during those chaotic months in early 1979 when he'd become estranged from Linda Welborn, and she had fled from him a few months later, after he'd laced his raw whiskey with cocaine, grinned his demon-appeasing grin and waved his loaded pistol around her one time too often.

"He was like another person," she recalled of his first night back from the darkness. "He was in real good spirits, like a child—like a forty-eight-year-old child."

Still, it alarmed Linda when she noticed that his speech was more rapid than usual, and that his shotgun eyes were once again dancing with pinwheel wildness. After she prodded him, he finally confessed that he had stopped and bought himself a six-pack of beer on the way home from the hospital. Then when she found some cocaine in his bedroom, he owned up to the fact that he'd had some hidden away in the freezer, and had seen fit to thaw it out and take a little hit of it as well.

He assured Linda that there was absolutely nothing to worry about—that he felt so damn good about being straight, he just *had* to have him a little ole drink and a little ole toot to celebrate. He almost succeeded in convincing her that this would be both the beginning and the end of it all right here, that this was absolutely all the messing around with that awful stuff that he intended to do. After all, he'd already been to the brink of the abyss. He'd already stumbled on the precipice and stared down into the darkness, and then regained his balance just in the nick of time. He promised her that he was through with all this foolishness, and was finally ready to walk the straight and narrow. Linda believed him. She surely did.

After having finally gotten a passable vocal performance out of George, Billy Sherrill listened repeatedly to the unmixed tracks of "He Stopped Loving Her Today." He was pleased with the way veteran session musician Pete Drake's weeping steel guitar and Charlie McCoy's subtle harmonica shadings enhanced the song's inherent sadness. He'd even overdubbed a softly wailing soprano background vocal—sung by Millie Kirkham—that gave the song an added dimension of funereal poignance. It concerned him, though, that in the chorus of the song, there still seemed to be something missing—it bothered him that "it just kinda laid there and died."

Sherrill called veteran Nashville string arranger Bill McElhiney and a couple of dozen concert violinists and cellists and brought them in the studio. He overdubbed them all in unison, playing a full octave-and-a-half upward glissando in the song's chorus.

After "He Stopped Loving Her Today" was released as a single in early April, George lost his original $100 bet with his wily producer. The song sparked a flurry of excitement that even Sherrill, in his infinite shape-note, dollar-sign wisdom, could not have foreseen. It not only hit the number one slot and hung in the country charts for eighteen weeks; it kept right on selling until it sold more than a million copies—far more than any of the prodigal singer's hit records had ever sold before. *I Am What I Am,* the celebrated "come-back" LP on which "He Stopped Loving Her Today" appeared, met with similar success when it was released later that year. It, too, would eventually top the million sales mark.

Once again, the wave was rising with a vengeance and moving

forward at a frightful velocity. The people in whose hands George had carelessly placed his career could see that it was now time to crank up their own star-making apparatus to the max. They could see that the time was ripe to put the Real Thing back out under the intense scrutiny of the public eye.

Paul Richey, in order to churn the waters and fan the flames still higher, enlisted the services of yet another national wave-making and fame-enhancement megacorporation. He called in the Halsey Agency, a powerful Tulsa-based booking and management organization. It had already been handling certain aspects of Tammy's career, and was rumored to have impressive connections with the West Coast TV and movie industry.

One of the Halsey Agency's first measures toward raising the prodigal singer's profile amongst the masses of chronic TV gazers was to land him several spots on the addlebrained quiz show "Hollywood Squares."

The months rolled by and the Halsey Agency pressed on with its relentless efforts to pass the prodigal singer off on Hollywood (much as the geezers back in the Big Thicket had once tried to palm their bottles of purple-tinged crude petroleum off on unsuspecting tourists as a digestive balm). They engineered a real coup when they put together a deal for an hour-and-a-quarter-long Home Box Office (HBO) television special, entitled "George Jones: With a Little Help from His Friends."

The HBO special was, in many ways, another shining example of video in the hands of idiots. Musically, the show had its inspired moments. But far too much of the on-air time was squandered as the illustrious lineup of guests—Waylon Jennings, ubiquitous ex-wife Tammy (who bulged noticeably in a slinky, skintight outfit), Emmylou Harris and Elvis Costello, to name a few—were made to strut and fret across the stage, spouting tedious, cliché-ridden testimonials as to George's multifaceted greatness. George himself smiled patiently as he endured all this. But under the unblinking gaze of the video cameras, he appeared frighteningly wan. As he flailed awkwardly around the stage, mouthing his own good-natured malapropisms, he looked like a stranded fugitive, searching desperately for his lost car keys . . . or a bathroom window.

Though "A Little Help from His Friends" did not sweep any awards, it did serve its intended purpose. It succeeded in carrying the arcane greatness of the Possum out to the vast audience of cable

TV gazers: Soon, his name was spoken on more tongues where it had never been spoken before.

Other tongues were wagging furiously with the news of an impending revival of the "Mr. and Mrs. Country Music" road show—a revival which, to Jim Halsey, head of the huge Halsey Agency, had the taste of big money—a taste which he was already savoring deliciously, like an after-dinner mint melting on his tongue. Such a road-show revival, he declared to the press, "would be to country music what a Beatles reunion would be to pop music."

So it was not much of a surprise to anyone when, early in 1980, the Halsey Agency announced that George and Tammy were indeed planning to resurrect their tired passion play, and take their sad, stretch-marked masquerade back out across the country once again in a series of concert dates.

Tammy and her cowboy-hatted crew made little attempt to portray this professional reconciliation as anything more than their own modest, self-effacing contribution toward helping a friend (George) rejuvenate his ill-starred career. But since George was now hotter than ever, while Tammy's own recording career was growing colder by the minute, there were more than a few questions raised as to who was really helping whom.

The Halsey Agency launched their multifaceted game plan of publicizing the George-Tammy revival with yet another misdirected field-goal kick in early February. Its rumored West Coast connections helped the agency land the freshly united musical odd couple a spot on "The Tonight Show."

The appointed evening of their "Tonight Show" rendezvous rolled around. George showed up with an ill-suited "uptown" hairdo that had been slapped on him at the last minute by some image consultant, and which made him look like something off the set of *Night of the Living Dead.* Under the harsh, unrelenting glare of the live TV monitors, he and Tammy sang their hit duet, "Two Story House."

As the Halsey Agency wizards realized too late, live television was a medium in which George was morbidly uncomfortable—a medium which seemed to always draw his festering insecurities to the surface, like moist heat drawing the pus out of a blister. Before the two of them were even halfway through the song, George stopped suddenly, without warning, and confessed sheepishly to the vast live TV audience that he'd forgotten the words. The cameras panned briskly away. The programmers broke for a dog-food commercial, and the Possum was seen no more that night.

As Paul Richey watched all these glorious media events unfold, one by one he made still more plans and executed still more megabuck deals—deals for more TV shows, more concert tours, more records, more interviews . . . he even began laying the groundwork for another brainchild—an overdubbed duet album which would consist of the wayward singer singing along with the disembodied, prerecorded voice of the long-dead dark archangel of despair, Hank Williams. It was an album which Richey hoped to call either *Two Legends* or *The Legends*.

As members of George's new management team hurriedly wheeled the singer around—from recording studio to tour bus and from one television taping to the next—pushing him like a wooden prop from one ill-planned, hastily executed project to the next, confusion set in. The troubled singer could be seen reeling and staggering, gasping to catch his breath as the earth beneath him and the firmament above him once more reeled dizzily. Like a lost child, he could be seen rubbing his eyes confusedly, as if he had been rudely awakened and thrust much too quickly before the cold light of day.

But there was to be no rest for the weary. The call of the road was louder than ever now and no sooner would one month-long string of $15,000–$20,000-a-night road shows be over than another would begin.

More potbellied, gold-chain-bedecked factotums were enlisted to shield the dazed, exhausted singer from the multitude of whiskey-swilling backslappers, dope-snorting groupies, amphetamine-breathed deejays, cocaine-dealing promoters and all the other assorted weasels, jackals and freshwater vultures who are drawn, with crablike precision, to the pallid backstage incandescence of fame, money and impending doom.

The wave, with its strange and awesome new dimensions, rolled on. On the evening of August 18, as a light drizzle fell on the gray sidewalks outside, George—after several previous no-shows—finally made it to New York to perform at the prestigious Bottom Line club. In the hours before the show, he became so nervous and distraught over the prospect of facing the strange wall-to-wall audience of sun-pale, bland-faced music biz intelligentsia and show business elite that he shed quiet tears of desperation. When he took to the stage, he was troubled by yet another dark omen: his trembling hands clutched a borrowed guitar—a poor substitute for his tried-and-true twenty-year-old Martin, which felt so warm and comforting to his touch and which had been stolen a few days earlier at a show in North Carolina.

He began to sing and felt his fear and trepidation gradually fade off into nothingness; his powerful voice, with all its resonant undercurrents of ghostiness, outrage and the sadness with no name, once again worked its mysterious magic. The audience, which included Andy Warhol, David Frost, Linda Ronstadt and Bonnie Raitt —the latter two of whom joined him onstage for a couple of numbers—clambered to their feet, and many of them stood atop their chairs and whistled, applauded and cheered with abandon.

Now the wheels of the star-making machinery whirled with renewed fury. Still, George, the Good Samaritan, found the time to throw his energies into yet one more project where his talents were needed. He took it upon himself to organize a benefit concert for a good friend of his, David Johnson. Johnson, a record producer, had been severely injured in an automobile accident on a downtown Muscle Shoals street. He had sustained twenty-seven separate bone fractures and suffered a severe concussion. He lay in a coma for fourteen days and was hospitalized for the next 106 days, unable to return to his livelihood for nearly a year. The end result was $28,000 in medical bills. Due to his forced inactivity, his studio and production company faltered on the verge of bankruptcy.

George—never one to turn his back on a friend in need—worked tirelessly and used his own considerable influence to secure the talents of the Oak Ridge Boys and several other popular country acts. With Peanut Montgomery's assistance, he also lent a hand in otherwise organizing and publicizing the September 30 benefit show, which was to be held at the Florence-Lauderdale Coliseum.

"The only one who didn't actually make it onstage that night was George himself." Johnson laughed warmly as he recollected the concert, the proceeds of which enabled him to turn his life and his business back around again. "He was so drunk that he couldn't physically get off his bus. He thinks I hate him over that, and he apologized every time he saw me. But George put all that together for me on his own, even though he didn't have to. And I'll always love him for it."

CBS released a second single from the *I Am What I Am* LP, one written by artist-writer Tom T. Hall and entitled "I'm Not Ready Yet." It was a song seemingly tailor-made for George—a statement about a man who'd wrestled with the sinister forces of death and despair but was not yet ready to give in to them. As the neurasthenia-ridden singer was once more stalked by those very same cruel shadows of depression, exhaustion and paranoia that had pulled him down into that black, bottomless well once before—the record quickly rose to the number two spot.

On the evening of October 13, the powerful Country Music Association, after having virtually ignored George's very existence for more than a decade, finally bestowed upon him its coveted Male Vocalist of the Year award. George was not even in Nashville when the announcement was made at the glittery, nationally televised awards ceremony. He was far away, in a lonely hotel room in Sparks, Nevada, dressing to play yet another road show. It was by long-distance telephone that the news of his long-overdue victory finally reached him. He was also informed that his runaway hit "He Stopped Loving Her Today" had precipitated a virtual sweep of the prestigious awards: Song of the Year, Single of the Year, along with Album of the Year—for the *I Am What I Am* LP.

"I'm sittin' here on the side of the bed with my pants half down, one leg in and one leg out, and I just don't believe it," he told one of the first reporters to reach him through the hotel's fiercely buzzing switchboard. "I guess, well, I just can't express myself too good right now.

"I've been through a lot, and I've put my friends through a lot," he added. "But I'm on my way back. The Good Lord's been good to us."

But even as he spoke, the axis at the center of all things was beginning to tear loose and fly asunder once more; the earth and the firmament gyrated wildly out of their orbs. Once more the poisonous serpents, with their Medusa heads, were stirred awake by the dark forces of whiskey, cocaine and mortal confusion.

Out on the concert trail, exhaustion and disillusionment settled in like a choking fog. Loud voices, full of anger and recrimination, could be heard issuing from behind closed motel-room and dressing-room doors, hurling accusations and recriminations back and forth at each other. Though George was now commanding concert fees in the top-dollar range, the road musicians found themselves working more shows than ever while being paid a fraction of their usual salaries. George himself, chain-smoking nervously, face rivuleted with fatigue, was put on a $1,000-a-week draw, since the bankruptcy court had given him back his guitars, seized more of his jewelry and begun attaching the rest of his income to service his immense debts. The prodigal singer, despite his ever-increasing fame, found that his pockets were once again empty, found that he was once again, like the organ grinder's trained monkey, dangling helplessly on a string.

"We really felt sorry for him," recalled David Burns, a steel guitar player who accompanied George on the road during these long months. "A lot of times, he'd have nothing, and he'd have to borrow five or ten bucks off of me or one of the other guys in the band. We'd be at a gig, and he'd be hungry, with no money, and we'd go out to the hot-dog stand and buy him a hot dog."

On the night of December 5, an unseasonably warm and clear evening in Nashville, the seething cauldron finally exploded. Several hundred of the country music industry's most celebrated and jewelry-bedecked leaders gathered at a nightclub called the Exit Inn for what had been billed as "Nashville Loves George Jones Night." It was to be a benefit concert performed by the singer, along with a select group of his illustrious musician friends, the proceeds of which were slated for the Nashville Songwriters' Association. George, who'd reportedly had a heated dispute with one of his management minions earlier in the day, was said to have last been seen, bottle in hand, fleeing town in a chartered plane, headed for the breezy isles of the Bahamas.

Ex-wife Tammy, who'd stood him up at one of their scheduled shows the month before when she'd been rushed to the hospital, purportedly for "removal of a cyst," was called to stand in for him at the last minute.

"George was drunk," she told a reporter who later visited her at her Nashville pleasure palace, where she was once more abed. (She had just returned from yet another hospital stay, reportedly for treatment of injuries she'd received after falling down the stairs in her office.)

"I don't know any other way to put it," she added. "He gets off and gets these wild, weird . . . I guess when he's strung out . . . that he thinks the FBI's chasin' him and he has to hide out and all these things. And it's so pathetic. Got a million-dollar voice and can't use it."

Once again, George and Linda Welborn renewed their plans to tie the connubial knot, and they set a date for their wedding. "I was going to take my son [from her first marriage] to school, and then I was going to meet George at ten A.M., down at the clinic in Florence, so we could get our blood tests. I waited out in my car for over an hour. George ended up runnin' off with some friends, and never did show up."

On the occasional Sunday when George was home off the concert merry-go-round, he and Peanut would sometimes attend the local Baptist church together. Even though Peanut was still resting safely in the arms of Jesus, he still felt a strange itching within him. Soon this itching told him that he had a higher calling: it told him that he must further serve the Lord by helping to spread His word.

Peanut went down to WBTG, a 3,000-watt all-gospel station located on Main Street in nearby Tuscumbia, Alabama, and got himself a half-hour-long daily radio show. Soon Peanut's own perfervid brand of salvation was echoing out over the airwaves, out across the northern Alabama wilds. Day after day, Peanut would preach up a storm. He preached of George's blasphemy, and apostasy, and he condemned these acts. He preached of Legion, the demon-infested man who dwelt in the tombs at Gadara, and he likened George to him. He preached of Satan's temptation of Christ in the wilderness, and he likened these devilish temptations to those that had been laid at George's feet in his now immense worldly fame. He preached about how the Roman governor Agrippa, after listening to the words of the Apostle Paul in the city of Caesarea, had told him: "Almost thou persuadeth me to be a Christian." Brother Peanut likened this to the rainy Sunday morning when he and George had ascended the mount at Hawk Pride, and George's soul had seemed to hang in the balance.

Peanut brought his sister-in-law Linda Welborn on the radio and she testified, at Peanut's insistence, how she had attended a tent revival, and how she'd seen the light and fallen down on her knees before the altar and been saved. She confessed as to how she'd lived in sin with the prodigal singer for far too long, and she testified that she would live in sin with him no longer.

Day in and day out, week after week, Peanut preached on,

preached till he was blue in the face. Sadly, though, Peanut's preaching did not raise the seventeen dollars a week in mail-in contributions that were required to keep his show on the air, so in December 1980 his fleeting career as a radio preacher came to an end. Linda once again returned to living in sin, and neither she nor George would return to the tent revivals with him.

Peanut still remained steadfast in his faith and eventually had himself ordained as a full Baptist minister. He finally saw his lifelong dream come true in May 1981, when, with the help of a $5,000 donation from George, he opened his own humble all-denominational church, a small brick chapel located on the Jackson highway in Sheffield, Alabama. Peanut called his church the Lord's Chapel. The attendance was sparse when it first opened—no more than three or four people on some nights. Peanut had faith, though, faith in the Lord's assurances in the Bible that "For wherever two or three are gathered in my name, there am I in the midst of them." With unflinching certitude, Peanut continued to preach for anyone who would listen—continued with his efforts to spread the Gospel According to Peanut.

The occasional light snow flurries of February 25 whipped up and down the cold New York streets as George surfaced at the twenty-third annual Grammy Awards ceremonies at Radio City Music Hall. He was being presented a Grammy for the Best Male Country Vocal Performance of 1980, for the million-selling single "He Stopped Loving Her Today." He sang the song and received a standing ovation. As he stood under the glare of the live TV cameras clutching the small trophy awkwardly, reporters from all media surrounded him, anxious to get a word from the "new" George. Confusion abounded. As if uncertain as to where he was, much less what he was doing there, George replied as he looked down at his shuffling feet, "Shoot . . . I'm just an old country boy"—not knowing quite what else to tell them.

On this same uneasy trip to Gotham in late February, a fidgeting, restive George spoke to a writer, Mark Rose from *The Village Voice*. The two of them sat together at a Formica table—much like those found in bars everywhere. George ordered an iced-tea glass of cold water and sat staring darkly into it, hoping to fend off the demons that he heard singing loudly in his blood, and hoping to shake himself free from the cruel fate spelled out by their prophecies.

After effacing himself once more as "just an ignorant country boy who never had much schoolin'," he looked more deeply within himself than usual. He offered up a fleeting and uncharacteristically vivid insight into the troubling conundrum of his abiding despair and its disturbing connection to his vast emotive talents.

"All I can say is that I put it all, everything, into one thing, singin'," he revealed uneasily. "Call it heart, call it soul, call it what you want. I don't know. . . .

"Then again, maybe my singin' might be the cause of a lot of my problems," he added tentatively as he warmed slightly to the subject. *"You might be a bastard in other things you do, you might be a sorry son of a gun, but as long as they relate to you in your songs, it seems to be all right. I don't show a lot of affection. I have probably been a very unliked person among family, like somebody who was heartless. I saved it all for the songs. I didn't know you were supposed to show that love person to person. I guess I always wanted to, but I didn't know how. The only way I could would be to do it in a song."*

In early March, there came yet another violent assault against the frayed strands of his sanity. A twenty-six-year-old woman named Carol Kissman Rosenbaum, whom George had "dated for a while" and who had visited him several times in Nashville in 1981, was brutally murdered in an apparent robbery at the Okey Dokey Country & Western Nightclub in Austin. She was found with her hands tied behind her back and her face stuffed into a mop bucket. She had been drowned. She had last been seen, in the early morning hours before her death, counting the receipts from the previous evening's show.

George pulled himself back together temporarily and went back into the Columbia studios with producer Sherrill, and recorded an upbeat anthem of survival and enduring love called "The Same Ole Me," which had been written by Paul Overstreet. All four members of the famous gospel quartet turned country music superstars, the Oak Ridge Boys, dropped by the studio to contribute some powerful background harmonies. Released later that year, the song went to number two in the singles charts.

The short-lived George-and-Tammy realliance was now coming unraveled once again. "The crowd wants us back together. That's all they talk about," Tammy drawled to a reporter from the Nashville *Banner*. "They just scream, 'George and Tammy!' [But] I've got my other George [Richey], and that's the only George I want.

"I think," she added, extending some unsolicited advice to her third ex-husband, "if he [Jones] would commit himself to a good hospital or go to some AA meetings, he'd come out so much better."

George's singles continued to race up the charts, one after the next, while Tammy's persisted in fading quickly from sight, like sinking stones. "That," George later told friends, in reference to their last hit duet single, "Two Story House," "is the last goddamn time she gets a free ride on my coattails!"

And indeed, it would be. .

The wave roared on. On May 1—at yet another nationally televised ceremony—George was presented with the Male Vocalist of the Year award by the West Coast-based Academy of Country Music.

The waters rose higher.

> *"The finest, most riveting singer in country music. . . . Mr. Jones has a way of accenting a key word or note in a melody that can enliven an entire song."*

John Rockwell, New York *Times*

> *"He is so awesomely and elementally human that his music can be not just heard but felt to issue from flesh and hot blood. . . . He could well prove to be The Last Country Singer . . . the last great spiritual descendant of the field's archetypal demigod, Hank Williams."*

Jack Hurst, Chicago *Tribune*

CBS records continued their efforts to saturate the market with the record products of the Real Thing. In late May, an internal CBS memo circulated to all departments of the huge transcontinental star-making and fame-enhancement network, calling for an advertising, merchandising, promotional, publicity and sales "blitz," geared to "make people feel their record collection is incomplete without George Jones being represented."

The earth and the firmament swirled crazily onward in their collision course. The snakes writhed in dark places, and "the Duck" and "the Old Man" were loosed from the bottomless pit. Chaos waved its double-bladed scepter of nausea and fear, and the sadness with no name fell like a shadow of famine across the dark, troubled landscape.

In June, George was sued for $10.1 million by the owners of a music park in Ohio where he'd failed to appear for a show several weeks earlier. Enraged fans had started a riot that resulted in seven arrests and a deputy sheriff's being seriously injured. Officials of the 1981 Ohio State Fair then canceled an upcoming appearance that the troubled singer was supposed to make there. "We try to run a family affair," a spokesman explained, noting that George had also missed a scheduled show in Columbus that February. "We can't take a chance on something happening."

The night had now devoured the day, like a headless serpent devouring its own entrails. "The Duck" and "the Old Man" squawked on with renewed fury. The Antichrist, loosed from the depths, slouched on toward Bethlehem, and the thin-lipped Possum grin widened once more into a soundless scream.

On July 2, George performed at the Palace, near Beaumont. He gave a lively show, but when it was over, he did not—as was customary—bid the audience adieu and disappear into the shadowy backstage corridors. Instead, he jumped frantically off the stage—practically into the laps of those sitting in the front rows—hoping against hope to make his escape from the demons who now assaulted him from all sides. He now believed "the devils" in his management team were holding him prisoner, holding him hostage for whatever top-dollar ransom could still be wrung out of the steadily ascending dollar signs attached to his ever-increasing fame and notoriety.

After his jump, the troubled singer fled into the night, spirited away by his sons, Bryan and Jeffery, who had been waiting patiently for him to make his move.

A day or two later—his whereabouts till then a mystery—George surfaced in nearby Vidor. It was a holiday, and a large group of his kinfolk—some of the now countless progeny of the old patriarch, Frank Jones—had gathered at a house in the shadow of Interstate 10. One by one, these Joneses came forward and spoke to the prodigal singer, the pride of their bloodline. Their words were bland and unthreatening, but George could see that their faces were grim and unsmiling; he could see that they were the bearers of bad tidings. When a police car and an ambulance turned in the driveway, he grabbed his trusty little shaving kit and he fled on foot, running toward the nearby interstate. He knew he could make his escape by maybe thumbing a ride somewhere—though he knew not where.

The familial multitude ran after him, grabbed at him and pulled him toward the ambulance, which had been summoned to take him to the Baptist Hospital in Beaumont.

"All right, all right!" he shouted over and over again as he climbed into the ambulance, waving his middle finger menacingly in the faces of these, his newest persecutors, and fighting back bitter tears of betrayal. "All right, I'll go," he cried. "I'll go! But when I die . . . I don't want none of you all t'come to my funeral!"

The Baptist Hospital could not hold the Possum for long. Nor did it hold "the Duck" and "the Old Man." A couple of days later, he was released. Shortly afterward, he showed up at the home of his sister Ruth with sixty-four cents in his pocket. Back in Alabama, his checking account had been frozen, his credit cards revoked and his phone temporarily disconnected. In a voice riddled with confusion and sadness he pleaded with Ruth to give him a ride back to his home in Alabama.

Back into the jaws of the beast.

In the troubled years since they'd lost their mama and daddy, Ruth had watched her younger brother sink deeper and deeper into his seemingly bottomless confusion. During those grim, fallow years, she had been no stranger to hard times herself. She'd divorced, remarried and redivorced her husband, Buster, and she was now living in common law with him. In late 1976, she'd been hit by a truck, a rather serious accident which left her with a "hysterical reaction," accompanied by a temporary psychosomatic speech impairment. Though she'd undergone sodium pentothal treatments and was ministered to with "nerve medicine" and various other nostrums, there were some in her family who believed she'd never fully recovered.

After Ruth's efforts to unravel the elusive mystery of Rollie Jones's oil wells had dead-ended, she'd turned her mind to other, similarly perplexing matters. She'd read in the *National Enquirer* about how John F. Kennedy, though deformed and an invalid, was still alive and secretly held prisoner in a Swiss sanitarium where he patiently awaited an eventual reunion with Jackie. When Ruth pondered the meaning of this, her thoughts led her to the plight of her little brother. She believed that he, too, was now being held prisoner—a prisoner of fame.

"My brother George Glenn is a white slave," she'd tell anyone who would listen. "He's being held captive by a bunch of Mafias.

They keep him drugged, and they move him from state to state, from one hell to another, and they've got control of his mind."

Ruth knew that the others in the family called her "Crazy Ruth," but she knew that to her brother George she was still "Ruth the Truth." It was he who suggested that she come back to Alabama and stay with him and take care of him for a while. Naturally she accepted his offer, certain as she was that time was running out on George. She quickly took it upon herself to free him from "the devils" whom he insisted were trying to destroy him.

When they arrived back in Alabama, Ruth the Truth saw that things were worse than she had imagined. She was certain that all the telephone lines that her brother talked over were tapped. Thus, she began tape-recording all incoming and outgoing phone calls, particularly the ones that he made. She spoke to her brother incessantly about her fears and suspicions, much as Peanut had once spoken to him about the face of Jesus. She fed his paranoia relentlessly with her theories about the "white slavers" who were controlling his thought patterns and were out to kill him, and "the Duck" and "the Old Man" along with him.

George listened to Ruth and tears of desperation glistened in his eyes. One day, he picked up the phone and called the Florence Police Department. "Come and get me," he told them wearily. "I've had it, boys. I can't run no more!"

The local police furrowed their brows, scratched their heads, sighed a collective sigh, and explained to him that they couldn't really do that, since they were unaware that they had been looking for him in the first place.

On July 8 a news crew from WNGE-TV Channel 2 in Nashville had gotten wind of the fact that George was now a fugitive from his own management team and was once again adrift in a sea of personal problems. Unable to find any dogs riding on cars or armless mandolin players in their own backyard, the trolling television journalists decided to cross state lines and venture on down to Alabama on a Possum hunt. They were finally able to track down the enraged, uncooperative singer and corner him at Jimmie Hills's barbershop in Florence.

"I have two hundred and thirty-seven dollars, they tell me, in my banking account," George lamented bitterly. "I went to Texas last week and tried to work [some shows] and they [the managers] lied to me again and stuck the money in their pockets, and wouldn't give me a cent. . . . I have nothing to my name . . . but this pair of blue jeans and this shirt."

George and Ruth the Truth knew now that their cover had been blown, and that members of the management team would soon be scouring the Alabama back roads for him once again. So in mid-July the two of them fled, fled for their lives. They jumped in one of George's sleek new pleasure machines and headed out across the great green expanses of Frank Jones's long-lost Confederacy, heading southward, toward the safer shores of their native East Texas.

Near the Alabama-Mississippi line, Ruth and George paused briefly from their harrowing flight. They stopped at a roadside fruit stand and bought a big watermelon. As they cracked it open and ate it with their fingers, they laughed and joked, and for just a little while, it was just like the good old days when they were both carefree teenagers back in Beaumont. Night fell and they drove on. As they were driving, Ruth the Truth, who was at the wheel, noticed that George was no longer laughing, but that he was having trouble breathing and was coughing and convulsing like a drowning man. His mouth was no longer smiling, but had once more fallen open into a silent scream; he pressed the palm of his hand tight against the window, as if that window were the fragile, cracked vessel of his own sanity, and he was trying desperately to keep it from shattering into a thousand pieces.

Upon seeing George's state of desperation, Ruth the Truth now fell on the verge of hysteria herself. Panic-stricken, she stopped at the Twin Oaks Motel, on Highway 72, near Walnut, Mississippi, and checked in. When her brother's condition worsened, Ruth lost control and called "the devils"—some management minions—who quickly made the drive from across the Alabama line to their motel near Walnut. When the minions arrived, Ruth believed everything to be all right. She went out to buy some Maalox antacid tablets for her brother, thinking that might be the answer to his problems. When she returned, she discovered that she'd been tricked. The management minions had double-crossed her and spirited her brother away in the big blue Cadillac which they had arrived in about an hour earlier.

Still on the edge of hysteria, Ruth fled back to Vidor, where she called the FBI and urgently explained to them that her famous brother had been kidnapped. An "all-points bulletin" was quickly issued on George. Ruth the Truth went on to explain to the FBI all her theories about the "white slavers" with their mysterious drugs and the invisible Mafias with their interstate mind-control organization. The law enforcers listened patiently, for hours in fact, then assured her they would find her "missing" brother.

The FBI tracked the errant singer down to a house in Fort Worth, Texas, where he was preparing to strike a deal with yet another manager. A strangely calm and collected Possum assured the FBI that he was not being held against his will. The confused FBI agents scratched their heads, furrowed their brows, sighed wearily, then called off their manhunt.

On an unusually cool, cloudy evening in late July, George showed up in Nashville. At a small supper club called Pee Wee's in a particularly dreary northern section of town, he played what was being billed as his "Farewell, Nashville" performance. A press conference was held beforehand. George, looking surprisingly dapper in a brown silk suit with gold-and-orange suede cuffs, stood before the assembled crowd and enumerated his troubles. He announced the formal termination of his association with Paul Richey and the striking of a new managerial deal—this one with a man named Billy Bob Barnett, a burly six foot, seven inch former Dallas Cowboys football player turned owner of Billy Bob's in Fort Worth, Texas. His club had the somewhat dubious distinction of being the world's largest honky-tonk.

On hand for the occasion was a motley collection of yawning, sweating, beer-swilling print media journalists and TV reporters. Despite the abundance of free liquor, this gaggle was only roused slightly from its collective occupational torpor and chronic boredom by the rumored possibility of a violent confrontation between the embittered singer and the jilted Paul Richey. The smell of potential violence, in fact, hung heavily in the still humid air like thick smoke from cigarettes and overcooked hamburgers.

"I made more money last year than I have made in my whole life, and I don't know where the funds are." As George spoke to the reporters, he seethed with barely contained anger. "I haven't seen no receipts, I haven't seen nothin' regarding my last eighteen months with Paul Richey."

"Is there a woman in your life?" inquired one of the torpid, glassy-eyed reporters.

"There's always a woman." Loud belly laughter bellowed out from the ragpickers and beer swillers. "You know, boys, you can't live with 'em and you can't live without 'em." (Nancy Sepulveda, an attractive, dark-haired thirty-three-year-old Cajun divorcée whom he'd only recently met was George's latest flame, but he didn't dare relate that to the hungry press, lest Linda Welborn find out.)

"Why you leavin' Nashville, George?"

"I'm a Texan, I'm from Texas," the prodigal singer replied. He was further bombarded with questions about his plans with Billy Bob Barnett of Fort Worth. "I just wanta get back to Texas, where home is, and continue with whatever career I have left."

But even as George was speaking, Paul Richey and Billy Bob Barnett were hard at work slicing up the pie every which way. The two of them had struck a deal which bore George's signature. Under their new arrangement, Richey would receive from Barnett a "consulting fee" of $100,000, "to be paid from . . . fees received from personal appearances by Jones." Their written agreement also specified that Barnett and Richey would work together on the production of the overdubbed duet album that Richey had earlier planned for George to do with the disembodied voice of the late, great Hank Williams. For his participation in the completion of this LP, Richey was to receive "fifteen percent of the proceeds, until the sum of $100,000 was reached." Richey and Barnett also outlined similarly grandiose plans for a book and a movie based on the prodigal singer's life. Of the anticipated profits from these two projects, it was agreed that "fifty percent of the net proceeds will be paid to Richey, and fifty percent to Barnett, with Jones to receive his income from the fifty percent . . . being paid to Barnett."

Their agreement also specified that "complete ownership of the proprietorship of [music publishing companies] known as Jones Songs [BMI] and King George Music [ASCAP], which are now owned entirely by Richey, will be transferred to Barnett." Barnett found a house for George in Fort Worth, and had the singer's few worldly possessions—including his music awards and his treasured pictures of his mama and his daughter Tamala Georgette in their expensive wormwood frames—moved there from Alabama. He even bought a shiny new silver Mercedes-Benz pleasure machine for the Possum to drive.

At the very last minute, perhaps after grasping the full implications of his new management deal, George balked at this new arrangement as well. Once again, he fled. He failed to appear at a scheduled show in Wichita Falls, Texas. He had been last seen leaving Nashville—where his deal with Billy Bob was to have been formally consummated—in a borrowed limousine. The car was later found deserted, with the windows rolled down, in a pouring rainstorm, illegally parked in front of the passenger terminal of the Huntsville, Alabama, airport.

As fate would have it, in the midst of George's disappearing act, record company officials were busy trying to find the Possum themselves. They wanted to present him with his first gold album award for his half-million-selling *I Am What I Am*. George didn't hear about it until weeks later and the accomplishment was only noted in the record company's files.

Back in Fort Worth, angry creditors impounded George's precious awards and wormwood-framed pictures of his mama and daughter. Later they were auctioned off in order to satisfy the singer's remaining indebtedness in that city.

After his disappearing act, the Possum finally reappeared back in Alabama with a mysterious lump of cash money. He made a down payment on yet another big, fancy house—a $130,000 Spanish-style job on Marietta Drive in Muscle Shoals. He made another down payment on $22,000 worth of new furniture to furnish it with, then he moved his on-and-off-again fiancée Linda Welborn in with him. As a little surprise he bought her a shiny new baby-blue 1981 Lincoln Town Car.

Once they were settled, the madness swirled with renewed fury at the new Marietta Drive pleasure palace, taking on ever darker and more sinister hues. The snakes writhed and the worms turned in silent places. Sister Ruth moved in with George, as did "the Duck" and "the Old Man." Soon, a host of uninvited companions and associates—many of them bearing copies of keys to the front door, which George, in his weaker moments, had given them—descended with termitelike glee. Day after day, strange cars choked the driveway; loud drunken voices and the occasional sound of gunfire shook the late-night silence. Expensive household items—guns, televisions, stereos and the like—inexplicably grew legs and crawled off and disappeared. An antique 1939 Buick coupe which George had bought (and which he soon sold to his ex-brother-in-law Buster for the bargain-basement cash-and-carry price of $1.00) was found to have all four of the bolts in its steering column mysteriously loosened. Ruth was even more certain than ever that there were sinister forces at large that were out to kill her brother. She began searching the phone lines for wiretaps again and tape-recorded all incoming and outgoing calls. She busily gathered evidence against the interstate mind-control organization.

George himself now dwelt, night and day, in a spectral haze of depression, fear and nervous, rat-in-the-maze exhaustion. His hair had now turned silver, and all the strife-torn years showed heavily again on his haggard, wrinkled face. His health had once again deteriorated to its hellish pre-Hillcrest low. He was pallid and sallow, suffering from bronchitis and occasional bouts of laryngitis, and was still chain-smoking Virginia Slims cigarettes. Malnutrition, bleeding gums, abscessed teeth and other related maladies haunted him. His thoughts would not focus; sleep eluded him, and when he did sleep, the face of Jesus with its brightness like the holocaust visited him often. For little or no reason, he would fly into rages, smash furniture and hurl objects through windows. Some nights, as the invisible ethers swirled through the room, he would sit and weep about the pictures of his dead mama that he had lost somewhere in Texas.

"I'm trapped!" he'd sob pathetically to Ruth the Truth. "I know they're beatin' me outa millions of dollars, but I . . . I can't, can't escape! They all think I'm crazy and no one will listen to me. They know everything I *do*. They have me bugged!"

Frantically, he would pull down ceiling tiles, roll back rugs and move furniture, and with the eager help of Ruth (who now had absolutely no doubts that her brother's thoughts were indeed being monitored by outside forces), he would search in vain for the hidden microphones that they were sure were concealed in the walls or crevices somewhere in the house on Marietta Drive.

Ruth the Truth watched her now gray-haired brother as he nervously mixed himself a drink, stirred it with his little finger, and sat alone in an armchair in front of his huge Advent TV and cried softly to himself. She reflected on the irony of it all: the sad and painful fact that he'd now literally reached out and touched millions through his music; yet he himself remained unreachable and alone —lost and *utterly* alone.

Still, the worms turned, the termites chewed and the snakes writhed.

Just four days short of his fiftieth birthday in September, George surfaced for a show at the Pequea Silver Mines Club near Lancaster,

Pennsylvania. He'd failed to appear for scheduled concerts there on five previous occasions. As the crowd sang "Happy Birthday" to him, he took to the stage, grim and unsmiling. Dressed all in black, with his bloodshot eyes hidden behind dark glasses, he had the grim, tragic demeanor of death itself. A huge plywood cake was wheeled onto the stage and fifty multicolored balloons were released from a trapdoor. They floated skyward toward a huge banner that, in bold letters, also bade "Happy Birthday" to the beleaguered singer. But George was lost in his sorrow and paranoia, numb to this adulation, and insensate to the celebratory atmosphere that surrounded him. After playing a dispirited forty-five-minute set, he stalked offstage and refused all requests for an encore. Retreating to his bus, he sank back into his sadness and solitude. He granted no interviews (because his attorneys had advised him not to) and he signed no autographs.

On October 3, Epic released another single by George. "Still Doin' Time (in a Honky-Tonk Prison)" quickly hit the number one spot and hung in the country "hot 100" for seventeen weeks.

As the strangulated chorus of madness grew louder, and as his *I Am What I Am* LP moved inexorably on toward the million-sales platinum plateau, he staggered drunkenly onstage at the "Grand Ole Opry" House in Nashville and received his second consecutive Male Vocalist of the Year award from the Country Music Association.

He'd never kissed ass before, and he wasn't about to start now. Two nights later, he vanished from his backstage dressing room at the Opry House and failed to make a scheduled appearance before 4,000 deejays, record company execs, music biz dignitaries, and assorted nonfunctionaries who'd gathered for CBS Records' annual Country Music Week artists' showcase.

He got sky-high and sideways in a Virginia motel room, broke several lamps and was unable to fulfill his contractual obligations at a show at the Salem-Roanoke Civic Center. Wayne Oliver, yet another manager, explained that "George is . . . a very sick man . . . he's too sick to perform." He went on to say that George would soon be hospitalized again.

On November 24, the Possum caught a jet plane out to Los Angeles, for the signing of a new five-year, ten-LP contract with CBS Records—a contract which was reportedly the second most lucrative record deal ever extended by that label to one of its country artists.

(Willie Nelson's was said to be higher.) The contract—described by one high-ranking label executive as "a top-drawer, superstar deal: enough to pull him out of all his [financial] problems"—guaranteed him cash advances on each of his LPs which (based on a complicated formula) would range from $50,000 to as much as $300,000. He was also given an exceedingly healthy album royalty rate (on LPs sold through retail channels) of nearly 20 percent (a dollar or more an album).

The same month, he was nominated in *Playboy*'s December readers' poll as the year's best male vocalist in the country and Western category. Around the same time, CBS released an album recorded earlier that year, called *The Same Ole Me,* which included the hit single of the same name as well as the chart-topping single "Still Doin' Time." It sat pretty in the country album charts for twenty-five weeks, eventually reaching the number three position.

George struck a deal with yet another manager in early 1982. The new rep was Gerald Murray, a thirty-three-year-old Muscle Shoals mobile home sales entrepreneur. They had first met one night in the mid-1970s in nearby Russellville, Alabama, at the grand opening of the George Jones Steakhouse—another short-lived enterprise which, only a few months after its inception, came unraveled in a flurry of bizarre cross-litigation which resulted in its closing.

When the prodigal singer failed to appear for a performance in Jackson, Tennessee on January 10, a minor riot ensued. Fans stormed the box office for ticket refunds and the police had to be called in to subdue them. The following Friday night, he performed in a show in nearby Memphis. After the show that night, he threw a bottle through the sliding glass doors of his room at the Holiday Inn Rivermont, near the banks of the wide Mississippi. "You can hear all kinds of rumors," he replied when a reporter inquired about the unusually large hotel bill with which he was presented upon his departure the next day. "We have been trying to get over [a] virus," he added, lapsing momentarily into the flatulent imperial plural favored by doomed royalty in Shakespearean tragedies. "I had manager trouble and, you know, personal problems."

Back home in Alabama, the Possum started buying and selling fancy cars again like a kid spending quarters at a penny arcade. He decided to buy himself a pleasure machine unlike any other pleasure machine he'd had before: a completely customized 1982 Chevy pickup truck complete with a torso-built seat and all the other doodads that made it a genuine "Possum Mobile." With "the devils" and the invisible Mafia on his tail, he fled again in his new machine—fled down the long, dark ribbon of interstate and did not tell anyone where he was going. For five whole days he did not return. Scheduled appearances were canceled; an APB was almost issued; vague, contradictory rumors of his death circulated.

Alone, with the setting sun as his only compass, he headed southward down the highway, without destination, without purpose. His trip would eventually put 3,000 miles on the odometer of his new pickup. Time slowed down and spread out like raindrops on the windshield. The hours crawled by until night became day and the sepulchral grimness of winter slowly gave way to subtropical balminess. As the first spectral fingers of darkness once again began reaching up into the sky to devour the day, he could feel the soothing pleasance of his whiskey-and-cocaine buzz beginning to wear off, and once more he could feel the world coming back into focus and the sadness with no name settling in on him like a mist.

When he pulled over to the side of the highway to have him a little drink and a little snort to try and make things right again, he did not see the black man standing there with his thumb out. Did not see him at all until the man—who assumed that the shiny new pickup had stopped for him—came over and opened the door on the passenger's side and slid in beside him.

"Where the hell you goin'?" the prodigal singer asked.

"*Foht Mey-uhs,*" the man replied, referring in his thick-lipped patois to the large Florida metropolis that lay just to the south.

"*Fohty miles!?*" George responded in his own thick, slurred East Texas brogue as a wicked gleam came into his eyes. "How the hell am I s'posed to know when we gone *fohty miles!?* That's the damnedest thing I ever heard!"

"I'm goin' to *Foht Mey-uhs,*" the black man repeated calmly, without raising his voice or changing his demeanor. He said no more. George handed him a whiskey bottle; he merely drank from it deeply and shuddered. "*Hot damn!*" Then, together, they roared off down the highway.

"You think we done come *fohty miles* yet?" George sneered a short time later as they headed through a particularly grim and desolate stretch of countryside. "You want out here or don'cha?"

The black man took another slug of whiskey and once again

struggled with his syllables. "No, man, I'm goin' to *Foht Mey-uhs* . . . Foht *Mey-uhs!*"

"Hell with it! I done told you: how the hell am I s'posed ta know how far *fohty miles* is!"

The black man reached over quietly and turned on the radio. "All right!" George mumbled disjointedly as he pulled the truck back over to the side of the highway. "All right, just for that, you can ride in the back of the truck for a while! . . . No, wait," he added scornfully as he had second thoughts. "*Fohty miles* is *fohty miles*. Get your ass out! I've had my fun!"

Before he tore off back down the highway in a spray of gravel and screeching tires, disappearing into the sunset, he reached into his pocket and pulled out a thick wad of hundred-dollar bills and stuffed them into the man's hand.

After his little trip, George soon grew tired of his new customized machine and wandered back to the familiar shores of northern Alabama. George and Linda Welborn had, by now, again parted ways, and now he was keeping constant company with Nancy Sepulveda. "She hung on to him like a rusty fishhook," Gerald Murray recalled. "She was just a down-home, homebody-type person who was not into drugs at all and hardly even drank. At first, she didn't seem to fit into his way of life at all. But I guess that's why she was so good for him."

One afternoon in early March, the Possum and Nancy were out in his new 1982 Lincoln roaming the vast interstate system, rambling southward on the way to visit some of Nancy's kinfolk in southern Louisiana. With Nancy behind the wheel, George, who was already in a semicomatose state, took a slug of whiskey and felt the soothing fingers of warmth spreading through his entrails. Without warning, the caressing fingers suddenly turned to cold icicles and stabbed at his insides. Seized with terror, he turned and looked over his shoulder. He saw the wave of such horrible dimensions was no longer merely behind him: he saw that its murderous waters were now churning beneath him, all around him, and were about to pick him up and hurl him bodily over the edge of earth and into the dark abyss. He screamed a dry-mouthed animal scream at Nancy, and soon the two of them were roaring down Interstate 55, hurtling onward toward a final rendezvous with the prodigal singer's own unutterably dark vision of the Götterdämmerung—descending into that blinding, fiery finality where the gods war among themselves until the world and the universe are destroyed.

Before the world had time to come to an end, and before the gods had time to unsheathe their lightning bolts, George and Nancy were yanked back from the brink by a Mississippi state trooper who pulled them over at about 1 P.M. some twenty miles south of Jackson. He'd clocked their speed at 91 miles an hour. As the trooper stood by the car exchanging pleasantries and presenting them with a clipboard full of his own sinister-looking, multicolored documents and petitions to be autographed, he could not help but notice the carnival pinwheels dancing in George's eyes. With his curiosity now aroused, he glanced around the interior of the car more carefully, and he spied a suspicious powdery substance on the back seat and the floorboards of the shiny Lincoln. A narcotics-sniffing dog was summoned to the scene. After the canine investigation, the dog barked loudly, snorting up a storm, until its eyes gleamed, too. Nancy and George were then hauled off to the Hinds County Detention Center. After the mysterious trace of white substance was taken to a crime lab and tested, the Possum was charged with public drunkenness and possession of cocaine—a felony in Mississippi good for three years in prison and $30,000 in fines. Nancy was charged with speeding. Late that afternoon, both were released on their own recognizance.

"It was all a setup-type deal," George—who pleaded innocent to both charges—later told an Associated Press reporter. "That's the way it is when you're in the limelight."

Then—not twenty-four hours later—around two o'clock the following afternoon, the prodigal singer was once again back behind the wheel of his tan 1982 Lincoln, roaring down a lonesome stretch of highway, again running from his invisible pursuers, again fleeing from his inchoate visions of doom. With Nancy still at his side, he came roaring through rural Monroe County, Mississippi, some ten miles from the Alabama line. Fearing for George's life as well as her own, Nancy made him stop the car and she got out at a roadside restaurant near Hamilton. In desperation she called the police, advising them that they should stop George before he killed himself, along with whoever else might happen to get in his way.

Raging on alone, George barreled down U.S. Highway 45, running several other cars off the road along the way. The police, who were momentarily in pursuit, clocked him moving at over 90 miles an hour.

Thinking that the times told of in Revelations, where the world would end in a lake of fire and the giant fulcrum of time and eternity would swing back upon itself, had finally arrived, George fled onward, rushing headlong, eagerly into the awaiting jaws of doom. Moving at a more than impressive velocity, he suddenly turned off the paved highway onto a narrow gravel farm road. He lost control of his car, and felt the world turn sideways, felt the darkness engulf him. The shiny Lincoln, which still bore the sheen of factory newness, turned, flipped several times, crashed into two embankments, slid 307 feet and then came to rest—though nearly demolished—once again right side up.

Trembling terribly, he opened his eyes and was startled to see that the world was still bathed in daylight. He wriggled his fingers and toes, and was similarly amazed to discover that there was still sensation in them. He was utterly astounded—and perhaps slightly disappointed—that he was *not* dead, and that the world had *not* ended.

Arriving on the scene shortly thereafter, Monroe County Chief Deputy Pete Shook noted that the driver—a man whom he did not at first recognize—had crawled out of the twisted wreckage of the '82 Lincoln, and was lying in a roadside ditch. Shook, who also found a half-empty bottle of vodka in the car, observed that the man had sustained minor facial lacerations and was "totally bombed . . . he didn't even know where he was."

The officer summoned an ambulance, which carried the dazed singer off to the nearby Aberdeen–Monroe County Hospital. He was tied down on a stretcher with restraints and a neck brace for the trip. George was charged with driving under the influence, reckless driving, driving without a license and—since Monroe County was a dry county—illegal possession of alcohol.

Realizing now that George could run no further, his manager Gerald Murray, along with Ruth the Truth and some other kinfolk, went to a probate judge in Jefferson County, Alabama, and had legal papers drawn up to try and have the prodigal singer committed. On April 1 he was transferred by ambulance from the Aberdeen–Monroe County Hospital to Hillcrest Psychiatric Hospital in Birmingham, where he stayed for nineteen days.

During his short stay, the $300-a-day psychiatrists at Hillcrest once again probed George's troubled psyche. With their eyes subtly trained on their time-clock wristwatches—as if these were their taxi meters and George was their fare—they issued stern paternal and medical warnings that if he did not mend his ways this time, he would surely die. The Possum nodded his head and grinned his wide, lopsided grin as if he understood. He'd been through it all before, and he told them all the things that they wanted to hear. Told them that he'd finally seen the light this time, and assured them that everything would be rosy from here on out.

But friends who came to visit George at Hillcrest saw that nothing had changed. They saw that he still flew into unprovoked rages in his hospital room, and talked incoherently for hours, jerking and flailing his hands wildly all the while. "I don't think the hospital helped at all [this time]," recalled Gerald Murray. "Basically, he spent nineteen days in there for nothing."

When George was released he returned to Muscle Shoals. The hospitalization and medical advice had had little effect. Once more engulfed in madness, the Possum raged wildly on.

In outward defiance of any authority, he failed to appear at a scheduled TV taping in Nashville, he missed a scheduled show in Birmingham and the next night he stood up a capacity crowd of 4,000 that had gathered to hear him sing at the Florence-Lauderdale Coliseum.

Gerald Murray, George's fourth manager in less than a year, unable to harness George, resigned. He was left with debts amounting to $100,000, his three-month-old marriage fractured, and a headful of gray hairs that he had not had before.

In early May, two women psychics, one from Chicago and the other, a black lady, from the South, insinuated their way into this ever-dizzier dance of madness. They had been bombarding Gerald Murray with a flurry of dire prognostications and urgent instructions via long-distance telephone. One of their first Hecate visions was: "The king [George] is in deep depression . . . He told a lie . . ." A few days later, the Chicago seer called to warn Murray that "death is all around [George]. He will not live long. . . . An evil person is around him." Eventually, the phone calls ceased, and the psychics disappeared as mysteriously as they had appeared.

There came yet another round of bizarre litigation in late May: George was sued for $250,000 by the promoters of the show he'd missed at the Florence-Lauderdale Coliseum on May 1. In an attached affidavit, the complainants advised the court that the Possum was "an elusive person . . . and has been known to use fictitious names in order to avoid the public." The plaintiffs warned that "unless a special process server who has knowledge of his whereabouts is appointed . . . it will be impossible to serve the defendant." Taking heed of this advice, the court appointed an unusual summons server: an eighteen-year-old woman named Betty Lee Head, who "is acquainted with the defendant and has knowledge of his whereabouts." After several futile attempts, the papers in question were finally served on George at a Florence bowling alley that he often frequented (usually in no condition to bowl).

When George received a $100,000 advance for a duet album he was preparing to record with his friend, singer Merle Haggard, a termite swarm of creditors quickly surrounded him to get their due. Nonetheless, George hesitantly went about his business with Merle and producer Sherrill in Nashville. In rounding out the album, George and Glenn Martin composed "No Show Jones," a little tune about George's now infamous reputation of nonappearance. As the song continues, Merle's chorus yields to George's refrain but . . . as typified by the Possum's actions, he had left the studio, and Haggard was left to sing the song—asking for George in the process —by himself.

On the cloudy, rain-swept evening of May 25, another roving TV camera crew, this one from WSMV-TV Channel 4 in Nashville, was out trolling for car-riding dogs and armless musicians. Around 6:30 P.M. the news crew got wind of an even better catch: a Possum. This particular Possum had shotgun eyes and was behind the wheel of a shiny silver 1982 Cadillac traveling southward down Interstate 65, just outside Nashville, at an impressive rate of speed. The local police got wind of this Possum, too, possibly after having been tipped off by the TV news people, who were not above stirring up a good piece of sensationalism when they saw one in the making.

The police—with the Channel 4 camera crew hot on their heels— were soon in pursuit of George's weaving Cadillac. The car had no rear license plate, but merely a piece of cardboard stuck in the rear window that had scrawled on it: "Plates Stolen: POSSUM 3."

The police pulled George over near the town of Franklin, Tennessee, and after issuing a citation for speeding, they found a half-empty fifth of Jack Daniel's on the front seat. George offered no resistance, but refused to take a breath test. After he failed a simple

finger-to-nose coordination test, the arresting officer noted that
"his eyes were bloodshot, he was swaying back and forth, and he
kept mumbling. . . . He had a wad of money on him that would
have choked a horse. . . . He was very courteous. . . . He told me
he was drunk, and he was glad I pulled him over before he killed
somebody."

During these proceedings, one of the WSMV cameramen got out
of the news truck, walked up to within a few feet of George and
zoomed his camera in on the debauched contours of George's sor-
rowfully rivuleted face. When George realized what was happening,
he suddenly exploded with the rage of a wounded, cornered animal.
He lunged repeatedly at the cameraman, and tried his best to kick
him in the groin. "Take me to jail!" he bellowed at the police officer,
who was finally forced to physically restrain him as he continued to
vent his fury against the harassments of the trolling camera crew.
"Tell them to get the hell away from me!" he screamed. "Take me to
jail now!" That sensational footage was aired that night, along with
the usual parade of bloody mishaps and grotesqueries normally
seen on the ten o'clock news.

The raging bull was then formally placed under arrest, and a
wrecker was called to tow away his shiny Cadillac. Under restraint,
in the back seat of the patrol car, he hung his head forlornly in his
hands and shed more quiet tears of desperation. The arresting
officer quickly whisked him away to the Williamson County jail,
where he spent an obligatory four hours in a holding cell. "He'd
raise hell a while, then he'd laugh a while," noted another officer,
who kept an eye on him during his brief incarceration. Around
midnight, he posted a $500 cash bond and was on the loose once
more, raging wild once again in the Tennessee night.

The snakes writhed and the worms turned. Chaos wielded her
double-bladed sword of confusion and despair. He was sued by the
Commerce Union Bank in Nashville for $91,194 in unpaid loans. A
few days later, a check written by the beleaguered singer to cover
the $737 in fines that he incurred in the Mississippi wreck bounced,
and authorities in that state threatened to issue an arrest warrant.

Back in Alabama, George kicked his new girlfriend Nancy out of
his spacious Marietta Drive pleasure palace. Then he called Linda
Welborn, from whom he'd been estranged for many months, and
summoned her to meet him at 3 A.M. at Big Daddy's, a Muscle Shoals
music club. Once again, he told Linda that he loved her and wanted

her to marry him. "I'm gonna quit all this messin' up. I've got it all together now."

Linda believed him this time, she truly did. She returned with him to Marietta Drive, and stayed there with him for a week and a half. For a few days, he kept his promise to stay straight, but then, finally, after sending her to the kitchen to mix him yet another double whiskey, Linda realized that nothing had really changed.

Time after time, the phone would ring. Linda would run to answer it, and it would be Nancy. Linda told her repeatedly that George did not want to talk to her. George took the phone from Linda after one of these calls and bellowed angrily into it at Nancy, "Don't you call me back no more, you hear!" Then he hung up.

One time, shortly after Linda hung up, the phone rang again and she again ran to pick it up. This time it was a man's voice that she heard, low, cruel, menacing. "The Mafia's comin'!" the anonymous caller told Linda. "They're on their way down from Nashville. Get outa the house! They're gonna kill you both!"

The anonymous call "scared the fire" out of Linda. Before leaving the house, she urged George, who was pacing nervously, near his wit's end, to come with her. He decided to stay.

An hour later, after Linda had returned to the safety of her own house, she thought it best to call George and see if he was all right. When she rang the number, it was not George who answered, but Nancy. The rusty fishhook had already ensconced herself with the prodigal singer once again, and she quickly gave Linda the brush-off.

For a few days peace reigned, then George turned on Nancy again. He cussed her and hit her and turned her out of his car along a lonesome stretch of interstate highway. But she returned to him. Finally he instructed his Alabama attorney to send her a letter ordering her to vacate his house and not come back.

Nancy was beside herself with grief and desperation. She took an overdose of pills and ended up in the hospital, where her stomach was pumped. Back at home a short time later, she was still lost in her sorrow. She took a second overdose, and was rushed to the hospital again. "I just don't wanta live without that man," she sobbed to her friends. "I just wanted to cook buck-eyed peas and cornbread for that man. That's all. I didn't care about any big ole house or big ole car. I don't care if we live in a shack, as long as we're together."

Still, George eluded Nancy and could not accept her love. He hid from her where she could not find him or reach him by phone. Unable otherwise to penetrate the concentric circles of death dancers and sycophants who now surrounded him, she tape-recorded an anguished message and—as a last resort—gave it to Ruth the Truth to give to him.

"I love you, I'll always love you," she told him in a surprisingly strong, even voice. "You're gonna see that for once in your damn life somebody's gonna love you, somebody's gonna take care of you, and it's gonna be me. I love you. Let's just find us a whole new life and start over. If you don't wanta sing, then I'll go to work and support you. I love you, baby."

The tape never got to George, but the message did. He set aside his anger, and soon the two of them were inseparable once again.

The Possum decided to buy himself a big motorcycle—an 1100-cc Honda Interstate which he purchased from Brother Peanut. At the Universal Cycle Shop in Florence he bought a $2,500 "Vetter" sidecar for the motorcycle, for Nancy to ride in. After all fears had been buried and George had actually learned how to guide his new machine, he and Nancy rode that motorcycle down to Augusta, Georgia. He drew 5,000 people to a show at the Augusta–Richmond County Civic Center, only to storm off the stage after singing seventeen songs.

Afterward, a group of fans—apparently angry over the relatively brief musical offering—followed George back to his motel, and began messing with his new motorcycle, which was parked in the parking lot outside his room. When his longtime friend Pee Wee Johnson, a Nashville nightclub owner who had also come along for the ride, tried to run them off, one member of the angry mob hit him in the face. He was rushed by chartered plane back to a Nashville hospital, where he was treated for a broken jaw.

A week or so after the Georgia incident, the Possum, with Nancy once again in tow, took himself another motorcycle ride, down to his home state of Texas, where he was to play a show in San Antonio. He was two hours late when he finally staggered onto the stage around 11:30 P.M. The crowd of 2,000, who'd paid ten dollars apiece to hear him, booed and heckled him loudly. "Hey, I'm drunk, but I love y'all!" he assured them in his whiskey-slurred East Texas brogue as he muffed the lyrics and mangled the melodies to a few of his greatest hits. Then he sang the mournful Hank Williams lament, "I Can't Help It If I'm Still in Love with You" twice, back to back. By the time he finally gave up the ghost around 1 A.M., all but 450 of the audience members had angrily walked out on him. The Possum was last seen weaving off into the night on his big Honda motorcycle, with Nancy and a bottle of tequila in the sidecar.

He failed to appear for a scheduled show in Odessa, Texas, a city some three hundred miles to the northwest, the very next night. The 5,500 fans who'd bought tickets to see him at the Ector Country Coliseum were left holding the bag.

A couple of weeks later, he pulled yet another no-show, this one in Tullahoma, Tennessee. "If I could get ahold of him, I'd kick him in the ass!" said one indignant fan who'd stood in line several hours to buy a ticket.

Yet another character sidestepped her way into this ever more elaborate tapestry of intrigue and suicidal confusion. This one was a self-appointed fan club official from the West Coast who had taken it upon herself to spin out feverishly composed and widely disseminated "news letters." Her dispatches urged George's fans to take into their own hands the awesome task of rescuing the troubled singing star from the death and destruction which now seemed to be written in the stars for him. She urged George's fans to write their congressmen and attempt to secure the services of those high government officials in freeing George from his alleged demons and tormentors, who, she charged, made him sing "when he can't even stand up or *preform* [sic]. . . . I have seen him *manhandeled* [sic] myself when I went on tour with him earlier this year," she testified. "[His] girlfriend has even threatened the life of others who have dared to befriend him or try to help him. . . . We have been to the FBI and the Criminal Intelligence [sic] . . . Maybe this human *travisty* [sic] can be stopped before George Jones becomes a DEAD legend!"

A backwater radio station, WIRJ-AM, in the small western Tennessee hamlet of Humboldt, decided that it would get in on the act, decided that it would single-handedly attempt to hold back the wave and quell the tide that now surrounded everything that George Jones touched. In a move probably geared more toward drawing attention *to* the tiny station, rather than *away* from George, station manager Gary Neese proclaimed that henceforth the prodigal singer's records—on account of his persistent no-shows and his shabby legal battles—would be banned from the air and would be heard no more on his station's feeble 250-watt broadcasts. "I have a sixteen-

year-old and a thirteen-year-old [child], and I don't want them looking up to someone like that," Neese declared.

Hardly anyone noticed. George had been once again nominated
for the Country Music Association's Male Vocalist of the Year
award. *A Taste of Yesterday's Wine,* the duet album that he'd recorded
with Merle Haggard back in May, was released in August, and both
the LP and the accompanying single—"Yesterday's Wine," an old
Willie Nelson original—soon hit the number one spot in the charts.
The *I Am What I Am* LP now hovered just a few thousand units short
of the million-sales platinum mark. In the midst of his trials and
tribulations, the sad, spent and exhausted singer managed to
squeeze in a few more trips back to the recording studio. Working
with Sherrill, he struggled wearily to complete the vocal tracks for
yet another solo LP, *Shine On,* which, when released the following
year, would yield still more number one singles.

Tammy Wynette, whose once supple body was now beginning to
sag as badly as her records were sagging in the charts, emerged
from yet another trip to the hospital. Upon her release, the aging
First Lady announced to the world that she was about to become a
grandmother. Later in the month, she made the news again when
she was forced to cancel out of a guest appearance on the TV show
"Love Boat" in order to undergo yet another operation. It seemed
that Tammy was spending more time in the hospital than on the
stage. Not long afterward, she admitted to a dependency on the
pain-killer Demerol. "She [was] taking enough to kill most people,"
one associate admitted.

Tammy made the national gossip columns again when she an-
noyed the *real* First Lady, Nancy Reagan, by giving her hubby, Ronnie, the President, a big old sloppy fever-blister kiss on the mouth
while the two of them stood onstage together at a fund-raising
concert in Jackson, Mississippi.

Then on September 8 came yet another frantic dispatch from
George's fan club official—this one in the form of a letter to the
editor of the Nashville *Banner:* "This is an urgent plea. . . . George
is being given drugs by persons on the inside, members of his tour
group. They won't let anyone who is clean and decent get near him.
They know he can't *preform* [sic] anymore, yet they force him to go
on stage . . . either drunk or drugged senseless . . . and make a
fool of himself, and if he tries to get off stage, they beat on him. . . .
One [of George's] sisters was even *manhandeled* [sic] leaving bruises

on her arms . . . WHY? We want straight answers and NOW???????!!"

George played a concert in Salem, Virginia, on October 25, and as he stepped offstage he was greeted by County Sheriff Everett B. Obenshain, the bearer of still more bad tidings. A $25,000 court judgment had been levied against the errant singer after his failure to appear for a concert there the year before. The sheriff seized the gold watch off George's arm, the diamond ring off his finger (worth an estimated $5,000) and $10,000 in gate receipts. Obenshain also attempted to impound the singer's buses, but could not; they were leased. The watch and the ring were later auctioned off at a public sale at the Salem courthouse.

With the worms turning, the snakes writhing and the darkness now encroaching from all sides, George could smell the terrible acrid smell of death burning in his nostrils, suffocating him. He again felt the horrible roar and deadly crushing weight of the drowning waters as they pressed against his shoulders and rose to his chin. He screamed another twisted, dry-mouthed scream, grabbed Nancy, and together the two of them jumped into one of his pleasure machines and fled for their lives.

Their painful, twisted memories of northern Alabama trailed off behind them like torn banners as they fled the wave and all its cruel flotsam and jetsam which threatened to choke them and pull them apart. They fled the tattooed cocaine dealers, they fled the Mississippi grand juries and they fled the conniving ex-managers with their visions of ascending dollar signs and grandiose five-year plans. They fled the idiot-wind astrologers and doomsaying fan club officials. They fled the TV preachers and they fled Peanut Montgomery and the blinding light of the face of Jesus. They fled Ruth the Truth, "the Duck," "the Old Man" and the imaginary Mafia; the process servers, the $300-a-day psychiatrists, the sensation-mongering TV camera crews, the backstage whiskey swillers and the rouge-and-lipstick-besmirched groupies. They fled all the other silk-jacketed, gold-chain-bedecked music biz flunkies and various and sundry self-appointed Possum hunters and carrion-eating vultures who now dogged his every move.

With his principal demons still ripping at his flesh and gnashing at his heels, he and Nancy searched desperately for high ground. They fled to southern Louisiana, and then onward to George's beloved

East Texas piney woods, where, on March 5, 1983, they were married in a simple ceremony performed by a backwoods Baptist preacher. There, in what they knew to be the prodigal singer's eleventh hour, they made one last stand against the darkness.

Epilogue

OUT OF THE
DARKNESS
AND INTO THE LIGHT

When he awoke once more, like a swimmer emerging from sleep's dark, bottomless depths, he found he was bathed in a light sweat. Outside, he could see that it was still night. A light rain was falling, and once more he could hear the wind ghosts whispering in the boughs of the tall pines, which had taken root there generations ago.

The weight of sleep was still heavy upon him, and his mouth was dry, as if it were full of sand. He wriggled his fingers and toes, discovering that there was still sensation in them. He smiled softly to himself, because he knew he'd survived once more.

He arose in the darkness, went to the window and stared out into the vastness of the night. Somewhere in the far-off distance, beyond the soothing veil of shadows, he thought he could faintly discern the sound of distant thunder.

He now knew that the wave, with all its horrible, crushing turbulence, had—for the time being at least—swept by him and gone crashing on to wreak its destruction elsewhere, washing its grim, lethal cargo of corpses and bones against some other treacherous shores, far off, beyond the windswept horizon. He could see now that he'd been swept up on dry land again. He was now far away from Nashville's fool's-gold glitter and northern Alabama's suicidal cacophony of madness; he was back on the familiar shores of his beloved East Texas. Even though he was bruised, scarred and tarnished, he was still intact and shining—still a shining diamond in the rough.

The prodigal singer had come full circle now. The autumnal gray had come into his own hair; the older of his own children were full-grown, some with children of their own. Age was beginning to gather in his own face, just as it had gathered in the faces of old George Washington Jones and Uncle Litt Patterson and all the others who'd come before him. He'd once more returned to the abiding solitude and ghostiness of the Big Thicket, with its primeval pine forests, where he'd drawn his first breath a half century ago.

There in the Thicket he found his own good piece of high ground, the highest point in all of Tyler County and one of the highest points in all the surrounding forest. There he wrestled with his principal demons and railed against the encroaching darkness. There, in the possum- and armadillo-infested piney woods of Tyler County, not far from that place in the forest where he was born, he bought himself a double-wide trailer for him and Nancy to live in. He rekindled his long-standing dream and raised his hands anew, and set about building yet another country music entertainment park with his own name on it. He called it, simply, Jones Country.

In the strange faraway cities, his records still ran to the top of the charts; his recording career, having spanned three decades, moved inexorably onward, toward the fourth. His voice, as always, was still powerful and precise, full of raw conviction and preternatural clarity —still a formidable instrument which, with its resonant truths of mortal confusion, human suffering and the hope of redemption, parted the waters and lit a pathway through the darkness for all the other wayward pilgrims who walked there.

Then he picked up the telephone and, after hesitating briefly, dialed the digits of a once familiar number. Standing there in the shadows, he listened to it ring again and again as it tore at and shattered the profound pre-dawn silence in the darkness of some other small room many, many miles away. When a voice, sleepy and bewildered, a voice that he knew, finally answered, he did not answer back. He merely listened—listened to the confused familiar voice as if it were some frail connection with his own ever more distant, ever receding past. But no. All that was so long ago . . . *too* long ago . . . too long . . .

He hung the phone back up without speaking, and sighed softly to himself. As he lay back down in the darkness, beside his fourth wife, Nancy, he again thought he heard the distant anger and confusion of the faraway thunder. But whether it was moving toward him or merely echoing off and dying in the distance, he could not tell.

He lay listening to the soothing sound of the rain and the wind ghosts in the ancient pines. Sleep beckoned to him again, offering him solace; solace in its warm, soundless depths . . . and a peace beyond.

A peace that will hold? Maybe.